Great Artists
of the
Italian Renaissance
Part III

Professor William Kloss

THE TEACHING COMPANY ®

PUBLISHED BY:

THE TEACHING COMPANY
4151 Lafayette Center Drive, Suite 100
Chantilly, Virginia 20151-1232
1-800-TEACH-12
Fax—703-378-3819
www.teach12.com

ISBN 1-56585-911-1

William Kloss

Independent Art Historian, The Smithsonian Associates,
Smithsonian Institution

Professor Kloss is an independent art historian and scholar who lectures and writes about a wide range of European and American art. He was educated at Oberlin College, where he earned a B.A. in English and an M.A. in Art History.

Professor Kloss held a teaching fellowship at the University of Michigan, was awarded a Fulbright Scholarship for study in Rome, and was an assistant professor of art history at the University of Virginia, where he taught 17th- and 18th-century European art and 19th-century French art. His courses were highly rated by both undergraduate and graduate students.

A resident of Washington, D.C., Professor Kloss has had a long association with the Smithsonian Institution as an independent scholar and lecturer for the seminar and travel program, presenting more than 100 courses in the United States and abroad on subjects ranging from ancient Greek art to Impressionism. He has also been a featured lecturer for the National Trust for Historic Preservation and for The Art Institute of Chicago. He is a guest faculty lecturer for the American Arts Course, Sotheby's Institute.

Professor Kloss serves on the Committee for the Preservation of the White House, a presidential appointment he has held since 1990. He is the author of several books, including *Art in the White House: A Nation's Pride*, and most recently, co-author of *United States Senate Catalogue of Fine Art*. He has also written articles published in *Winterthur Portfolio*, *Antiques*, *American Art Quarterly*, and *Antiques and Fine Art*.

Table of Contents
Great Artists of the Italian Renaissance
Part III

Great Artists of the Italian Renaissance

Scope:

This course of 36 lectures introduces the art of the Italian Renaissance—the epoch that was the genesis of the next 500 years of Western art. This survey will extend from about 1400 to about 1520. The artistic language associated with the late Middle Ages began to be replaced with a radically new style around the beginning of the 15th century, and the chosen terminus date permits the inclusion of the complete careers of Leonardo da Vinci and Raphael while acknowledging the radical shift in style that occurred in the 1520s. The dates, therefore, cover the art historical periods commonly called the Early Renaissance and the High Renaissance.

The focus will be on central and northern Italy, with central Italy considered first. Instead of integrating the artists of north and south, the course makes clear the strong contrasts between the two regions. The city of Florence in central Italy was the birthplace of the Renaissance and the location of most of its defining moments and monuments. Rome, though then a somewhat moribund city, was the seat of the Catholic Church and, therefore, of great power and influence. Other sites where notable artistic events occurred, for example, Arezzo and Orvieto, will also be included. Northern Italy had many cities with strong individual traditions, notably Padua, after the arrival of Donatello to work in the pilgrimage basilica of San Antonio, and Mantua, the court of the d'Este family. Venice, dominating the north on the Adriatic, was the birthplace of a distinct artistic tradition whose influence has never ebbed.

From Masaccio to Raphael, from Donatello to Michelangelo, from Piero della Francesca to Leonardo da Vinci, and from Giovanni Bellini to Titian, more significant artists were born and more epochal art created in Italy in the 15th century than in any comparable place and century in the history of art. In this course, we will look at some great ensembles of world-renowned art, such as the Brancacci Chapel in Florence or the Sistine Chapel in Rome, and at single masterpieces, such as Titian's *Assumption of the Virgin* or Botticelli's *Primavera*. No later Western art can be discussed without reference to the Italian Renaissance, its rediscovery of the achievements of classical antiquity, and its own artistic inventions. Above all, a canon of beauty was established—with many variations—that served artists for centuries. Humanism—an ideal synthesis of human intelligence, dignity, and spiritual vigor—was the basis for that canon. The paintings, sculptures, and buildings of the Renaissance continue to astonish us by their harmonies of drawing, color, and proportion and in their embodiment of humanism. As already noted, this course will conclude at the beginning of the 1520s, with the Protestant Reformation and the beginnings of the Catholic Counter-Reformation, when radically new political and social conditions brought with them a radically new art.

As the title suggests, most of the lectures are on individual artists, presented in roughly chronological order, and the emphasis is on the style and content of their paintings and sculptures. Essential elements of the political, social, and intellectual milieu in which the artists worked will be introduced throughout the lectures, but this is not primarily a course on those subjects. There is an enormous literature on the civilization of the Renaissance, which the bibliography can only suggest. The artist-centered approach of the course is, perhaps, slightly unfashionable these days. But in these art historical lectures, when limited time dictates a choice between art and history, art will dominate.

Beginning in Florence in the late-Gothic period, into which the founding artists of the Renaissance were born, we look at such artists as Lorenzo Ghiberti, whose style is divided between Gothic and Renaissance. Filippo Brunelleschi and Donatello are the principal founders of the Renaissance style. Architecture is mostly beyond the scope of these lectures, but the early Renaissance in Florence cannot be properly understood without looking at Brunelleschi's buildings. When his dome for the cathedral was completed around 1434, "rising above the skies, ample to cover with its shadow all the Tuscan people" (wrote Leon Battista Alberti), the primacy of the "good modern manner" was established. The influence of Donatello's sculpture was unequaled before that of Michelangelo. The greatest painter of the early Renaissance, Masaccio, is studied in two lectures, in which he is also compared to Giotto, the great "proto-Renaissance" master of a century earlier. One lecture is devoted to the Brancacci Chapel, one of the most influential works of European painting.

More than 40 artists are included in these lectures. Here, we will anticipate only the most famous. The greatest artist of mid-century,

Piero della Francesca, did not work in Florence, and indeed, his fame was established only in the 20th century. We will look at the work of a handful of the gifted sculptors between Donatello and Michelangelo. Botticelli, whose wistful grace gave way to anguished expression, is studied in two lectures. The triumvirate of artists whose names are, for many, synonymous with the Renaissance will be examined in seven lectures. Leonardo, Michelangelo, and Raphael are artists of the High Renaissance, and their influence and fame has scarcely waned from their day to our own.

Our transition to northern Italy is by way of Urbino, which offers us a microcosm of the cultured Renaissance city-state. There, the arts and learning were honored by a professional soldier whose small dukedom fostered remarkable achievements. Further north, in Padua and Mantua, we will look at the famous frescoes of Andrea Mantegna. Venice, the proud center of culture in northern, Adriatic Italy, will be the focus of eight lectures, beginning with its Byzantine-accented glories in architecture and decoration. The self-reflexive character of this city, whose daily life and public spaces were so often painted, will be observed in work by Carpaccio and Gentile Bellini. The introduction of the oil medium into Italian painting will be studied in the pivotal short career of Antonello da Messina, a visitor to Venice, and the long career of Giovanni Bellini, the first of the great Venetian masters of the Renaissance. From Giovanni's workshop came a generation of important artists who defined the Venetian High Renaissance. They included Giorgione, whose few surviving paintings, all agree, altered the development of Western art, and Titian, who blended the achievements of Giorgione, central Italian painting, and his own coloristic genius into a style of stirring beauty and six decades of influential art.

We have alluded to the enormous political and religious upheavals in Italy during the early 16th century that disrupted the ideal moment of the High Renaissance. The long later careers of Michelangelo and Titian can only be touched on as we summarize the course of Renaissance art from 1400 to about 1520. Theirs were not the only lives and careers that collided with the much-changed world of post-Reformation Italy. Thus, finally, we will look briefly at the artistic maelstrom that mirrored the historical one swirling during the remainder of that century.

Lecture Twenty-Five
Urbino—Microcosm of Renaissance Civilization

Scope:

Today, Urbino seems a magical world tucked away in its own hilly landscape, an escape from modern civilization. But in the 15th century, owing to the ruling house of Montefeltro, it commanded a larger territory and an outsize importance. The Montefeltro was a dynasty of *condottiere* ("mercenaries") since the 12th century, whose apogee was the short career of Federico da Montefeltro (1422–1482), first count, then duke (1474) of the stronghold in the Marches. Its location near the Adriatic meant an awareness of different political and cultural centers (Venice, Dalmatia). Federico was an almost equal blend of soldier and scholar, an ideal Renaissance balance of the active and contemplative lives, and that was the key to the richness of his court. Within their palace-fortress, he and his redoubtable wife, Battista Sforza, surrounded themselves with beauty and culture. His reputation and wealth enabled him to summon artists and architects to Urbino—from Dalmatia, from Flanders, from Florence and Siena. And he had one great artist in the neighborhood: Piero della Francesca, who became intimately associated with Federico's court. The gem of the palace is the small private study of the duke, the *Studiolo*. This refuge nourished the intellectual resources of the duke, yet he had only to walk a few steps to his loggia to view the territory he governed, and beyond the hills lay the wider world in which he led armies.

His successor, Guidobaldo, with *his* refined duchess, Elisabetta Gonzaga, continued the culture of the court. It was there that the young Baldassare Castiglione spent many evenings in late-supper conversation, which served as the setting for his book *The Courtier* (1527). Alas, the book appeared long after the early death of Guidobaldo (1508), when Urbino was losing its independence.

Outline

I.   Our examination of the art of Raphael offers a nice segue to a lecture on the place in which he was born, the extraordinary city-state of Urbino. Had he been a generation older, Raphael would certainly have been in the artistic service of the famous duke of

Urbino, Federico da Montefeltro, whose dedication to culture made his court one of the most refined in Italy.

A. Piero della Francesca was patronized by Federico, and his portraits of the duke and duchess of Montefeltro were discussed in Lecture Ten. The reverse sides of these portraits are also painted, with allegorical *Triumphs* of the couple. Such imagery was popularized by the poetic "triumphs" of Petrarch. The duke's chariot, drawn by a pair of white horses, carries the seated duke in full armor, crowned by Fame and accompanied by the Four Cardinal Virtues. The duchess, recently deceased, is accompanied by Faith and Charity and reads her prayer book while flanked, perhaps, by Youth and Age; her carriage is drawn by two unicorns, symbols of Chastity. The landscapes are very like those on the front and mirror that of Urbino's countryside.

B. Federico and Battista Sforza created the renowned ambience of their court together, but in the first instance, the ducal palace is a fortress signifying the duke's renown as a *condottiere*. Its huge mass crowns the rock around which the town gathers for protection.

II. Like most palaces, it took form over many years and under many architects. Parts of it were never finished, such as the north and east façades facing onto large piazzas, where only a little of the marble revetment was attached to the brick walls.

A. The most admired part of the palace is an inner courtyard in the purest Renaissance style, designed by the Dalmatian architect Luciano Laurana around 1465. His presence here reminds us of the proximity of Urbino to the Adriatic and the considerable movement of artists and others from one shore to another.

B. On the western façade, graceful superimposed loggias (open galleries) framed by two round towers (*torricini*) punctuate the long, massive, outward wall of the palace. This famous ensemble is also owed to Laurana, who however, left Urbino in 1472. He was replaced by the important Sienese architect and artist Francesco di Giorgio Martini.

III. The vast interior is today the National Museum of the Marches and, therefore, largely devoid of furnishings. This makes it difficult to envision the welcoming quality that these sometimes cavernous rooms must have had.

A. The elegant vaulting and elaborately decorated fireplaces help the imagination. The long Throne Room, in the photograph we see, has some tapestries on the walls, which were, of course, standard practical decoration in palaces—practical because they diminished the cold emanating from the masonry walls and partly muffled the echoing spaces.

B. The Hall of Angels (*Sala degli Angeli*) is named for the small dancing and music-making angels on the frieze of the great fireplace. The work of one Domenico Rosselli, these white and gold angels on a blue ground are reminiscent of Donatello's animated *putti* on the *Cantoria*.

IV. The *Studiolo*, or small study, of the duke of Urbino is one of the most famous rooms of the Italian Renaissance. Arranged and decorated between 1474 and 1476, it was the duke's refuge, his place of study, reflection, and correspondence. It held, as well, his wardrobe, cupboards for scientific and musical instruments, and a famous library (which, we are told, he regarded as "the crowning glory of his great palace"). Everything was on shelves concealed behind doors decorated with intarsia *trompe l'oeil* designs, some of which were themselves illusionistic replicas of the books, instruments, and armor they enclosed.

A. The closets and their woodwork doors covered the lower walls of the *Studiolo*. Although nothing certain is known about the artists involved in the intarsia designs, several artists, including Botticelli, have been associated with the room, and skilled Florentine craftsmen, possibly from the workshop of Giuliano da Maiano, have been credited with the actual execution.

  1. The objects depicted in *trompe l'oeil* often seem to have been selected for their geometric or perspective complexity. Thus, the *Bird Cage and Clock* of one cupboard are marvels of mathematically precise illusionism.

  2. Elsewhere, standard *trompe l'oeil* effects are created, such as doors slightly ajar or a terrace glimpsed between piers with a landscape in the distance.

3. Of course, everything is in the natural tones of the woods used, not painted, so that there is no question of a complete illusion of reality, only constant astonishment at the artists' skill.

B. Above the woodwork, the wall is hung with two tiers of portraits of famous learned men from antiquity to the duke's day. Justus of Ghent, a Flemish artist, was invited to Urbino to paint the portraits.

1. No particular logic governed the choice of the 28 illustrious men so honored. Christian and Hebrew and pagan, writers and popes and philosophers, some were friends or patrons of the duke. In sum, they represented a broad intellectual range, and we may assume that they were Federico's personal choice.

2. After 1474, Pedro Berruguete, a Spaniard from Castile, was brought in to complete portraits that Justus had left unfinished, for unknown reasons. Berruguete reworked the unfinished paintings completely, also changing the architectural settings.

3. All were removed in 1632 after the death of the last duke. Today, 14 are in the Louvre, and 14 have been reassembled in the *Studiolo*.

C. No small part of the appeal of the *Studiolo* is its location within the palace. If he so desired, Federico da Montefeltro had only to take a few steps from his place of seclusion and he could be standing on the loggia of his twin-towered façade, master of all the tranquil landscape that lay below and beyond. Once more, the interplay between the active and the contemplative life so much discussed in the Quattrocento, and so completely exemplified by Federico, is apparent.

V. The Cappella del Perdono in the palace has been tantalizingly suggested as the original location of Piero della Francesca's *Flagellation*, which we discussed in Lecture Ten. It could not have been the altarpiece, but it could have been the altar *frontal*, a step above floor level. The measurements agree and the low vanishing point of the perspective works smoothly from the slightly high point of view of one standing on the floor of the chapel.

VI. The exalted air of the double portrait of *Federico da Montefeltro and His Son Guidobaldo* (c. 1477) marks it as a state portrait (it is still in the ducal palace, in the museum), consciously reflecting the dignity and diplomatic achievements of the duke.

   A. He wears the collar of the Order of the Ermine, bestowed by the king of Naples, and the Order of the Garter, from the king of England. His dynastic pretensions are embodied in his young son, born in 1472.

   B. Guidobaldo married Elizabetta Gonzaga, and it was the famously cultured conversations stimulated by her salon that inspired Baldassare Castiglione to write *The Book of the Courtier*. In the rooms of the duchess, together with music and dancing, "sometimes intriguing questions were asked" or "there would be a sharp exchange of spontaneous witticisms."

   C. It is also appropriate to look for a moment at a painting called *The Ideal City*, whose date and authorship are unknown. This painting is also today in the museum in the palace. Whether it is by the architect Laurana, as has been proposed, or someone else, this essay in perfection is believed by most to have originated in Urbino, in this circle of cultured idealists who were also men and women of the world. It resembles a strikingly rational stage set, to be *looked at*, but its vacantness is also apt to prompt some "intriguing questions."

Works Discussed:
Raphael:
~ *Self-Portrait*, probably 1506, Galleria degli Uffizi, Florence.

~~ *Count Baldassare Castiglione*, c. 1514–1515, Musée du Louvre, Paris.

Piero della Francesca:

Portraits of Duke Federico da Montefeltro and Battista Sforza, Duchess of Urbino, and reverse, c. 1465–1472, Galleria degli Uffizi, Florence.

The Flagellation, c. 1460, Galleria Nazionale delle Marche, Urbino.

Various artists:

The Studiolo of the Duke, and details, 1474–1476, Galleria Nazionale delle Marche, Urbino.

Justus of Ghent with Pedro Berruguete:

Homer, Solomon, and *Moses*, panels in the *Studiolo*, Galleria Nazionale delle Marche, Urbino.

Pedro Berruguete:

Federico da Montefeltro with His Son Guidobaldo, c. 1477, Galleria Nazionale delle Marche, Urbino.

Attributed to Francesco di Giorgio Martini:

Guidobaldo da Montafeltro, 1490s, Galleria Nazionale delle Marche, Urbino.

Artist unknown:

View of an Ideal City, late 15th century, Galleria Nazionale delle Marche, Urbino.

Essential Reading:

Adams, chapter 9.

Hartt, chapter 14.

Supplementary Reading:

Castiglione, Baldesar. *The Book of the Courtier*. Trans. by George Bull. New York: Penguin Books, 1976.

Osborne, June. *Urbino: The Story of a Renaissance City*. Chicago: University of Chicago Press, 2003.

Questions to Consider:

1. What was the profession of Federico da Montefeltro, duke of Urbino?

2. What was the duke's *Studiolo*, and why was it so significant?

Lecture Twenty-Five—Transcript
Urbino—Microcosm of Renaissance Civilization

This lecture is a departure from our usual examination of the work of one or more artists. Until now, we have chosen not to treat individual Italian city-states other than Florence; Urbino offers us a compact opportunity to do so. Today the city Urbino seems a magical world tucked away in its own hilly landscape, an escape from modern civilization (despite its busy university). But in the 15th century, Urbino commanded a larger territory and an outsize importance. This was due to the ruling house of Montefeltro, a dynasty of condottiere (soldiers of fortune, mercenaries) since the 12th century, whose apogee was the short career of Federigo da Montefeltro, who was born in 1422 and died in 1482. He was first count, then duke, in 1474 and after, of the stronghold in the Marches.

Its location near the Adriatic, which you can see on your map, meant an awareness of different political and cultural centers (Venice and Dalmatia) across the Adriatic. Federigo was an almost equal blend of soldier and scholar, an ideal Renaissance balance of the active and contemplative lives, and that was the key to the richness of his court. Within their palace fortress, he and his redoubtable wife, Battista Sforza, surrounded themselves with beauty and culture. His reputation and wealth enabled him to summon artists and architects to Urbino—from Dalmatia, from Flanders, from Florence and Siena. Our just-concluded examination of the art of Raphael offers a nice segue to a lecture on the place in which he was born.

You're looking at Raphael's self-portrait, painted in Florence probably about 1506. Raphael was born in this significant city-state of Urbino; had he been a generation older, Raphael would certainly have been in the artistic service of the Duke of Urbino, whose dedication to culture made his court one of the most refined in Italy. The Duke did have one great artist in the neighborhood, Piero della Francesca, who became intimately associated with Federigo's court, as we've already seen. We already looked at these wonderful portraits, the paired portraits by Piero della Francesca of Battista Sforza, the wife of the Duke, and Federigo da Montefeltro.

Battista Sforza and Federigo da Montefeltro, painted between 1465 and 1472, they're not dated, and in these two profile portraits, we notice the classical purity of the profile pose, which was still the pose that portraits were painted in at this point; it hadn't changed to the three-quarter pose that we have since seen in Raphael, among others. The landscape of their territory is seen behind and below them, as though they were standing on one of the balconies of the palace. It is noticeable that the landscape behind Federigo is marked by a lake and a river, which may suggest his professional activity in the world beyond Urbino—a means of travel beyond Urbino—suggesting that he was not landlocked in his duchy at Urbino. The landscape behind these two is a continuous landscape essentially, despite that variation in the water.

We glanced briefly at the reverse sides of these portraits, and I show them to you again, with the allegorical triumphs of the couple. Such imagery had long been popularized by the "triumphs" described in Petrarch's poetry in the 14th century. Here in the left panel, which is the back of his portrait, the Duke's chariot, drawn by a pair of white horses, carries the seeded Duke, who is dressed in full armor here at the back. He's crowned by Fame, the white-robed figure with wings that stands behind him, and he is accompanied by the Four Cardinal Virtues, who have hitched a ride on the wagon as it processes across the painting.

The Duchess, recently deceased, is accompanied by Faith and Charity as she reads her prayer book. She's seated here, and she's reading her prayer book; Faith and Charity are in the front of the carriage, and she's flanked by figures. It's uncertain what allegories they are, but they may perhaps represent Youth and Age, specifically since she had recently died. Her carriage is drawn not by the white steeds that we saw, but by a pair of unicorns, and you recall that unicorns are symbols of chastity. We encountered them in Pisanello's bronze medal of Cecilia Gonzaga. The landscapes here are very like those on the front, and again they mirror Urbino's countryside, and again it's interesting that Federigo's triumph is associated with a body of water, while Battista Sforza's is not.

Federigo and Battista Sforza created the renowned ambiance of their court together, but in the first instance, the Ducal Palace is a fortress, signifying the Duke's renown as a condottiere. Its huge mass crowns the rock around which the town gathers for protection. It is an extraordinarily imposing mass from this view; I'll move a little closer to the same and point out some of the elements in the complex of this palace. On the left, because it is dominant, I will begin with the bell tower and dome of the cathedral. They're not physically adjoining, but they abut the palace; they're very close, and you have the domed cathedral, the bell tower beside it. This is the apse, obviously, of the church, with the semicircular shape of the wall, and then as you move across, and we are looking from the west-southwest; that is the side of the palace that we see, and you have the bulk of the palace here moving across, and then a very famous element, which we will return to, and that is the tower façade, the small tower façade, the small circular towers that flank a very beautiful set of superimposed loggias.

Like most palaces, this one took form over many years and under many architects. Parts of it were never finished, such as the north and east façades, facing onto large piazzas, where only a little of the marble *revetment*, the clothing, the covering of the brick, was ever achieved. Here is the east façade on the left and the north façade in shadow here on the right. If you look at the east façade in sunlight to the left, it's the earliest. It was begun in 1447, and it still has, though you can't really tell it from here, but it still has the late medieval details. The windows are curved tops, but they are divided into two lights by a calumniate in the middle, and this is a Florentine style, which had already been well established in the late Middle Ages, and it has not been replaced here yet with a Renaissance window, and as you see, that side, the sun side is completely lacking in the *revetment*, that word meaning "clothing" or "covering" for the brick walls, or also for rubble walls if you were talking about Roman architecture, for instance.

This is a very large piazza facing that long wing. On the other hand, on the shadow side here, the north façade faces a small piazza between the palace and the nearby cathedral. You can just see the portico of the cathedral at the right-hand side of the image here. It has, this side of the palace has, Renaissance windows; you can see that these are Renaissance-style windows with a horizontal pediment and calumniates. These are really pilasters flanking the windows and not divided by a column in the middle, but by a single light. Of course, we see modern windowpanes in there now, but this was a single opening, no architectural central member. A very small amount of marble revetment does cover the lower part of this wing, but it never got beyond that. The windows look lonely up here because they're highly finished in stone, and around them is simply this brick façade awaiting the marble that never wants to be placed upon it.

This Renaissance façade, and this is the first Renaissance motive we've seen on the side, this Renaissance façade is owed to the architect Luciano Laurana, who came from Dalmatia across the Adriatic. I'm going to show you the most admired part of the palace, which is also his work, and that is the interior courtyard, the *cortile*, begun about 1468. It's an inner courtyard in the purest Renaissance style. This enters directly off that shadowed façade that we were looking at through the portals that you saw there, and then into this wonderful courtyard. His presence here, Laurana's, reminds us of the proximity of Urbino to the Adriatic and the considerable movement of artists and others from one shore to another. People often worked more and supplied trade as well across the Adriatic than they did across the mountains and the spine of Italy, for instance, which were more of a hindrance than the seas sometimes proved.

I want you to notice while looking at this image of the courtyard, however, that there is an alteration, and an unfortunate one in terms of the purity of the architecture. The upper two stories, those attic stories, even though they sit back, they are recessed in space from the lower two—they are additions. They are not by Laurana, and they do (unfortunately) temper the absolute balance and proportion of this courtyard, so if you can think them away, the upper two levels, or block them out with your hand, you will get a much better idea of the elegance of the elevation, which stopped at the crown—large-crown cornice of the second story, right across here if we're looking at the end of the courtyard.

There is an elegant inscription; in large Roman capitals, there is an inscription that runs across both levels, both the first above the first arcade and above the pilasters on the second arcade, and it is a composition of words in praise of the Duke of Urbino's undoubted virtues. More than that, it really helps the architecture because you can't appreciate it at such a distance here, but the capitals are so clearly spaced, carefully spaced, that they actually further the harmonious effect of the architecture. Nothing was done here carelessly at all.

While we have this one, I will show you another view in a moment, a lower view, but we can see the corners here, which you can't otherwise see easily, and if you're looking at them, you see that he has very successfully achieved a resolution of what happens in the corner of the courtyard. Previous Renaissance palaces, such as the Medici Palace in Florence, in the courtyard had the arches in the corner, from this wall and then from this wall, meeting on a single column. They had to share a landing point, if you will, and it was awkward, unresolved. Here, he's very carefully built the corner out (you can see it on both sides) with a larger pier and a column for the arch here, and another one, a separate one, for the arch coming down the side. It's very smoothly achieved. Here's a view from the court floor point of view. You see you still are aware of the upper two stories, though not quite so strongly, but one should try to ignore them if possible.

This courtyard, which is known as the Court of Honor, has since its completion been regarded as one of the most perfect Renaissance courtyards anywhere, with columns and capitals of truly classical purity. They compare well with Roman columns in Rome, which may have served as models. The white stone pilasters of the second story, looking up again, these white stone pilasters, have capitals that harmonize with those of the columns below, and these pilasters are placed against an only slightly darker brick wall, and it's a wonderful lightness that is achieved by not having dark colors or great heaviness on the second story. The lightness both of tone and of weight, which carries from that lightness of tone, seems easily supported visually by the graceful open arcade below this. The cornice above the arcade wraps completely around the courtyard, unifying the space entirely.

We saw the small courtyard, the small tower façade on the other side, and I'll go back to it now; it's called in Italian the *facciata dei Torricini* (small towers); so, we have this two-towered, small-towered façade on the western façade, commanding a view of the town and the countryside, and marked by these graceful superimposed loggias. A loggia is an open gallery, and it can be applied to a long row of arcades on the ground level, but here it applies as well to the superimposed balconies on the west side. This extraordinarily gracious ensemble punctuates that long massive outer wall that we saw of the palace. This is also the work of Luciano Laurana. For reasons we don't know, Laurana left Urbino in 1472, dying in 1478. He was replaced as court architect (of course, there was much more work to do inside and out) by the important Sienese architect and artist Francesco di Giorgio Martini, whose sculpture we have seen in an earlier lecture.

I want to show you this small tower façade scene from below as well. The middle loggia of the three that you see here is the one on the level of the *piano nobile*, the "noble floor," the second floor, but the principal living level of the palace and behind that, flanked by the towers, are the Duke's quarters, behind this balcony. His bedroom, wardrobe, audience chamber, private chapel, and above all his private study are nestled in the center of his apartment complex. The vast interior of this palace is today the National Museum of the Marches, and therefore largely devoid of furnishings. This makes it difficult to envision the welcoming quality that these rooms had—so cavernous to us frequently today, but they must have seemed very welcoming when they were new.

I'm going to quickly show you three of those rooms. The Throne Room is what we're looking at now, an enormous room as you see, with elegant vaulting and elaborately decorated fireplace here; there's another at the end of the room, and it is a room that in this photograph does have some tapestries on the walls, and these, of course, were standard practical decoration in palaces, practical because they diminished the cold that emanated from the masonry walls. They also partly muffled the echoing spaces. Another room in the ducal apartments is the Sala degli Angeli, the Hall of Angels, which is a reception hall introducing the suite of the Duke's apartments. Its name comes from the small dancing angels, the dancing and music-making angels, on the frieze of this great fireplace. They're done by a sculptor whose name was Domenico Rosselli. These white and gold angels on a blue ground are reminiscent of Donatello's animated putti on the *Cantoria*, the "singing gallery" that we saw earlier.

No photograph can encompass the compact space that is the gem of the palace. It is this small private study of the Duke, known as the Studiolo, known everywhere as the Studiolo. Shelves and wardrobes holding his renowned library, his scientific and musical instruments, and even his armor were concealed by doors, which are decorated with superb *trompe-l'oeil* inlaid woodwork. *Trompe-l'oeil* of course is the French phrase for "deceive the eye," and these are some of the most remarkable examples of *intarsia* (inlaid) wood. These inlaid doors, which we will return to, were surmounted by a double row of portraits, and you can see the bottom row above, of famous men of the past and present. This private study, this refuge, nourished the intellectual resources of the Duke. His chapel adjoined it, and adjoining that was the loggia that we looked at, which overlooks his territory, a territory that he governed, it was said, with unusual benevolence. He had, it appears, the common touch.

The Studiolo, or small study, of the Duke of Urbino is one of the most famous rooms of the Italian Renaissance. Arranged and decorated between 1474 and 1476, it was the Duke's refuge, his place of study and reflection and correspondence that held also parts of his wardrobe, cupboards for scientific and musicals instruments, and a famous library (which, we're told, he regarded as "the crowning glory of his great palace"). Everything was on shelves concealed behind doors decorated with these designs. Some of these designs are themselves illusionistic replicas of the things that one found inside. You see that doors are shown ajar. Look in this photograph at the bottom; this seems to be open. This is all a flat surface; this latticework door just seems to be opened. It is all inlaid wood on a flat surface.

Nothing certain is known about the artists involved in these designs, though several names have been associated with it, suggested, including Botticelli's as a designer, and skilled Florentine craftsmen—possibly from the workshop of Giuliano da Maiano— have been accredited with the actual execution, but there's very little documentation. I want to show you a series of the individual inlaid wood pieces that we're looking at. There is, for instance, this *Bird*

Cage and Clock. The birdcage is on your right; the clock is this open mechanism. Here is the long pendulum hanging from it. It looks as though you're looking right through the door; it's wonderfully effective. The objects depicted were probably selected for their geometric or perspective complexity. It's playing games and setting up the game in a very amusing and clever fashion.

This particular door is a marvel of mathematically precise illusionism. Then, there is the open cupboard with books on your left, door wide open, and a niche with an allegorical figure here on the right. It looks like we have a niche with a sculpture in it—the allegorical figure of Hope—and below, on this lower level, there are instruments, musical instruments, lying upon a shelf. Or there is the door, which has the bookshelves on it, both doors open and showing wonderful bookshelves, one with an hourglass atop it, a symbol of mortality, transience of life right there, with the symbols of knowledge, very interesting pairing there.

The Duke's famous library, which was in this room, is now part of the Vatican library. This became a papal property later. Here is another; this is a reading stand on the desk. You see it; it is the kind of reading stand that you could put books on four sides, another one leaning against its pedestal down here, a table below that. It's as though we had a small study within the small study. Or this terrace; here it is as though you glance to your right and you see a pair of columns or flat pilasters here, and then a terrace with a squirrel and a still life in a basket, and then across the terrace a view through an arcade onto the landscape around the palace. Of course, everything here in this woodwork is in the natural tones of the wood used; it's not painted, so there's never any question of a complete illusion of reality, only constant astonishment at the artists' skill. But it's still astounding to see the effects that the artists have achieved.

Above the woodwork, the wall is hung with two tiers of portraits of famous learned men from antiquity to the Duke's day. Justus of Ghent, a Flemish artist who was invited to Urbino, painted most of the portraits. In our very first lecture, we saw his portrait of *Petrarch*; here is his blind *Homer*. No particular logic governed the choice of the 28 illustrious men so honored. So as far as we can tell, they are Christian and Hebrew and pagan figures, writers and popes and philosophers. Some of them were friends or patrons of the Duke; some of them are from the distant past. In some, they represented the broad intellectual and historical range of the Duke's interests, and we may assume that they were his personal choice. Here is Solomon, King Solomon, seated, who in the Studiolo is directly beside Moses.

By 1475, Justus of Ghent was apparently in Rome, leaving some of these portraits unfinished. We don't know the circumstances of his departure, but after 1474, Pedro Berruguete, a Spaniard from Castile, was brought in to complete the unfinished work. Berruguete extensively reworked the unfinished paintings, even changing the architectural settings. All the paintings were removed from Urbino in 1632 after the death of the last duke, and today 14 are in the Louvre, and 14 have been reassembled in the Studiolo together with photographs of the rest of them.

No small part of the appeal of the Studiolo is its location within the palace. If he so desired, Federigo da Montefeltro had only to take a few steps from his place of seclusion and he could be standing on his balcony of the twin-towered façade, master of all the tranquil landscape that lay below and stretched to the horizon, and beyond the horizon lay the wider world in which he led his army in the service of other rulers. Once again, we see the interplay between the active and the contemplative life, so much discussed in the Quattrocento and so completely exemplified by Federigo da Montefeltro.

The Cappella del Perdono (a beautiful, small chapel built probably about 1476) means "the chapel of pardon or forgiveness." On the ground floor of the palace, beneath the apartments we've been looking at, this was where sacred relics belonging to the Montefeltro family were kept. I show it to you because it's been tantalizingly suggested that this was the original location of Piero della Francesca's enigmatic *Flagellation*, which we discussed in Lecture 10 and which we see here again. It could not have been this painting, an altarpiece above the altar, but it could have been the altar frontal, mounted on the face of the altar, one step above the floor level.

The dimensions match—the dimensions of the painting and the dimensions of the altar frontal here on the left match—and the perspective would work smoothly to somebody standing on that lower level (not up where the photograph was taken) and looking at this painting whose perspective is otherwise somewhat unusual. It's also fascinating to know that the room parallel to the Sacred Chapel was a room called the Small Temple of the Muses, pagan mythology balancing Christian faith, yet another indication of the reach and balance of the Duke's mind and temperament.

I've mentioned Pedro Berruguete, the artist from Castile. Here is his portrait of *Federigo da Montefeltro and his Son Guidobaldo*, painted about 1477. The exalted air of this double portrait is owed to the fact that it is a state portrait. It's a formal state portrait, and it's still in the Ducal Palace, in the museum now there. This painting consciously reflects the dignity and diplomatic achievements of the Duke. Federigo wears the collar of the Order of the Ermine, which was bestowed by the King of Naples, and he wears the Order of the Garter, which was given to him by the King of England. His dynastic pretensions are embodied in his young son (standing to the left), Guidobaldo, who was born in 1472.

Here is a profile portrait in stone of Guidobaldo, done probably in the 1490s and attributed to Francesco di Giorgio Martini, who was working there as an architect. Guidobaldo succeeded his father in 1482, and in due time—with his refined Duchess Elizabetta Gonzaga—continued the traditions of the court at Urbino. It was then that the famously cultivated conversations stimulated by Elizabetta's salon inspired the young Baldassare Castiglione to write a book. Here he is as a somewhat older figure. The young Castiglione spent many evenings in late-supper entertainment and conversation where, as he put it, "sometimes intriguing questions were asked." Those dinners served as the setting for his book, titled *The Book of the Courtier*, which appeared in 1527, alas long after the early death of Guidobaldo, childless, in 1508. By then, also, Urbino was losing its long independence.

This is also an appropriate place to look for a moment at a painting called *The Ideal City*, whose date and authorship are unknown, although it's surely from the last third of the Quattrocento. It is one of three paintings that are closely related, this one remaining in the palace today—all three presumably coming from the same source.

But we don't know who made it. It has been variously attributed to the architect Laurana, to Piero della Francesca, and to Alberti, Leon Battista Alberti…in other words, you've got three men there who all practiced architecture, including Piero, at some time, and who would seem to fit the image here, and others, other people, have been advanced as possible artists of this really striking painting.

Regardless, this essay in perfection is believed by most people to have originated here in Urbino, in this circle of cultured idealists who were also men and women of the world. It resembles a strikingly rational stage set, to be looked at, but its mysterious vacantness has also caused some "intriguing questions" to be asked.

Lecture Twenty-Six
Andrea Mantegna in Padua and Mantua

Scope:

This lecture takes us to Padua and Mantua. The expulsion of the Medici from Florence in 1494, followed by the turmoil surrounding the charismatic preacher/reformer Savonarola, resulted in a displacement of artistic development to other cities. Rome drew great artists for specific papal commissions, as we have seen, but no Roman school of artists emerged from their activity. Cities in the north of Italy had become increasingly important, innovative centers of art. Andrea Mantegna (c. 1430/31–1506) was born near Padua and apprenticed there until 1448. The strongest influence on him was Donatello, then at work in Sant'Antonio. The great bronze reliefs on the high altar, with their compelling illusion of pictorial space, inspired Mantegna to master perspective and foreshortening. He also developed a lifelong passion for classical antiquity, aided by continuous archeological discoveries on the Venetian mainland. Mantegna's great Paduan achievement was the frescoes in the Ovetari Chapel in the Eremitani Church, almost entirely destroyed by bombs in 1944. His *San Zeno Altarpiece* in Verona combines the monumentality and spatial conquest of the frescoes with prominent ornamental swags already part of the Paduan tradition.

In 1460, Mantegna moved to Mantua, where he would remain for the rest of his life as court painter to the Gonzaga family. His most famous work there is the *trompe l'oeil* fresco decoration of the *Camera degli Sposi* (*Room of the Bride and Groom*) in the ducal palace. When finished in 1474, it had no equal in the field of illusionistic architectural painting. Giovanni Santi, Raphael's father, reported that the frescoes made the visiting "Duke of Urbino stop in stupefaction." They remained a powerful influence on artists for centuries. Mantegna's startling foreshortening of *The Dead Christ* has many echoes in later paintings. Late in the century, the remarkable Isabella d'Este (wife of Francesco Gonzaga) commissioned Mantegna, among others, for paintings to adorn her *studiolo*, which housed her collection of precious objects.

Outline

I. Andrea Mantegna (c. 1430/31–1506) is one of the most individualistic artists of the late Quattrocento. The innovations of the Florentine Renaissance affected him strongly, but so did the qualities of color and stylization of the Venetian and Byzantine art amidst which he grew up. He was an avid archeologist, and his active involvement with the large numbers of Roman remains, architectural and sculptural, that were being unearthed in northern Italy accounts in great part for the notably tactile surfaces of everything he painted.

II. Trained in Padua, Mantegna naturally adopted certain elements of the established Paduan style, including the device of decorative swags or garlands of fruit and flowers. But the most powerful influence on his art was the work of Donatello (whom he may even have known) in Sant'Antonio, which was drawing to a close in 1453 at just the moment when Mantegna, whose apprenticeship in Padua had begun around 1440 and concluded by 1448, inherited his first great commission.

A. He had been part of a team of young painters assisting the Venetian artists Antonio Vivarini and Giovanni d'Alemagna and the Paduan Niccolò Pizzolo in the decoration of the Ovetari Chapel in the Church of the Eremitani in Padua. The older painters died or withdrew from the project, as did some of the younger ones, and Mantegna found himself entrusted with the rest of the fresco cycle (1454–1457).

   1. The remaining subjects were four scenes from the life of Saint James, culminating in his execution. They reflect the artist's close study of Donatello's reliefs on the Santo High Altar and the brilliant perspective schemes they exhibit.

   2. *Saint James Led to Execution* is remarkable for its command of foreshortening and perspective, as well as its archeologically convincing setting of a Roman arch decorated with sculptural reliefs.

a. Because the bottom of the fresco was slightly above eye level, Mantegna paints the figures as seen from that viewpoint. The principal figures of the saint, the soldier, and the cripple are placed at the front edge of the scene where they can be viewed whole, while other figures further back are cropped below the ankles as the receding space seems to tilt downward.

b. A command of perspective does not mean that the perspective system is consistent. On the contrary, artistic command or control of perspective means mediating between the desire for illusionistic re-creation of reality and the demands of the reality of the painted surface. The architecture in this fresco should also be drawn with lines that converge as the structures rise, but this would create the impression that the buildings were tipping into the space and severely compromise the visual stability of the chapel. Thus, Mantegna compromised a system for the sake of pictorial cohesion.

c. That the image we must study is an old black-and-white photograph is the consequence of the disastrous accidental bombing of the church by a U.S. warplane in 1944, which destroyed the Ovetari Chapel. A valiant attempt was made to reconstruct the frescoes from the flakes of painted plaster buried in the debris. It could have been worse, art historically, because the Arena Chapel, with Giotto's masterpiece, stands only a few hundred yards beyond the Eremitani.

B. While engaged on the Eremitani frescoes, Mantegna received a major commission for an altarpiece. It was for the high altar of the imposing Romanesque church of San Zeno, in nearby Verona, whose abbot was a member of the aristocratic Correr family of Venice. This vast basilica terminates in the east with a raised sanctuary above the crypt, creating a prominent stage for the painting.

1. The *San Zeno Altarpiece*, finished in 1459, appears at first glance to be a conventional triptych. But closer examination reveals the boldness of Mantegna's invention. The sumptuous classical frame was conceived as a sort of real portico for the unified painted space behind it, a courtyard defined by stone pillars carrying an architrave, beyond which crystalline clouds in a blue sky are seen. The space is inhabited by the *Enthroned Madonna and Child*, with child angels, flanked by four saints on each side. It is a major example of the *sacra conversazione* type, of which we have seen earlier examples by Fra Filippo Lippi and Domenico Veneziano.

2. The three *predella* panels are unusually large and may have been directly inspired by Donatello's large reliefs on the High Altar of the Santo in Padua. Two of them have been separated from the altarpiece and are in museums but have been replaced by copies.

   a. One is in the Louvre: the *Crucifixion*, which was the center panel. It is bold in color, precise in drawing, and spatially expansive. The body of Christ is modeled like sculpture; because the top of the cross nearly touches the frame, the crucified figure isolated against the sky presses dramatically toward us.

   b. One of the *predella* panels showed Christ on the Mount of Olives with the apostles sleeping below. Probably just afterward, Mantegna painted a slightly smaller independent version of the subject. Now in London (National Gallery), *The Agony in the Garden* is a powerfully expressive work. It features an extensive landscape, but one dominated by rocks. The apostles are stretched in sleep on the barren ground; Christ kneels in prayer on a rocky mount with an altar-like rock table in front of him. Above the background city (Jerusalem), two conical mountains rise. In the middle distance, Judas leads the soldiers to their quarry. All of this unyielding stone underlies the implacable progress of the narrative of Christ's Passion.

C. Mantegna moved from Padua to Mantua in 1460, at the invitation of Ludovico Gonzaga. The city, unattractively situated in a swampy plain near three lakes, had always had to import its artists, but the Gonzaga family had cultural pretensions and importuned many talented painters, architects, composers, and writers to grace their court (and Mantua had been the poet Virgil's birthplace).

1. In his first decade at the Mantuan court, Mantegna painted portraits, small paintings, some frescoes for a chapel, tapestry designs, and other decorative work typical for a court artist. He also made his first trips to Florence (where he saw Gozzoli's chapel in the Medici Palace) and to Pisa, apparently in study preparation for the decoration of a room in the ducal palace, the *Camera degli Sposi*.

2. The *Dead Christ*, a powerful painting, is undocumented and there is no consensus on its date. It has been dated as early as 1466–1467 and as late as 1500, because the painting was in the artist's possession at his death in 1506. We are using a recent dating of c. 1470–1474.

3. Many artists retain their work for personal reasons; that alone is not enough reason to date this painting late. On the other hand, the softer, gentler modeling suggests a stylistic change that is apparent in the frescoes in the ducal palace in Mantua. The question is well worth considering, because it directly affects our understanding of Mantegna's stylistic development.

4. It has been correctly observed that the two mourning heads at the left are unconvincing: They are crowded into the space, their faces are too harshly linear in comparison with the figure of Christ, and they distract from rather than enhance the effect. They may well have been added posthumously. Viewers may judge for themselves by blocking the figures out with a hand.

III. One project above all signifies the achievement of Mantegna during his Mantua years: the fresco decoration of the so-called *Camera degli Sposi* (*Room of the Bride and Groom*), probably begun in 1471 and completed in 1474. This room is one of the triumphs of Renaissance painted ensembles, charming and dignified by turn, perfect in scale, compelling in its many portraits, and representing a new level of achievement in *trompe l'oeil* effects and spatial illusionism.

A. The name by which we know the room was given by a 17th-century writer, probably on the basis of the large inscription over a doorway trumpeting the names of Ludovico and his wife, Barbara. By contemporaries, it was known simply as the *camera picta*—"painted room"—and it was used for banquets and entertainments.

B. There are two principal scenes on adjacent walls. The larger is the extraordinary group portrait of the family of Ludovico III Gonzaga, in which the artist incorporates the large fireplace on that wall as a sort of podium on which the duke and duchess sit, surrounded by their attendants, while others mount a staircase or stand on the mantle!

C. The smaller scene depicts the meeting of Ludovico and his son, Cardinal Francesco Gonzaga, on a shallow terrace opening onto an extensive landscape quite different from the marshes of Mantua. It has fertile fields near in and hills climbing behind, with a walled city and much classical architecture and sculpture.

D. In the center of the vault is a painted oculus, an illusionistic opening to the sky surrounded by a parapet, over which adult women peer at us while *amoretti* both look over and stand in front of the parapet, painted in the sharpest foreshortening. This foreshortening, called *di sotto in su* ("from below up"), is the earliest important Renaissance example of extreme illusionism on a ceiling, and though modest in size, it became the prototype and inspiration for three centuries of such decoration.

IV. At court, other members of the Gonzaga family employed Mantegna during his long years there. The Marquis Francesco Gonzaga became the husband of Isabella d'Este. A learned and art-loving woman, she commissioned Mantegna for two paintings to decorate her *studiolo* cum treasury (she called it a *grotta*, or "cave") in the Castle of Saint George, where she kept the rarities she amassed. One, *Pallas Athena Expelling the Vices from the Garden of Virtue* (c. 1500–1502), is an allegory remarkably stressing the role of a woman—a goddess, but probably a surrogate for the duchess—in protecting the realm of virtue in her highly cultured domain.

V. Mantegna's late style is sometimes criticized for dryness, but the unflinching intensity of *Christ as the Suffering Redeemer* (c. 1495–1500) is the epitome of a late masterpiece—all superfluous elements are eliminated. There is, nonetheless, a backward-looking character that is undeniable. The painting has the overawing immediacy of a Byzantine mosaic of the Pantocrator. It is not known for whom the painting was made, but one wonders if the fact that Mantua possessed a famous relic that attracted many pilgrims—a drop of Christ's blood saved by Longinus, the centurion at the Crucifixion—influenced the presentation of the subject. Granted, the wounds of Christ are notably bloodless, but they are starkly presented.

Works Discussed:

Andrea Mantegna:

Saint James Led to Execution, c. 1455, destroyed, Ovetari Chapel, Church of the Eremitani, Padua.

Saint Zeno Altarpiece, 1456–1459, Church of Saint Zeno, Verona.

Crucifixion, predella from the *Saint Zeno Altarpiece*, 1456–1459, Musée du Louvre, Paris.

Christ on the Mount of Olives (The Agony in the Garden), c. 1460, National Gallery, London.

Dead Christ, c. 1470–1474, Pinacoteca di Brera, Milan.

Camera degli Sposi, c. 1470–1474, Palazzo Ducale, Mantua Pallas.

Pallas Athena Expelling the Vices from the Garden of Virtue, c. 1500–1502, Musée du Louvre, Paris.

Christ as the Suffering Redeemer, 1495–1500, Statens Museum for Kunst, Copenhagen.

Essential Reading:

Adams, chapter 12.

Hartt, chapter 15.

Supplementary Reading:

Camesaca, Ettore. *Mantegna*. New York: Scala/Riverside, 1992.

Questions to Consider:

1. What are the principal stylistic characteristics of the early paintings of Andrea Mantegna?

2. Can you describe Mantegna's innovations in the *Camera degli Sposi* in the ducal palace in Mantua?

Lecture Twenty-Six—Transcript
Andrea Mantegna in Padua and Mantua

During the flowering of Urbino, the cities of northern Italy had matured as artistic centers, and this lecture takes us to Padua and Mantua. The expulsion of the Medici from Florence in 1494, followed by the turmoil surrounding the charismatic preacher/reformer Savonarola, resulted in some displacement of artistic development to other cities. Rome drew great artists for specific great papal commissions, as we've seen, but no Roman school of artists emerged from their activity. Cities in the north of Italy had become increasingly important, innovative centers of art.

Andrea Mantegna, who was born about 1430/31 and lived until 1506, is one of the most individualistic artists of the late Quattrocento. He was born near Padua and apprenticed there until 1448. Naturally, he adopted certain elements of the established Paduan style, including, for instance, the device of decorative swags or garlands of fruit and flowers. The distinctive qualities of color and stylization of Venetian and Byzantine art amidst which he grew up affected him strongly, but so too did the innovations of the Florentine Renaissance. The strongest influence upon him was probably that of Donatello, then at work in Padua in Sant'Antonio. The great bronze reliefs on the high altar, which we have seen, with their compelling illusion of pictorial space, inspired Mantegna to master perspective and foreshortening. He was an avid archaeologist with a lifelong passion for classical antiquity, a passion that must have been stimulated by the scholars of Padua's already famous university, where classical antiquity had long been studied.

Mantegna's active involvement with the large numbers of Roman remains, architectural and sculptural, that were being unearthed in northern Italy accounts to a considerable degree for the notably tactile surfaces of everything that he painted. Since Mantegna's apprenticeship in Padua lasted from about 1440 until 1448, he may well have known Donatello, whose decade working in and near the shrine of Sant'Antonio was drawing to a close in 1453. That was at just the moment when Mantegna received his first great commission.

He had been part of a team of young painters assisting the Venetian artists Antonio Vivarini and Giovanni d'Alemagna and the Paduan artist Niccolò Pizzolo (not a name to conjure with) in the decoration of an important chapel, the Ovetari Chapel in the Church of the Eremitani in Padua. Since the name of the church is unusual it may interest you to know that *eremitani* means "hermits," but that here it refers to an order of Augustinian friars, originally a congregation of hermits, who by the Renaissance had forsaken the contemplative life for the active life, although they remained rather austere. Many of the painters working on the Ovetari Chapel decoration had died or withdrawn from the project, and suddenly Mantegna found himself entrusted to finish the rest of the fresco cycle, which he did between 1454 and 1457.

The principal remaining subjects, there had been work finished of course, but the principal remaining subjects were four scenes from the life of St. James, culminating in the execution of St. James. In their brilliant use of the perspective, these frescoes reflect the artist's close study of Donatello's reliefs on the Santo High Altar. The image you're looking at, *St. James Led to Execution*, depicts a specific moment as the saint is led to the place where he will be decapitated. According to *The Golden Legend*, along the road there lay a paralyzed man who called out to James, begging him to cure him. James said to him, "In the name of Jesus Christ, for whose faith I am led to execution, stand up cured and bless your creator." The man stood up and blessed the Lord.

Perhaps Mantegna imagined that the man had in fact been lying by the road and had already begun to rise. I suggest it because the Roman soldier appears to raise his hand in surprise. Here's the paralyzed man below, the formerly paralyzed man, or perhaps the soldier is merely objecting to James's intervention. St. James stands here. In any case, his hand, that of the soldier, is an effective foil or counterpart to that of James. This is very nice, this play of open palms across that empty space above the head of the man to be cured. The composition is remarkable for its command of foreshortening and perspective, as well as for its archeologically convincing Roman arches decorated with sculptural reliefs. The saint and the other figures are also sculptural, the lines and planes of their faces carved by the brush, as it were; a close-up of the face of St. James looks virtually like a painted sculpture.

Because the bottom of the fresco was slightly above eye level if you were standing in the chapel, the bottom of the fresco was slightly above eye level, Mantegna painted the figures as seen from that viewpoint. The principal figures of the saint, the soldier, and the cripple are placed at the front edge of the scene, where they can be viewed whole, entire, while other figures placed further back are cropped below the ankles—here, for instance, in the center, as the receding space seems to tilt downwards, and downwards and backwards. A command of perspective, however, does not mean that the perspective system is consistent. On the contrary, artistic command or control of perspective means mediating between the desire for illusionistic recreation of reality, and the demands of the reality of the flat, painted surface.

For example, here the architecture in this fresco should also be drawn with lines that converge as the structures rise. The triumphal arch, the line should be converging, but that would create the impression that the buildings were tipping into the space and severely compromise the visual stability of the wall surface, indeed of the whole chapel. So, Mantegna, as Masaccio and others had done before him, compromised a system for the sake of pictorial cohesion.

That the image we have been studying is, as you've of course noticed, an old black and white photograph is the consequence of the disastrous accidental bombing of the church by a U.S. warplane in 1944, which destroyed the Ovetari Chapel, together with most of the east end of the church. A valiant attempt was made to reconstruct the frescoes from the flakes of painted plaster buried in the debris. One earlier fresco had been removed at an earlier time because of its bad condition and wasn't in the church anymore, and so it, in an already poor condition, survived the bombing. Mantegna's great Paduan achievement was this fresco cycle in the Eremitani, and old photos show us what we lost. The result of the bombing could have been worse, art historically speaking, since the Arena Chapel with Giotto's masterpiece stands only a few hundred yards beyond the Eremitani.

While engaged on the Eremitani frescoes, Mantegna received a major commission for an altarpiece. It was for the high altar of the imposing Romanesque church of San Zeno, in nearby Verona, whose abbott was a member of the aristocratic Correr family of Venice. This vast basilica terminates in the east with a raised sanctuary above the crypt, creating a prominent stage for the painting. The *San Zeno Altarpiece*, finished in 1459, appears at first glance to be a conventional triptych, as you see. But the sumptuous classical frame was conceived as a sort of real portico, an entrance opening into the unified painted space behind it, where there is a courtyard defined by stone pillars carrying an architrave here, the pillars here, the architrave with carved figures upon it, beyond which if you look through the pillars behind, you can see the sky, white crystalline clouds floating in a blue sky beyond.

The space, this courtyard that he has painted behind the real columns of the altarpiece, is inhabited by the *Enthroned Madonna and Child* in the center, together with the child-angel musicians, very charming figures around her, and flanked on either side in their own columned space, but again part of a continuous space behind those columns of the altarpiece. You have four saints on each side, four on the left and four on the right, and then those figures are arranged intelligently in the space. Prominent ornamental swags, I mentioned them, the Paduan idea or decorative device of hanging swags of flowers and fruits, you see them here in the foreground, painted as though hanging across from the very edge of the room. These were already part of the Paduan tradition; you find them constantly in Paduan art, and they're painted here at the top of the painting.

The monumentality and the spatial illusion of the Eremitani frescoes is also found here. Let me show you a detail with the central section. A striking foreshortening of the marbled pavement in these frescoes, it's a very shallow floor space, the Madonna and Child monumentally seated and raised above the ground level. Here you see the clouds in the sky and even a touch of landscape better in the distance behind, and you also see behind the head of the Madonna, just above the head of the Madonna, the frieze, which has a gilded background and seems to be a sculptured frieze with putti on it. This is a wonderful change of different kinds of reality.

You have real columns here in the foreground in this detail, the real columns of the altarpiece itself. Behind that, you have painted columns that seem to extend from them. The painted swags seem to be very real, right in front of your eye and almost part of the altar frame itself, and then the space, the frieze, behind that, and the Madonna and angels within that, and then the space beyond into the landscape. It's a very complex and very skillful arrangement spatially. On the left-hand side, you have equally successful perspective recession. Here you see clearly the tiles, but your viewpoint is so low, you see it's virtually down at knee level or below here, just above their feet, so we're just seeing the tops of those tiles, and yet he's able to lay them out according to the rules of perspective.

The color in Mantegna is striking, strong colors, the strong yellow and red of St. Peter in the foreground here. We have St. Peter next to him, St. Paul with his sword, and then we have the figure of John the Evangelist and finally the Bishop in the background is St. Zeno. The skillful arrangements of these saints in perspective recession, the monumentality, sculptural monumentality of the figures, and the striking color all aid in the total strong effect of this piece, which carries the length of the church. It's remarkable what strength it has visually to carry down a huge space. Here's the whole altarpiece again; in fact, this time, you see the front of the altar table and below. This is the altar itself, where the Host would be placed.

I'm going to call your attention in a moment to the three predella panels, the footer panels here below the main scene, but I will point out before turning to them to the fact that if the Host, if the Eucharist, were placed here, the crucifixion would be directly above it, and of course, the Madonna and Child directly above that, again the emphasis on the body of Christ, on the Corpus Christi that we've seen elsewhere. By the way, this altarpiece with its saints gathered around the Madonna in a single coherent space is another example of the Sacred Conversation, the Sacra Conversazione, type that we have seen before in examples by, among others, Fra Filippo Lippi and Domenico Veneziano.

The three predella panels are unusually large. They're about three feet wide, and they may have been directly inspired by Donatello's only slightly larger reliefs on the High Altar of the Santo in Padua. Two of these predella panels have been separated from the altarpiece and are in museums, but have been replaced in the church by copies, so you have all three, but only one of them is original. The one I'm going to show you now is in fact today in the Louvre, so what you see on the altar is a copy, and that is the *Crucifixion*. It was the center panel, and it is wonderfully bold in color, very precise in drawing, and spatially expansive, both in terms of a distant landscape, with these wonderful rocky mountains above, and the sky. Again, it becomes very typical for Mantegna; his clouds have a sculptural quality to them as well. As brilliant and airy as the sky is, it is also a very structural sky.

The body of Christ is modeled like a piece of sculpture, just to take one figure in the painting. Since the top of the cross, where the plaque with I-N-R-I, the Jesus of Nazareth King of the Jews, which was mockingly placed there, where that plaque is, it nearly touches the top of the frame. It gives the effect that the crucified figure is not only isolated against the sky, but is pressed dramatically close to us. You see at the base of the cross, we see how far back it sits from the front of the painting, but there is something contradictory that happens in perspective when you run this right up to the top. Associated with the edge of the painting, with the frame, it pulls it forward visually; that together with the sculptural quality of the body makes it very immediate. A very great Venetian painter, Tintoretto, would perhaps, borrowing from this, perhaps reinventing it, do something very similar in a work of his later on.

Another of the predella panels in the *San Zeno Altarpiece* showed Christ on the Mount of Olives with the Apostles sleeping below. Just after he did that altarpiece, he painted a slightly smaller independent version of the subject, so what I'm showing you now is not from the altarpiece, but a separate related piece that he did. *Christ on the Mount of Olives (The Agony in the Garden)*, as it is often called, a painting of about 1460, in London in the National Gallery, is a powerfully expressive work. This event, which I think we haven't seen before, followed the Last Supper. Jesus, accompanied by Peter, John the Evangelist, and John's brother James, went to the garden of Gethsemane at the Mount of Olives. Gethsemane signifies "oil press" in Hebrew; the garden was on the east side of Jerusalem.

Asking them to wait and watch for him—asking his Apostles to wait and watch—he drew a little apart from them to pray for release from the coming events. Agony, as we use it in this title in English, is probably poorly chosen because it's easily misunderstood. It comes from the Greek word *agon* meaning "contest." When we say we made an agonizing choice, that's closer to the meaning here because it signifies the struggle between the human nature of Jesus, which feared suffering, and the divine nature that accepted it, so that's the sense in which it's the agony in the garden. It's expressed in the words "Father, if Thou be willing, remove this cup from me, nevertheless not my will but Thine be done."

Mantegna's painting features an extensive landscape, but one dominated by rocks. The Apostles, all too fallible in their human nature, have fallen asleep, stretched out in sleep on the barren ground. Christ kneels in prayer on a rocky platform in front of him with a kind of buildup of rocks to the left of him, which looks almost like an altar or an altar table. Above the background city, which is understood to be Jerusalem, two conical mountains rise. In the middle distance, we have a procession of soldiers led by Judas to find their quarry. All of this unyielding stone underlies the implacable progress of the narrative of Christ's Passion.

Mantua is not far from Padua, and it was there that Mantegna moved in 1460, at the invitation of Ludovico Gonzaga. This map of the late 16th century gives you a pretty good idea of the city's layout, rather unattractively situated in a swampy plain near three lakes, easy to defend, however, but not pleasant to live in necessarily. They always had, the court at Mantua, always had to import their artists, but the Gonzaga family had cultural pretensions, and they importuned many talented painters, architects, composers, and writers to grace their court (and Mantua in ancient times had been the birthplace of the Roman poet, Virgil). Mantegna would remain in Mantua for the rest of his life, that's 46 years, as court painter to the Gonzaga family. In his first decade at the Mantuan court, Mantegna painted portraits, small paintings, some frescoes for a chapel, tapestry designs and decorative work of that sort that was quite typical for a court artist.

I want to show you a famous and startling painting, *The Dead Christ*, now in the Brera. *The Dead Christ* is powerful and undocumented in a sense; there's no consensus on its date. It's been dated as early as 1466 and as late as 1500, the latter because it was in his possession when Mantegna died in 1506, but since many artists have retained their work for personal reasons, I don't think that's enough reason to date it late. On the other hand, the rather softer, gentler modeling of the figure suggests a stylistic change that is apparent in the frescoes in the Ducal Palace in Mantua, which we will shortly see. We haven't talked too much about chronology and dating problems, but the question is well worth considering since it directly affects our understanding of Mantegna's stylistic development. Here I'm using a recent dating, which has been suggested of dating about 1470-74.

By the way, it's been correctly observed that the two mourning heads, the two heads that push in at the left, are unconvincing: they're crowded into the space; their faces are too harshly linear in comparison with the figure of Christ; they distract rather than enhance. They distract from the effect of the painting. I think they may well have been added posthumously. You can judge for yourself; block them out with your hand and see if you think that improves the effect of the painting. But the starling foreshortening of this painting, which forces us into a kneeling position at the feet of the dead Christ, is emotionally potent, and it was an invention that was borrowed by later artists looking for a similar effect.

During the 1460s, Mantegna also made his first trips to Florence, where he saw Bennozo Gozzoli's chapel of the Medici Palace, and to Pisa, and apparently these trips were done as study in preparation for the decoration of a room in the Ducal Palace, the room we know as the Camera degli Sposi—the Room of the Bride and Groom is the only translation. This is Mantegna's most famous work in Mantua. It is a *trompe l'oeil* fresco—an illusionistic decoration in the wing of the Ducal Palace, and when it was finished, it had no equal in the field of illusionistic painting in an architectural setting. Giovanni Santi, Raphael's father, reported that the frescoes made the visiting "Duke of Urbino stop in stupefaction," and they remained a powerful influence on artists for centuries after that.

Probably begun in 1471 and completed in 1474, this room is one of the triumphs of Renaissance painted ensembles. It's charming, it's dignified, it's perfect in scale, it's compelling in the many portraits of the court that are included in it, and it represented a new level of achievement in trompe l'oeil effects and spatial illusionism. The name—the Camera degli Sposi, the Room of the Bride and Groom—was given only by a 17th-century writer, probably on his misunderstanding of a large inscription over the doorway, which trumpets the names of Ludovico and his wife, Barbara. The room was not in honor of their wedding, as he may have thought. In any event, by contemporaries, it was known simply as the "Camera picta"—painted room—and it was used by the court for banquets and entertainments.

As you look at it, and these are the two basic painted walls, two principal scenes on adjacent walls, the larger is the one to the right, the extraordinary group portrait of the family of Ludovico III Gonzaga, in which the artist incorporates the large fireplace on that wall as a sort of podium upon which the Duke and Duchess sit, surrounded by their attendants and family, while others mount a staircase to join them on top of the mantelpiece, and I'll show you this in a moment, but let me show you the left-hand side here for just a moment. We'll be looking later at this fresco, which is the Cardinal Francesco Gonzaga returning home on the left-hand side, and some scenes that are essentially related to the hunt in the countryside, beautiful landscape area.

I should point out that Duke Ludovico, the Duchess (who was a Brandenburg by the way, Barbara Brandenburg), their children, the dwarf, etc., are to be found here. Here's the Duchess seated, the Duke talking to an advisor at this point, three of the Duchess's children—two young and the older, much older, boy standing behind a dwarf right here. This court, like many European courts, had dwarves, and here is a small woman at this point, the conjunction of real and painted architecture. This young man stands in front of an illusionistic pilaster. This is painted, and yet this corbel, which comes down from the vault, this is real architecture, so real architecture comes down to here, and is continued in fictive architecture, in front of which obviously this illusionistic young man stands. Curtains are pulled back, and a curtain rod is used all the way across to enhance that illusionistic effect, and on the right-hand side, people ascend the steps and are welcomed into the courtyard.

There is a certain similarity in noble dignity to the Piero della Francesca scenes of Solomon and Sheba at Arezzo, which Mantegna surely knew, but his aristocrats, Mantegna's aristocrats, are more approachable, more relaxed as befits real people in their own palace. Here is the arrival of the Cardinal Francesco Gonzaga. The smaller fresco depicts the meeting of Ludovico on the left now standing here, who we've just seen seated, and he's meeting his son Cardinal Francesco, who was elevated to that position in 1461 by Pope Pius II. They're on a shallow terrace that opens onto an extensive landscape quite different from the marshes of Mantua. It has fertile fields near in, close to us, and hills climbing behind, with a walled city and much classical sculpture and architecture. Cardinal Francesco had returned from Rome to visit Mantua in 1471 for the groundbreaking of the great Basilica of San Andrea designed by Alberti for the city of Mantua, and this scene may allude to that occasion.

The architecture and the landscape make numerous allusions to the city of Rome, and in the center of the vault of this room is a painted oculus, an illusionistic opening to the sky, surrounded by a parapet over which adult women peer at us, while amoretti both look over and stand in front of the parapet, painted in the sharpest possible foreshortening. This foreshortening—called *di sotto in su*, meaning "from below up" or "below upwards"—is the earliest important Renaissance example of extreme illusionism on a ceiling painting, and though modest in size, it became the prototype and inspiration for three centuries of such decoration. There is at least one thing you ought not to miss. There is a board or pole across this part of the open oculus and a huge, potted plant I suppose, a great tub here is balanced on that, giving a rather tentative feeling. Should the pole be removed, the plant will come tumbling into our space, but all of this, of course, is simply flat—one flat, painted surface.

Mantegna naturally painted individual works—many of them for specific patrons, and at the Mantuan court, other members of the Gonzaga family employed him during his long years there. Late in the century, the remarkable Isabella d'Este, wife of Francesco

Gonzaga, commissioned Mantegna, among others, for paintings to adorn her studiolo, which housed her collection of precious objects, and was therefore different from the studiolo in Urbino, which was principally a library and place of study. In that room is this (or was this) painting (it is now in the Louvre)—this painting by Mantegna. It is *Pallas Expelling the Vices from the Garden of Virtue*, and that was painted around 1499-1502. Isabella d'Este was a learned woman and an art-loving woman, and she commissioned Mantegna for two paintings for this room. She didn't call this a studiolo; she called it a *grotta*, a "cave." This was in the Castle of St. George, near the main castle, where she kept her collection.

One of these paintings, this one, *Pallas Expelling the Vices from the Garden of Virtue*, is an unusual allegory because it stresses the role of a woman in protecting the realm of virtue in her highly cultivated domain. To be sure, she's a goddess, but surely Pallas Athena is intended as a surrogate for the Duchess in this case. Lust stands just to the right of center, this mostly nude female, on the back of a centaur, and she seems heedless of the charge of Athena far left and her female attendants, who are going to expel Lust and all of the other vices, which are spread off to the right. Allegories, whether they're by Botticelli or by Mantegna, can be troublesome for modern taste, but they are important barometers of the intellectual climates of a particular court or culture, and fortunately, very fortunately, they have their beauties beyond their symbolic complexities.

Mantegna's late style is sometimes criticized for dryness, but the unflinching intensity of this *Christ Seated on a Sarcophagus supported by Two Angels* (painted in the 1490s, I would think as late as 1500) is the epitome of a late masterpiece—all superfluous elements are eliminated. There is, nonetheless, in this painting a backward-looking character; I think that's undeniable. The painting has, for instance, the awesome immediacy of a Byzantine mosaic of the *Pantocrator*, the figure of Christ in heaven ruling earth. It's not known for whom this painting was made; it's now in Copenhagen, but one wonders if the fact that Mantua possessed a famous relic that attracted many pilgrims—a drop of Christ's blood that had been saved by Longinus, the centurion, at the Crucifixion—influenced the presentation of the subject. Perhaps, I grant you that the wounds of Christ are notably bloodless, but they're certainly starkly presented to our view. A beautiful landscape extends behind it, rocky in Mantegna manner, but very expressive.

Andrea Mantegna is not quite like any other artist in the Renaissance, at least I think he's not. His special blend of intellect, archaeology, command of the vocabulary of perspective, and his narrative and symbolic intensity are generally speaking easily recognizable. He's not easily forgotten, and his influence was very long lasting.

Lecture Twenty-Seven
Venice—Byzantine, Gothic, and Renaissance

Scope:

Venetian art is inseparable from the city that inspired it, to a degree unparalleled elsewhere. Established on more than 100 islands in the vast Adriatic lagoon as a refuge from barbarian invasions in the 5th and 6th centuries, Venice elected its first *doge* (duke) near the end of the 8th century. She received the remains of Saint Mark in 829 (and, with them, religious prestige second only to Rome) and, by the 11th century, had become one of the greatest maritime trading powers in Europe. Although its mainland holdings in Dalmatia and Greece and on the nearby *terra firma* of the Italian peninsula were in constant dispute, Venice was one of the few states in Europe that was essentially free from conquest. The city as we still know it remained independent, and admired for its independence, for a millennium, until it was ended (in the name of liberty) by Napoleon Bonaparte.

At the core of the city are the ducal palace and the Basilica of San Marco, its patron saint. The huge, famous square in front of San Marco focuses on the Byzantine church, which is astonishing in its incrustation of marble slabs, columns, capitals, and sculpture, inside and out, much of it brought back from Constantinople after the Venetian sack of that great capital in 1204 during the Fourth Crusade. Chief among those treasures were the famous *Bronze Horses* and the enamel plaques for the *Pala d'Oro* (*"Golden Altarpiece"*), but the church itself was a marvel of Byzantine architecture and craftsmanship, with glowing mosaic decorations of surpassing beauty. The ducal palace was built in the European Gothic style; thus, the two buildings aptly represented Venice's place between those two worlds, between east and west.

From the beginning, Venetian painting was preoccupied with light, the light of glowing mosaics and the light of the sky reflected from the water on which the city seemed to float. The flashing gold grounds of late-medieval painting lasted longer in Venice than elsewhere in Italy, well past the mid-15th century. When the Renaissance came, it was at first tentative, and no great civic building in the Renaissance style arrived until the middle of the 16th century, in the form of Sansovino's Library. Painting, however, had a phenomenal development, and in the next seven lectures, we will introduce the most famous among the renowned artists of Renaissance Venice.

Outline

I. To understand Venetian art, one must understand the city that inspired it. This may be said of other cities and their art, but nowhere is it more essential than here.

    A. One must comprehend the improbable physical location of the city and how it came to be built.

        1. The barbarian invasions of the Goths and Huns in the 5th century drove inhabitants of northern Italy to seek refuge on small islands in the vast Adriatic lagoon. In the mid-6th century, the Lombard invasion caused a larger number of refugees to join them, and they fell under the protection of the eastern emperor in Constantinople.

        2. In the late 8th century, these settlers rebelled, prompted by the iconoclastic edict of Emperor Leo III, and sided with the pope. The first *doge* (the Venetian form of "duke") was elected soon after, initiating the 1,000-year history of the Venetian Republic.

        3. By the 11th century, Venice was a maritime trading power and had mainland possessions, but it was the security of its stronghold on the lagoon that guaranteed its independence.

        4. The lagoon can really only be grasped by flying over it or boating through it, when its extent and the challenge it presented to its settlers can be fully appreciated.

    B. The building of the city was the engineering work of centuries and involved driving thousands of huge pilings into the bottom of the lagoon and building the city on that foundation.

        1. In the process, more than 100 islands were connected to make a contiguous whole, while the countless canals that had been formed were spanned with hundreds of bridges.

        2. The Grand Canal is a broad serpentine waterway dividing the city that gives Venice its distinctive appearance on a map.

3. It was bridged at only one spot, approximately the midpoint, by the famous Rialto Bridge, which marked the commercial heart of this famous trading city.

4. As a center of trade uniting the eastern and western Mediterranean and northern and southern Europe, Venice became one of the wealthiest cities in the world. Its extensive maritime trade routes indicate the scope of its activity.

II. The civic and religious center of the city is at the mouth of the Grand Canal, where it opens into the Basin of San Marco.

A. From the basin or from the island of San Giorgio, the view of this administrative core of Venice is among the most famous cityscapes in the world. To the right, the gothic Doge's Palace is dominant; to the left, separated by the Piazzetta ("little piazza") is the library, and to the left of that is the mint. Behind these is the towering Campanile, and behind the Doge's Palace may be glimpsed the principal dome of the Basilica of San Marco.

B. The Basilica of San Marco, one of the greatest late-Byzantine churches, is fronted by the enormous Piazza San Marco, one of the most imposing public squares in Europe.

1. The Piazza San Marco did not have the huge, regularized form it has now until the 19th century, when some buildings, including a church, were demolished and the piazza was completed at the west end. However, it was always the civic center of Venice.

2. The basilica began its existence as the chapel for the Doge's Palace. The first structure was consecrated in 832, built to receive the supposed body of Saint Mark, brought from Alexandria to Venice in 829. Burned in 976 during a popular revolt, the basilica was promptly rebuilt.

a. The third and surviving church was begun in 1063; it was greatly augmented by the plunder brought back from the sack of Constantinople in 1204, during the Fourth Crusade, and after.

b. For more than seven centuries, the façade of the basilica was adorned with the famous gilded *Bronze Horses*, four magnificent Greek sculptures that had probably come from the Hippodrome in Constantinople. (They have been dated anywhere from the 3rd century B.C. to the 3rd century A.D.) In place on the façade by 1250, they were removed once by Napoleon, who vaingloriously took them to Paris, from whence they returned after Waterloo. In the late 20th century, they were permanently removed from the façade to save them from the acid rain and other pollution that assails Venice. Restored, they are now on the gallery inside the basilica.

3. The interior is clothed in sumptuous golden mosaics that, together with the volumes of the five domes and other vaulted spaces, create an effect of unrivaled splendor.

a. The mosaics are from many eras, but the most significant are from the 12th and 13th centuries. The *Creation of the World* (in one of the smaller cupolas in the atrium) displays the scenes in circular bands. Although they are at first difficult to distinguish, the individual scenes, like the stained glass in northern Gothic churches, become legible with practice (which was not necessary for contemporaries, who were familiar with the iconography of the stories).

b. The atrium contains a vast series of Old Testament scenes, originally created in the 13th century. Among them is a scene in which Noah sends a raven and a dove from the ark. The dove, which has not yet taken flight, will find that the flood waters have not receded and return. The raven has alit on a floating corpse, which it appears to eat as carrion. The single drowned body floating near the ark is as eloquent as the host of bodies in a nearby mosaic.

4. The plunder from Constantinople is further evidenced by the *Pala d'Oro* ("*Golden Altarpiece*"). It is a *retable*, a large rectangular surface mounted above the back of the altar table. It is encrusted with gold in which are set myriad gems, enamel plaques, and small medallions. The original *Pala* was made to order in Constantinople for Saint Mark's in the early 12th century. A century later, it was enlarged with plunder from the sack of Constantinople.

C. We will have more to say about the significance of the relics of Saint Mark the Evangelist for the Republic of Venice.

    1. A column stands on the Piazzetta near the water with a stone lion, the symbol of the saint, standing guard on its capital.

    2. The Doge's Palace, one of the greatest Gothic buildings in Italy, dominates the waterfront. For Venice, it has an unusually open situation, with two sides easily visible at once.

        a. The Doge's Palace was also the city hall, the seat of the highest magistrates of the republic and the site of the council chambers of the various governing councils.

        b. Earlier structures preceded the existing palace, beginning in 814. Fire destroyed that and a second palace. A 12th-century palace was enlarged in the mid-14th century, then torn down in 1424 to be replaced by an extension that exactly replicated the 14th-century portion. A devastating fire in 1483 required extensive rebuilding, and fires in 1574 and, especially, 1577 gutted major parts of the interior, also destroying many paintings. The palace was rebuilt in the same style each time, resulting in the complete stylistic unity in the largest civic structure in Italy during the Renaissance.

        c. Gracefully proportioned, the three-story structure is as open and airy as the Palazzo Vecchio in Florence is closed and massive. An open arcade is surmounted by an open loggia, and above that, the large expanse of wall is mitigated by pink and white stone in a large lozenge pattern. The elevation reverses the expected sequence of heavy supporting light. The palace seems to float above the piazza and the water.

d. Above the grand balcony on the Piazzetta façade is a sculpture group of Doge Andrea Gritti kneeling before the lion of Saint Mark.

III. Venice is pinned like a butterfly between water and sky, in a constantly changing, flickering light. It is a city whose ties to the Byzantine world filled many buildings with mosaics, in which a million cubes of colored stone and colored or gilt glass glistened with agitated light and color, reflecting the sun or lamps and candles.

   A. The gold ground painting of European Gothic art also flourished in Venice (and lingered longer), and the sheer brilliance of the gold seems magnified, perhaps influenced by the Byzantine models.

   B. Paolo Veneziano, one of the finest Trecento artists in Venice, painted the *Coronation of the Virgin* (c. 1358) for the no-longer extant church of Santa Chiara. The large central panel of the *Coronation* is flanked by eight smaller narrative scenes. The ensemble probably once had a painting of the Crucifixion above the Coronation.

   C. A remarkable amount of gilding is still found in the imposing triptych of the *Madonna Enthroned with the Fathers of the Church*, dated 1446, by Antonio Vivarini and Giovanni d'Alemagna. This painting also has an elaborate Gothic screen behind the figures. This is a quarter century after Masaccio had revolutionized Florentine painting and the "new style" was well established.

   D. In sum, Venetian painting is conservative by Quattrocento standards and would not change until the last third of the century.

IV. The tentative acceptance of the Renaissance style in painting and sculpture was even more remarkable in architecture. No great civic building in the Renaissance style was raised in Venice until Jacopo Sansovino's Library, begun in 1537, after the High Renaissance had been pushed aside in other Italian centers. Surprisingly, it was erected opposite the great Gothic Ducal Palace.

Works Discussed:

Various artists:

Basilica di San Marco and Replicas of *Bronze Horses*, façade, Venice.

Bronze Horses, Museo Marciano, Basilica di San Marco, Venice.

Dome showing the *Creation of the World*, with detail of Noah sending the dove from the ark, 13th century, Basilica di San Marco, Venice.

Pala d'Oro, Basilica di San Marco, Venice Doge's Palace, Venice.

Paolo Veneziano:

Coronation of the Virgin, c. 1358, Accademia, Venice.

Antonio Vivarini and Giovanni d'Alemagna:

Madonna Enthroned with Fathers of the Church, 1446, Accademia, Venice.

Jacopo Sansovino, Biblioteca Marciana, begun 1537, Venice.

Essential Reading:

Adams, chapter 13.

Hartt, chapter 15.

Supplementary Reading:

Hills, Paul. *Venetian Colour: Marble, Mosaic, Painting and Glass, 1250–1550*. New Haven: Yale University Press, 1999.

Howard, Deborah. *The Architectural History of Venice*. New Haven: Yale University Press, 2002.

Steer, John. *Venetian Painting: A Concise History*. London and New York: Thames and Hudson, 1970.

Zuffi, Stefano, ed. *Art in Venice*. New York: Harry N. Abrams, 1999.

Questions to Consider:

1. The spectacular geographical situation of Venice is world famous. How did it directly affect the appearance of Venetian art?

2. What artistic style do you think was dominant in Venice? Why?

Lecture Twenty-Seven—Transcript
Venice—Byzantine, Gothic, and Renaissance

I can't imagine anything more pleasant than introducing you to Venetian art and Venice; on the other hand, it's a complex matter. Venetian art is inseparable from the city that inspired it, to a degree that is unparalleled elsewhere. One must comprehend the improbable physical location of the city and how it came to be built there. The barbarian invasions of the Goths and the Huns in the fifth century drove inhabitants of northern Italy to seek refuge on small islands in the vast Adriatic lagoon. On the map, you see Venice's position at the head of the Adriatic, which I will remind you, was later frequently called the Gulf of Venice, representing its significance.

In the mid-sixth century, the Lombard invasion caused a larger number of refugees to join those who had fled to these islands in the first place, and they fell under the protection of the Eastern Emperor in Constantinople, thus established on more than 100 islands in the vast Adriatic lagoon as a refuge from barbarian invasions in the fifth and sixth centuries. These settlers thrived to some degree, but they were under the control of the Eastern Emperor, and in the late eighth century, they rebelled against the Eastern Empire. The rebellion was prompted by the iconoclastic edict, the famous edict of Emperor Leo III, and they, the residents of the lagoon, sided instead with the Pope in Rome. The first *Doge*, which is the Venetian form of "Duke," the first Doge was elected soon after, near the end of the eighth century, thus initiating the 1,000-year history of the Venetian Republic.

I want to show you a map of the trade routes. You can stare at this complex map for a few moments while I remind you that Venice received the relics, the supposed remains, of the body of St. Mark in the year 829, and with those relics came a Christian prestige, a prestige in the Christian world second only to Rome, where the body of St. Peter rested. By the 11th century, Venice had become one of the greatest maritime trading powers in Europe. Although its mainland holdings in Dalmatia on the other side of the Adriatic and in Greece and on the nearby terra firma of the Italian peninsula were in constant dispute, Venice was one of the few states in Europe that was essentially free from conquest. The city as we still know it remained independent, and was admired for its independence, for a millennium, until that independence was ended (in the name of liberty) by Napoleon Bonaparte.

As a center of trade, uniting the eastern and western Mediterranean and northern and southern Europe, Venice became one of the wealthiest cities in the world. This map showing extensive maritime trade routes indicates the scope of its activity. Here is Venice at the head of its great gulf, and, of course, there were lines that had nothing to do with sea routes. There were land routes from the north along rivers and across the mountains and into Venice in this area, fewer mountains to interrupt the flow of trade from the north, but it was the sea trade that went down the gulf, went along the Dalmatian coast, on down around over to Greece, up through the straits of Bosporus at Constantinople and on to the east there, down below the area of modern Turkey, down into the Holy Land, down into northern Egypt, across the whole top of the African continent, and, of course, along the southern coast of modern France and along Spain, and then out through the Straits of Gibraltar and following up to England and Scandinavia and so forth.

This was a vast trade route, and it had extraordinary possessions and extraordinary trade strength. Despite all of this extensive empire in terms of trading, it was the security of the Venetian stronghold on its lagoon that guaranteed its independence. It made it difficult to attack and helped its independence for those many centuries. I show you an aerial view here, which frankly only hints at it; so much water has been filled in by land, but nonetheless you begin to get some idea in this aerial view of waterways and the lagoon near Venice, some faint idea of the extraordinary territory that had to be dealt with. You can only really grasp this by flying over it or boating through it, sailing through it, when its extent and the challenge it presented to the early settlers can be fully appreciated.

The perspective map of Venice—which I show you now, dating about 1517, so very reflective of the period that we're studying— gives you an idea of the results of the building of the city. The building of the city was the engineering work of centuries; it didn't happen in 100 years or 200. It involved driving thousands of huge pilings into the bottom of the lagoon and building the city on that foundation. It's practically beyond comprehension. In the process, more than 100 separate islands were connected to make a contiguous whole, while the countless small canals that had been formed as a result were spanned with hundreds of bridges. The Grand Canal, the famous Grand Canal, is a broad serpentine waterway; it starts here at the top left of this map, a broad serpentine waterway dividing the city unequally, which gives Venice its distinctive appearance on a map.

Originally this waterway, the Grand Canal, was bridged at only one spot, approximately the midpoint, by the famous Rialto Bridge, which marked the commercial heart of this famous trading city. The civic and religious center is at the mouth of the Grand Canal down here, where it opens into the Basin of St. Mark's as it is known, the Basin of St. Mark's, the Bacino di San Marco, and there, just as the Grand Canal emerges into the Basin of St. Mark's, one finds the Ducal Palace here, the Basilica of St. Mark just behind it at this point here, the Campanile, and there the great Piazza of San Marco behind that. This is the center, which we will spend a good deal of time looking at.

Let me show you a view, and the view will be from an island, the Island of San Giorgio, San Giorgio where a famous church is built, looking back toward this area by the Ducal Palace. The painting is by Canaletto (made in the 18th century, in the mid-18th century) and it's a view including the Doge's Palace to the right, and then the Piazzetta, which is the small little piazza here between the Doge's Palace and the famous Library of St. Mark's, a Renaissance building that we will touch on later. This little Piazzetta goes down to the front of San Marco, which you see here, the Basilica, and the great piazza spreads off to the left behind these buildings on the waterfront. The other building on the waterfront here is the Mint, the Venetian Mint, and the tower; of course, behind it is the Bell Tower, the freestanding Bell Tower of the Campanile, the Bell Tower or Campanile.

Behind this as well, you can see at least one of the domes, the principal dome of the Basilica of St. Mark. I'll show you another Canaletto. Canaletto is invaluable for the study of Venice because these paintings were made for tourists who wanted to take home good proof of what they had seen and where they had been, and this is a superb painting from about 1740 of St. Mark's Square, now the view we saw before, over the building to the right. We're looking toward the Basilica of St. Mark, and you're looking at the many-domed Basilica. The Basilica of San Marco—one of the greatest late Byzantine churches—is fronted by the enormous Piazza of San Marco—one of the most imposing public squares in Europe.

The Piazza San Marco did not have the huge, regularized form it has now until the 19th century, when some buildings, including a church, were demolished and the piazza closed off at the west end, where we're standing in this picture. But it was always the civic center of Venice even before it achieved this final dimension. I'm going to move in on it, but before I do, just look to the right and you catch the left-hand side of the façade of the Doge's Palace here, so it adjoins on the other side of the Bell Tower, it adjoins the Basilica.

Moving in closer, the Basilica began its existence as the Chapel for the Doge's Palace, and the first structure of the Basilica was consecrated in 832. It was built to receive the supposed body of St. Mark, brought from Alexandria to Venice in 829. That early structure was burned in 976 during a popular revolt, but it was promptly rebuilt, and then a third church was built. Fires, of course, were the bane of architecture, and this continued for an awfully long time, and so you just kept rebuilding, and here we have the third and surviving church, which was begun in 1063, greatly augmented in terms of its decoration by the plunder brought back from the Sack of Constantinople in 1204, during the Fourth Crusade, and subsequently, because they continued to bring back spoil and booty from the east.

The square in front of San Marco focuses on the church, which is astonishing in its encrustation of marble slabs, of columns. Look at the multiplication of columns that are used on the front of it—capital sculpture here and on the inside, of course, much of it brought back from Constantinople, and above it mosaics. These are generally speaking later, but there were mosaics there from the 12th century, and the mosaic decorations above the doors and again high up on the façade of the church. Chief among the treasures brought back from Constantinople during the Fourth Crusade were the famous *Bronze*

Horses, and that's outside and inside, the enamel plaques that were mounted on the Golden Altarpiece, the Pala d'Oro, but the church itself was a marvel of Byzantine architecture and craftsmanship, with glowing mosaic decorations of very great beauty. You can just see here the four horses, not see them very clearly here mounted on the façade.

Let me show you a better view of them at an angle. What you're looking at are fortunately replicas of the *Bronze Horses* on the façade of San Marco. For over seven centuries, the façade of the Basilica was adorned with the famous gilded *Bronze Horses*, four magnificent Greek sculptures that had probably come from the Hippodrome in Constantinople (very appropriate, horses from a racetrack), and they have been dated anywhere from the third century B.C. to the third century A.D.; that's a lot of variation in possibilities of creation. They were in place on this façade by 1250. When they first came to Venice, they were mounted down in the arsenal and they were moved here, and they were here from 1250, removed only once historically by Napoleon, who vaingloriously took them with him to Paris, from whence they returned after Waterloo.

The *Bronze Horses*, I now show you the originals, which are inside now, no longer on the façade because, of course, of the acid rain and other pollution that assails Venice. They have had to be permanently removed from the façade and replaced by copies, but let me show you two views of these extraordinary horses, and they've been restored, of course, and the gilding, which for so long were simply covered up by the elements and by the changing of the surface, the gilding has been rediscovered inside. I show you the same horses from the other side. They're magnificent, and, of course, they were extremely influential on the development of sculpture, equestrian monuments during the Renaissance and later.

Let me show you the interior of the church. It always takes your breath away, even on a bad day. Even when the water floor is covered with water on high water days, it's an extraordinary experience. The interior of San Marco is clothed in sumptuous golden mosaics that, together with the volumes of the five domes and other vaulted spaces, create an effect of nearly unrivalled splendor. The mosaics are from many centuries, but the most significant are from the 12th and 13th centuries. You can understand that they've had to be repaired many times, and repair often meant changes, and so they are by no means a unified creation, but the effect of splendor is unified.

Let me show you one of the smaller domes; it's actually in the atrium at the front of the church, across the front of the church, where more of the oldest mosaics have survived. This is the dome with the *Creation of the World*, and it's in a small cupola in the Atrium, and it shows the scenes displayed in circular bands, one above the other, but all scenes from Genesis, from creation on. The scenes that we saw in the Sistine Ceiling are seen to some degree here in these much more naïve and earlier mosaics. At first, when you look at mosaics of this sort, the scenes are difficult to distinguish, but after a while it's like stained glass in northern Gothic churches. Once you have some practice looking at them, you can make out the scenes really quite easily without binoculars. It is a practice, however, that wasn't necessary to contemporaries because they knew the iconography of the stories; they knew how Adam and Eve looked in a particular scene, and that scene didn't vary much, and so they could recognize it quite easily. The same thing is true in stained glass as well.

Let me show you one of the scenes there; it's a scene from the *Flood*, and it is Noah who opens a window, as I recall, the only window (didn't the Ark have only one window and one door?); I'm still trying to figure out how they loaded and unloaded it, but in any event, there's the one window. He opens that; he sends a raven and a dove out. He's already sent the raven out; the dove he still has in his hands; he is just releasing it. The dove, which hasn't taken flight, will find that the floodwaters have not receded and come back to be sent out another time. The raven has alit upon a floating corpse, which it appears to be eating as carrion. To me, that singled drowned body floating near the ark is as eloquent as the host of bodies in the mosaic that is just beside it—just this one has tremendous impact.

In the choir of the church, we have (under a canopy) a famous golden altar— the Pala d'Oro, which means "Golden Altarpiece." It is here; it is actually a retable, a large rectangular surface mounted above the back of the altar table. It is encrusted with gold in which are set myriad gems and enamel plaques and small medallions. All of these or most of them are plunder from Constantinople. The original Palo was, in fact, made in Constantinople, the original one, for St. Mark's in the early 12th century. They ordered it and had it sent over; then, after the plunder of Constantinople, they enlarged it with the things that they took, so there's a certain historical irony here, I think. In another lecture, we'll have more to say about the significance of the relics of St. Mark the Evangelist for the Republic of Venice, but his presence is everywhere, and the specifics will have to wait for a while.

Let me show you in the exterior the Piazzetta of San Marco at dawn, with this marvelous column, standing quite near the water, and on the top of the column a stone lion, the symbol of St. Mark standing guard on the capital. The Ducal Palace, the Palazzo Ducale, the Doge's Palace, you may say all of those, this palace was built in the European Gothic style, and it stands beside the Byzantine Basilica of San Marco, which you can just glimpse to its left, and these two buildings together, therefore, aptly represent Venice's place between those two worlds, between east and west.

The Doge's Palace, one of the greatest Gothic buildings in Italy—rebuilt a number of times but in the Gothic style—dominates the waterfront. For Venice, it has an unusually open situation; you can see two sides at once. That doesn't happen very often in the crowded city, but here, of course, with the piazza in front of it and the water beside it, you can easily see the whole or a large portion of the block of the building. The Doge's Palace was also the city hall, the seat in the highest magistrates of the Republic and the site of the council chambers of the various governing councils.

Earlier structures preceded the existing palace, beginning in 814. Fire destroyed that one and the second palace. A 12th-century palace was enlarged in the mid-14th century and then torn down in 1424, to be replaced by an extension that exactly replicated the 14th-century portion. And then, in 1483, a devastating fire required extensive rebuilding, and fires in 1574 and even worse in 1577 gutted major parts of the interior, destroying many paintings as well. Each time, the palace was rebuilt in the Gothic style, thus the complete stylistic unity that we see in this enormous palace today, that was, by the way, the largest civic structure in Italy during the Renaissance.

Gracefully proportioned, the three-story structure is as open and airy as the Palazzo Vecchio in Florence is closed and massive, but the Palazzo Vecchio represented defense, and Venice on the water had water as its defense and so could express its power in a different way. An open arcade at the bottom is surmounted by an open loggia above that with smaller arches, so you have large arches here and what are two arches to every one below in the loggia above; above that, a large expansive wall is mitigated by pink and white stone. Every photograph shows the color slightly different, but they're essentially pale pink and white stone, set in a large lozenge pattern, which gives a great deal of activity and flickering of lights and so forth and color to the upper façade.

The elevation is odd because it reverses the expected sequence of heavy supporting light. Instead, we go from a light ground story to a slightly heavier to very heavy on the top, and yet it succeeds and the palace seems, no matter where you see it, it seems to float above the piazza and to float above the water so near to it. On the side, as you see on this long side facing the Piazzetta, there is a balconied window; let me show it to you—a balconied window with the lion of St. Mark again. It's a sculpture group, and it shows the Doge (at that time, Doge Andrea Gritti) kneeling before the Lion of St. Mark, and so this constant emphasis on the symbol of San Marco, of St. Mark.

Venice is pinned like a butterfly between water and sky, in a constantly changing, flickering light. It's a city whose ties to the Byzantine world filled many buildings with mosaics, in which a million cubes of colored stone and colored or gilt glass glistened with agitated light and color, reflecting the sun or reflecting lamps and candles. From the beginning, Venetian painting was preoccupied with light—the light of glowing mosaics, the light of the sky reflected from the water on which the city seems to float. Probably for these reasons, the flashing gold grounds of late medieval painting lasted longer in Venice than elsewhere in Italy, well past the mid-15th century. When the Renaissance came to Venice, it was at first tentative, and no great civic building in the Renaissance style arrived until the middle of the 16th century in the form of Sansovino's Library, which we will shortly see.

Painting, however, had a phenomenal development, and in the next seven lectures, we'll be introducing some of the most famous among the renowned artists of Renaissance Venice. In the 14th century, the Trecento, I want to introduce Paolo Veneziano and his *Polyptych with the Coronation of the Virgin* from about 1358. The sheer brilliance of the gold in Venetian Gothic painting seems magnified, perhaps influenced by Byzantine models. It seems golder than the gold in other gold ground paintings in Italy. Paolo Veneziano was one of the finest Trecento artists in Venice, and he painted this *Polyptych* for the church of Santa Chiara; it is now in the Academia Gallery. The Academia was created by Napoleon, and churches were closed and altarpieces taken from them and put into the museum; that is the formation of that gallery of that museum in Venice.

The large central panel here of the Coronation itself (with Christ crowning his mother—both of them clad in very beautiful robes) is flanked by eight smaller narrative scenes. There are also figures above, but I call your attention to the four larger narrative scenes on either side. The ensemble probably is incomplete today; it probably once had a Crucifixion above the Coronation on that same axis. Let me show you a detail of the four scenes to the left and simply identify them. Here is the *Nativity*, which takes place in a cave, which is a Byzantine tradition rather than the stable, which is the Western tradition. Here is the *Baptism of Christ*, with Christ in the water up to his chest here, in this very standard way of showing the Baptism. The lower left is the *Last Supper*, and here on the right we have a combination of Christ in Gethsemane praying, and below the immediately following scene of the capture of Christ.

Two painters worked frequently together; they were brothers-in-law: Antonio Vivarini and Giovanni d'Alemagna—the latter we really know very little about. Vivarini, who was from a famous family of artists, painted this work, the *Madonna Enthroned with the Fathers of the Church*, painted in 1446. It's a large painting; a great amount of gilding is still found in this imposing triptych; it also has a very elaborate Gothic screen behind the figures, behind the fathers of the church, the angels, and the Madonna. This was painted a quarter century after Masaccio had revolutionized Florentine painting and the "new style" (new Renaissance style) was well established.

I do not, however, want to sell this painting short. It is a very beautiful and a very important work in the Venetian Quattrocento. About 16 feet wide, it is an unusual combination of the theme of the Madonna in an Enclosed Garden—the phrase usually used is the Latin phrase *hortus conclusus*, "the enclosed garden"—which symbolizes the virginity of the Madonna. That theme combined with the Sacred Conversation of Saints sharing a unified space, something we've seen and discussed before. The Madonna and Child in the central panel are accompanied by four small angels—like an honor guard—and this central panel has a deep seriousness. The four Fathers of the Latin Church, those early writers who laid down the theological foundations of the faith, are: at the left, St. Jerome, nearest us, in his Cardinal's habit, and holding a model of the church of Santa Maria della Caritá, and St. Gregory the Great with his Papal Tiara; and at the right, St. Augustine, with the book and crozier, and St. Ambrose behind him. Ambrose, in a red robe, holds an unusual attribute by which he is often identified: it is a scourge, with three knots. The three knots represent the Trinity, and the scourge with the three knots represent St. Ambrose's defense of the Trinity, of the dogma of the Trinity, against the Arian heresy in the third century.

One oddity of this painting is the scalloped base or stage upon which the figures stand. It is painted in a very illusionistic way, but it is such an artificial element that it seems unrelated to the intuitive spatial logic that Vivarini gave the painting. The ornateness of the whole painting would have been even greater than it is before the original cornice—which it must have had—was lost. Remarkably, this painting is in a museum, but it is in the building that it was painted for at the same time because the School, or Scuola (or Confraternity) connected to the Church of Santa Maria della Caritá was converted during the Napoleonic occupation to the Academy, the Accademia, whose gallery now houses the greatest collection of Venetian painting, and this painting by Vivarini remains in the building for which it was made.

It seems remarkable that this painting was made while Donatello was at work in San Antonio in next-door Padua. For even if Donatello's revolutionary spatial innovations may have had some influence on Vivarini, it is more remarkable how slight that influence was. In sum, though there are Renaissance aspects to this beautiful painting,

Venetian painting is conservative by Quattrocento standards and would not change until the last third of the century.

The tentative acceptance of the Renaissance style in painting and in sculpture was even more remarkable in architecture. No great civic building in the Renaissance style was raised in Venice until Jacopo Sansovino's Library, begun in 1537, after the High Renaissance had been pushed aside in other Italian centers. Sansovino's Library is one of the great buildings of the Renaissance, and it was a source of great civic pride since it was one of the earliest public libraries of the Renaissance. It was ordered by the Venetian authorities in conscious emulation of the libraries of antiquity, as they were known from ancient descriptions, and principally it was constructed to house a priceless collection of Latin and Greek manuscripts given to the State by a private collector in the middle of the 15th century.

Architecturally it is distinguished by an open loggia on the ground level, like that of the Doge's Palace, surmounted by another arcade on the second story, also like that of the Doge's Palace, but all of this in the library done in the purest classical style. Its construction was not uneventful, for at one point in the very cold winter of 1545, the vault of the main reading room collapsed. Sansovino was immediately thrown into prison—the solidity and safety of architecture was not taken lightly. Only the intervention of his friend, Titian, among others, secured his release. However, he had to make the repairs at his own expense and he received no salary for two years.

Perhaps surprisingly, it was erected opposite the great Gothic Ducal Palace, but that has given posterity to three astoundingly beautiful and historic buildings in three contrasting styles—Byzantine, Gothic, and Renaissance—in a single location of the greatest imaginable beauty.

Lecture Twenty-Eight
Celebrating the Living City

Scope:

It is hardly surprising that a city as astonishingly situated as Venice—with its multitude of smaller canals framing the long serpentine of the Grand Canal and its numerous smaller piazzas complementing the vast Piazza San Marco and adjoining Piazzetta—should be addicted to public ceremonies and processions, both on water and on land. All of the cities of Italy had such public occasions and recorded them in paintings, but nowhere outside of Venice did the state and its leading citizens so compulsively commission artists to paint so many and such large canvases to trumpet the beauties and virtues of the city. The physical splendor of Venice and the close identification of the state with religion combined to foster the desire for grand ceremonial paintings, often in ensembles or cycles.

Vittore Carpaccio (c. 1465–c. 1526) and Gentile Bellini (1429–1507) were two of the principal painters of such scenes. When Carpaccio was at the height of his fame, he painted an imposing *Lion of Saint Mark* for the Ducal Palace, where it has become one of the most well known of the multitude of images of the symbol of Venice. The narrative cycles he composed were commissioned by *scuole* (literally, "schools")—confraternities, organized under religious institutions, whose activities were both charitable and social. Their meeting halls, whether small or large, were often decorated with paintings dedicated to their patron saints and were a focal point of Venetian artistic activity. Carpaccio's paintings for the confraternity dedicated to Saint Ursula are now in the Accademia museum. They relate in vivid detail the legend of that mythical saint and her 11,000 virgins, against a background that reflects, even when it does not portray, Venice. A smaller group of charming paintings decorated Saint Giorgio degli Schiavoni, a confraternity of Slavs from Dalmatia, one of the Venetian territories.

Gentile Bellini, so famous at 40 that he was made a knight of the Holy Roman Empire, followed the Venetian connection to Constantinople, where he was in the service of Sultan Mehmet II for two years. Upon his return home, he also painted large, multi-figured scenes of the civic life of Venice, one of which includes a famous representation of the Basilica of San Marco. At his death, he specified that a large unfinished painting of *Saint Mark Preaching in Alexandria* be completed by his brother, Giovanni.

Outline

I. In order to continue, in a sense, the tour of Venice begun in the last lecture, in this lecture, we will consider a notable category of Venetian art. This detour will briefly take us ahead of our story, to the end of the 15th century. The category in question is cityscapes—paintings of urban settings and daily life.

    A. Large Italian cityscapes had been painted before the Venetian scenes of the 15th century. The most important was the enormous fresco *Effects of Good Government in the City and in the Country*, by Ambrogio Lorenzetti, painted in the Palazzo Publico ("city hall") of Siena around 1340. These, however, are occasional efforts, whereas in Venice, the obsession with public ceremonies and processions, religious and civic, on land and on water, resulted in a more comprehensive body of cityscapes than was produced in any other city-state.

    B. Two of the principal painters of this subject were Vittore Carpaccio and Gentile Bellini. Carpaccio was much the younger, but we will discuss him first in order to place Gentile in closer proximity to his brother, Giovanni (Lecture Twenty-Nine).

II. At the pinnacle of his career, Vittore Carpaccio (c. 1465–c. 1526) was commissioned by officers of the republic to paint the *Lion of Saint Mark* (1516) for the Ducal Palace.

    A. A virtual billboard of the symbol of Venice, about 12 feet wide, it has become, perhaps, the best known among the hundreds created. The winged lion is the symbol of Saint Mark, deriving from the Book of Revelation (4:6–8). The painting depicts the lion, his right paw on an open book with the words "*Pax tibi Marce Evangelista meus*" ("Peace unto you, Mark my evangelist"), spoken to Mark on the eve of his martyrdom in Egypt. Behind him to the left is the city itself (the Ducal Palace), as seen from the island of San Giorgio

Maggiore, and at the right is an allusion to the Venetian naval power.

B. The Venetian institution of *scuole*, "schools," that were, in fact, confraternities with religious affiliations, was of the greatest importance for the patronage of artists. Among Carpaccio's patrons was the Scuola di Sant'Orsola (Saint Ursula), for whom he produced an extensive narrative cycle in the 1490s.

    1. The legend of Saint Ursula is fascinating, to say the least, because it involves the daughter of the king of Brittany, the son of the king of Britain, the pope, and 11,000 virgins. It is more like a fairy tale than a Christian epic, but it allowed for a great play of pictorial imagination.

    2. Although it does *not* take place in Venice at all, Carpaccio's cycle constitutes what has nicely been called a "fantasy on the theme of Quattrocento Venice." Architecture, decoration, costume, custom, and light all reflect the city he knew intimately.

C. A much more modest *scuola*, San Giorgio degli Schiavone, secured Carpaccio's services in the first decade of the 16th century.

    1. The confraternity, interestingly, was part of the important Dalmatian community in Venice (Schiavone = "Slav").

    2. On the ground floor is one of the most charming of such cycles (originally on the second floor, the paintings were moved in the 16th century). It includes scenes of Saints George, Jerome and Augustine, ranging from whimsical drama to spellbound meditation.

D. The Scuola of San Giovanni Evangelista (John the Evangelist) owned (since 1369) an important relic, a piece of the Holy Cross. Several artists contributed to a series of 10 paintings dedicated to this relic. Carpaccio painted *The Miracle of the Relic of the True Cross* (c. 1494), which is a rich portrait of a quarter of Venice and, at the same time, an indication of the sort of public celebrations that honored such miracles.

III. Gentile Bellini (1429–1507) had a remarkable international reputation, which led to his summons to Constantinople, where he was painter to Sultan Mehmet II for two years. Home in Venice, he turned his attention to large cityscapes with narratives, producing some of the best known examples.

A. Like Carpaccio, Bellini also contributed to the series of paintings for the Scuola of San Giovanni Evangelista. His large canvas *Miracle of the Cross at Ponte San Lorenzo*, painted in 1500, is similar to Carpaccio's but fuller of incident, because the event involved diving into a canal for the relic, which had been dropped there.

B. Unquestionably, Bellini's most famous canvas is the vast *Procession in Piazza San Marco* of 1496, nearly 25 feet wide, painted for the same *scuola*. It is a document of inestimable value because it shows the piazza and the basilica in precise detail. The event that it chronicles, a procession on the Feast of Corpus Christi in 1444, was known for the miracle that then occurred, when a Brescian merchant successfully invoked the aid of the relic of the Cross to save the life of his son.

C. Gentile was at work on another huge canvas, *Saint Mark Preaching in Alexandria*, for the hall of the governing council of the Scuola di San Marco, when he fell ill and died in 1507.

  1. The Scuola San Marco for which this painting was made was influential precisely because it was dedicated to the patron saint of Venice. When some Venetian merchant-adventurers brought back the supposed body of the evangelist to Venice, they set in motion an extraordinary, self-sustaining phenomenon.

  2. From the moment that the relics were in Venetian possession, they were regarded as the sacred and civic justification of the state. First, their existence in Venice constituted another act in the long-running dramatic conflict between the Moslem and Christian worlds over the status of Jerusalem and Constantinople. Second, it underscored the long reach of the Venetian Republic and its dominant navy.

3. The adoption of Mark's zoomorphic symbol, the lion, of course signified power. But it also announced the pacific intentions of the republic, because Mark was, after all, an apostle, a missionary, and bishop of Alexandria. The relics of Mark were to Venice what those of Peter were to Rome and considered second only to Rome in the dignity conferred.

4. The life of Mark, but especially the posthumous liberation of his uncorrupted body (as pious legend had it), was the iconographic centerpiece of Venetian art and architecture.

5. In his will, Bellini specified that his brother Giovanni finish *Saint Mark Preaching*. The softly fused colors of many of the figures are in Giovanni's style. The most striking feature, however, remains the fanciful "Alexandrian" architecture, which is surely owed to Gentile.

Works Discussed:

Vittore Carpaccio:

The Lion of Saint Mark, 1516, Doge's Palace, Venice.

Arrival of the English Ambassadors, Departure of the English Ambassadors, and *The Dream of Saint Ursula*, from the Saint Ursula cycle, 1490–1496, Accademia, Venice.

The Meeting of Ursula and Etherius and the Departure of the Pilgrims, 1498, Accademia, Venice.

Saint Jerome and the Lion in the Monastery, 1502–1507, Scuola San Giorgio degli Schiavone, Venice.

The Vision of Saint Augustine, dated 1502, Scuola San Giorgio degli Schiavone, Venice.

The Miracle of the Relic of the True Cross, c. 1494, Accademia, Venice.

Gentile Bellini:

Miracle of the Cross at Ponte San Lorenzo, 1500, Accademia, Venice.

Procession in Piazza San Marco, Venice, 1496, Accademia, Venice.

Gentile Bellini and Giovanni Bellini:

Saint Mark Preaching in Alexandria, 1504–1507, Pinacoteca di Brera, Milan.

Essential Reading:

Adams, chapter 13.

Hartt, chapter 15.

Supplementary Reading:

Brown, Patricia F. *Venetian Narrative Painting in the Age of Carpaccio*. New Haven: Yale University Press, 1990.

Humphrey, Peter. *Painting in Renaissance Venice*. New Haven: Yale University Press, 1997.

Muir, Edward. *Civic Ritual in Renaissance Venice*. Princeton: Princeton University Press, 1986.

Pedrocco, Filippo. *The Art of Venice*. New York: Scala/Riverside, 2002.

Questions to Consider:

1. What is the connection of Saint Mark the Evangelist to the Venetian state?

2. How did the s*cuole* (confraternities) of Venice employ Venetian art?

Lecture Twenty-Eight—Transcript
Celebrating the Living City

It's hardly surprising that a city as astonishingly situated as Venice, with its multitude of smaller canals framing the long serpentine of the Grand Canal and its numerous smaller piazzas complementing the vast Piazza San Marco and the adjoining Piazzetta, should be addicted to public ceremonies and processions, both on water and on land. All the cities of Italy had such public occasions and recorded them in paintings, but nowhere outside of Venice did the state and its leading citizens so compulsively commission artists to paint so many and such large canvases to trumpet the beauties and virtues of the city. The physical splendor of Venice and the close identification of the state with religion combined to foster the desire for grand ceremonial paintings, often in ensembles or cycles.

May I take just a moment to show you the map again? We have seen it, the Grand Canal again, the Rialto bridge halfway down, and as you enter the Basin of San Marco, you come to the Ducal Palace, the Piazzetta, the Basilica behind it, to the great Piazza San Marco in front of the Basilica. This is the largest public space, but far from the only public space in Venice. I didn't point out that further down, you see ships grouped here where we have the arsenal (the *arsonale*), this famous area obviously for defense and into which ships could sail and sail out of as well. It is a dense, a large dense area, but with many small pockets of piazzas and many smaller waterways, and there is a constant feeling of the movement of the Venetian populace in the city and on the water around and through the city in such celebrations.

In order to continue the tour of Venice that we began in the last lecture, I want to consider this very special and notable category of Venetian art. It will briefly take us ahead of our story, to the end of the 15th century. The category in question is Cityscapes—paintings of urban settings and daily life. Large Italian cityscapes had been painted before the Venetian scenes of the 15th century. The most important of those was probably the enormous fresco in the city hall of Siena, the *Palazzo Publico*, called the *Effects of Good Government in the City and in the Country* by Ambrogio Lorenzetti about 1340, but those are occasional efforts, whereas in Venice, the obsession with public ceremonies and processions, religious and civic, on land and on water, resulted in a more comprehensive body of cityscapes, usually conceived as narrative cycles, than was produced in any other city-state.

Two of the principal painters of this subject were Vittore Carpaccio and Gentile Bellini. Carpaccio was much the younger, but I'm going to discuss him first anyway in order to place Gentile in closer proximity to his brother, Giovanni, in our next lecture. When Vittore Carpaccio—who was born about 1465 and died about 1526—was at the pinnacle of his career, he was commissioned in 1516 by officers of the Republic to paint an imposing *Lion of St. Mark* for the Ducal Palace, where it has remained and has become one of the best known, perhaps the best known of the hundreds of images of this symbol of Venice. In fact, it's a virtual billboard of the symbol of Venice; it's about 12 feet wide.

The winged lion (you've seen it before in sculpture) the winged lion is the symbol of St. Mark. It derives from the Book of Revelation, from Chapter 4 of Revelation, as do the other symbols of the evangelists. It depicts a winged lion, his right paw on an open book with the words "*Pax tibi Marce Evangelista meus*," (Peace unto you, Mark my evangelist), words divinely spoken to Mark on the eve of his martyrdom in Egypt, in Alexandria. Behind the lion and to the left is the city itself. We are on the mainland and you are looking past the lion and his book, and you see the Ducal Palace, alluding to the city, and you can also see the Piazzetta on the top of the Campanile (the bell tower) as well.

At the right of the lion, you have these ships, a number of the ships, and a reference to the arsenal (to the *arsenale*), the Venetian naval power here, and I notice that the lion's back paws are in the water of the basin as well. The narrative cycles that Carpaccio and others composed were commissioned by Scuole (the singular is scuola)— Scuole, literally "schools" of Venetian institution; they were in fact confraternities, organized under religious institutions, and their activities were often charitable as well as social in character. Their meeting halls, whether they were small or large, were often decorated with paintings dedicated to their patron saints, and were a focal point of Venetian artistic activity, and they were of the greatest importance for artistic patronage.

I want to put this image up and talk to you about the great cycle, one of the greatest cycles of Carpaccio. Among Carpaccio's patrons was the Scuola di Sant'Orsola (St. Ursula), for whom he produced an extensive narrative cycle in the 1490s; the paintings are now in the Accademia Museum. The legend of St. Ursula is fascinating, to say the least, since it involves the daughter of the King of Brittany, the son of the King of Britain, the Pope, and not least, 11,000 virgins. It is more like a fairy tale than a Christian epic, but it allowed for a great play of pictorial imagination. Carpaccio's large paintings relate in vivid detail the legend of that mythical saint, and once again, one turns to *The Golden Legend* for details.

In brief, the pagan son of the King of Britain wished to marry Ursula, daughter of the Christian King of Brittany. She agreed on condition that he converts to Christianity and that there should be a three-year hiatus so that she might make a pilgrimage to Rome. She did not travel alone to Rome; she traveled with 10 female companions, and each of the young women was accompanied by 1,000 virgins. It is not only the modern male mind that finds this scene piquant. *The Golden Legend* relates, "From all sides, then the virgins flocked together and men hurried to see this great spectacle." They set out; I'm showing you some of the story that is not in front of you. They reached Rome, the 11,000, via Basil, but on the return they were besieged at Cologne by the Huns, who slaughtered all 11,000 Christian women.

The painting you've been looking at is the arrival of the English ambassadors at the court of Brittany. This canvas, set up in three parts, as we've so often seen in tripartite organization here, this canvas is nearly 20 feet wide. The ambassadors arrive at the left in the arcade by the water's edge, and then in the center they're received, and they present the proposal of marriage in the center, and behind them is a wonderful centrally planned temple that was not to be found, I assure you, in Brittany or Britain, but very much to be found in Italy, and that is true of the architecture that one finds here. It is, of course, recognizable Italian and often Venetian architecture.

On the right-hand side of this, you see a room—an elevated room—here. It's Ursula's bedchamber, and her father has joined her there, and she's telling him the conditions under which she will accept this offer of marriage, and I have to say that her father looks just a little dejected here, as though this is probably going to cause a war or something. He doesn't seem quite happy with this, and I won't have a chance to follow through on this. Nonetheless, this woman with a cane who sits at the steps outside at the feet, at the lower part of this elevated room, is an invention of Carpaccio's that you will see again in Venetian art, including in that of Titian. It's one of those little inventions, little footnotes that fascinated other painters and got quoted.

Although it doesn't take place in Venice at all, Carpaccio's cycle constitutes what has very nicely been called a "fantasy on the theme of Quattrocento Venice." Architecture, decoration, costume, custom, and—above all—light all reflect the city that Carpaccio knew intimately. For example, I show you a detail that in this large painting is tucked way over here. If you look out the arcade, you can see a gondola here, and I will show it to you now. It's so charming, it's almost lost on the detail, but it's purely Venice, of course; nothing like this in Brittany, and it is an exquisite scene. This gondola seen with the figure from behind, a foreshortening of it, is also charming. There's a kind of wit that runs throughout these paintings, regardless of the seriousness of their subjects.

The departure of the English ambassadors with the news that the son of the king will be accepted as a groom for the daughter of the King of Brittany, they're ready to depart, and this is simply a departure scene. They bid their respects to the king, but what a scene. It's the most wonderfully memorable, elegantly decorated architecture that you can imagine, with great paneled inlaid walls here, and wonderful color in the costumes as well—the oranges, many of the costume oranges, reds, greens—and also for the unity of space and light. This opens up into another area back here, with the staircase—a very tall high staircase—with a view through an archway beyond that, and even though it's dominated by the foreground, that foreground is flooded with light from a window that we don't see out of to the left, and that light floods across the space. It's a wonderful space for the ambassadors to take their leave in.

The meeting of Ursula and Etherius, the young man's name, is part of this scene, and the other part is the departure of the pilgrimage. It's another 20-foot canvas, divided more or less equally by the two sections by the flagpole here. Britain is on the left in the background here, very elaborate castle back here, and also a hill with a fortification on top of that hill. In the left foreground, we have Etherius bidding farewell—kneeling and bidding farewell to his father—the King of Britain.

On the right side of that pole, we have two scenes essentially. First, you should identify everything in the right-hand side as Brittany, with a more colorful or at least lighter in tone architecture, an architecture that is more clearly in north Italian style than the more medieval architecture on the left. Etherius is seen here greeting Ursula, and then the two of them to the right kneel before her father. Behind them, back in this area clear across the water here, some of the endless procession of virgins begin to enter boats—long boats here—that will ferry them out to the ships, and from thence they will take sail, and, in a sense, they already have. That's the indication of the ships moving into the distance.

By the way, the kind of thing that fascinated Carpaccio is to be found here in this ship, which is tipped not accidentally but intentionally. You tipped (or I think the word is careened) a ship in order to prepare it, no dry dock, but you could get it in a shallow area, tip it over, and cull the bottom—do whatever you had to do to repair the ship. This fascinates him. Remember, this is 20 feet wide, so he can show quite a lot of detail here, and if one is in front of the painting, if you're in front of the painting, you can very much enjoy the details of the men who are working on this repair. It also sets up a wonderful diagonal just cutting across the architecture here, and that diagonal is echoed by this diagonal running up the perspective, the buildings on the right-hand side, very carefully constructed.

Let me show you yet another scene from this; it's not precisely a narrative scene. It's the *Dream of St. Ursula,* and it occurs in a moment later in the story, when an angel appears in her dream; it's a kind of Annunciation, I suppose. The angel comes in from the right to inform her of her imminent martyrdom, so she is aware of this before they are attacked. Before they are attacked by the Huns, she is aware of this, and that means, of course, she's given an opportunity to escape this—so were the others, and *The Golden Legend* says only one of the 11,000 hid in her room, and then the next day got up the courage to sacrifice herself. The meaning of martyrdom is clear enough here.

This is one of the most lovely paintings in Venetian art. This cube of a room, this beautiful space, is geometrically clear and subdivided into geometric units: the cupboards; the windows; the bed; the way the light falls in very sharply defined ways, but falls very softly in terms of its atmospheric effect. It's a cube of space that melts in that light. The colors are delicate—the range of grays and blue-grays playing against the bedspread and so forth; the descriptive details are everywhere here. We have her shoes at the side of her bed here. At the foot of her bed is a crown; it's, of course, the crown of martyrdom, not merely the crown of a princess, but the crown of martyrdom placed there, and the angel is carrying a palm of martyrdom, a martyr's palm with her.

You can feast your eyes on the details of things that would've been in such a room, and there are a couple of odd details here that haven't been really explained. These are both classical statues over the doorways, nude classical statues, one of some sort of a water carrier and the other of a Venus, and their significance here has not really been explained, but what doesn't need explaining is the sense of wholeness brought about by a wonderful understanding of the architecture and suffused with this very poetic light.

A much more modest Scuola than that of St. Ursula also engaged Carpaccio. That Scuola is San Giorgio degli Schiavone, and it secured Carpaccio's services in the first decade of the 16th century. It's a very small confraternity in a small building, and the paintings that he made for it are smaller and have a greater poetic quality. They're lighter in meaning, in a sense. The confraternity is a fraternity of Slavs from Dalmatia; the word *schiavone* means "Slav," and that again shows you that the Dalmatian community in Venice from across the Adriatic was a very important one, as indeed it was. This cycle (actually three different subjects here) was originally on the second floor, but it was moved in the 16th century to the ground floor, where it is today. It includes scenes of St. Jerome and scenes of St. Augustine; there's one scene of St. George.

They range from whimsical drama to a wonderful kind of spellbound meditation that we found also in St. Ursula's dream. In this case, it is a lion that has limped into the monastery where St. Jerome is, terrifying all his fellow monks—the brothers—and they all flee, and these are just spectacular images of flight, just the way he's designed them with their cowls and their capes; it's just a beautiful forward movement as they rush off to the right-hand side. The elderly, obviously, saint, is trying to say, "It's all right, he's injured; he's not dangerous, and we should help him out." Of course, they do help him and they tend to his foot that (usually in the story) has a thorn in it, but, in fact, it is torn by thorns and, of course, the reference is to the Passion of Christ and the crown of thorns in something like this. In any event, the lion is tended to by St. Jerome and his fellow monks. There is a wonderful little sense of the monastic community here in the buildings that go with it.

A scene that is very reminiscent of the *Dream of St. Ursula* is the *Vision of St. Augustine*, signed and dated 1502, signed and dated right here on this *catolino*, an illusionistic piece of paper fallen on the floor in the foreground. This painting was thought for a long time to represent St. Jerome, but they have agreed that it is to be interpreted as St. Augustine writing a letter to St, Jerome, and they did have a real-life correspondence, and while he's writing he receives a visitation from Jerome in the form of light, telling him that he (Jerome) has died. There's also a related line in *The Golden Legend* where it's reported that Augustine wrote about Jerome, "By the nobility of his discourse, he is shone from the east to the west like the light of the sun," and that plays into this as well.

But like Ursula's room, this is the most astonishing cube of light-filled space, and the expectancy of the saint as he pauses in his writing, and no saint could be more associated with writing, he pauses and looks up, startled by what is apparently a flood of light that has suddenly illumined the room and entered the room, a room that is very large and has to be understood as a monastic study almost. It's certainly not a small room, but a large one in a monastery with all sorts of details that one would love to go into, but I shall resist the temptation.

In addition to the catolino down here, we have this utterly charming dog. The dogs in Carpaccio are *de rigeur*; he liked them, and he brings them into his paintings. Venetians in general introduced animals, and dogs in particular, into their paintings. Carpaccio loved them, but the way he's placed it is what's wonderful, right at the apex of that triangle of shadow that comes in. The shadow reaches across, the dog is lit, he looks up expectantly, and it starts a long diagonal moving up right through the arm of the saint as well. It's a beautiful piece of picture making; it's full of love and gentleness as well.

Another Scuola—the Scuola of San Giovanni Evangelista (St. John the Evangelist)—had owned (since 1369) an important relic, a piece of the Holy Cross. Several artists contributed to a series of ten paintings (over a period of years) dedicated to this relic. I'm showing you Carpaccio's *The Miracle of the Relic of the True Cross* of about 1494, which is a rich portrait, on the one hand, of a particular quarter of the city. You see real buildings—many of them could be identified—a bridge that had been built 40 years before, a wooden bridge that, in another 25 years, would be replaced by the stone bridge that is still there today, a wooden bridge that separated in the middle; it's a drawbridge to allow larger ships to pass through on the canal.

A wonderful gathering of gondolas on the lower part of this, and on this loggia at the top, a miracle is taking place, and the miracle is the healing of a man who was obsessed with a demon—was possessed by demons—by touching him or in some way using the relic of the Holy Cross to do so. Of course, there are many people who have gathered to witness this, and by that I mean members of the confraternity who are paying for it are down here in portraits of the lower part and perhaps in the upper one as well. The gondolas have brought many people to enjoy it, and here's a dog in the gondola as well in the foreground of this painting; here is a detail of that area at the bottom. There, you look back under the bridge and see much more going on on the far side. It's a wonderful image.

I'll turn now to Gentile Bellini (1429-1507), an artist who had a remarkable international reputation, which led to his summons to Constantinople, where he was the painter to Sultan Mehmet II for two years. We actually don't know much about what he did there; things have been claimed and dropped, but he was there. Home in Venice, he turned his attention to large cityscapes with narratives and produced some of the best-known examples.

One of them is from the same cycle of the Scuola of San Giovanni; it's the *Miracle of the Cross at Ponte San Lorenzo* (the Saint Lawrence Bridge), and at the San Lorenzo Bridge, somebody quite carelessly as they were in procession going across the bridge dropped the relic into the canal. Actually, one wonders if this sort of thing didn't happen a lot during processions, but it's dropped into the canal, and so everything stops until they are able to rescue it, and as you see, a number of people have gone in bathing in order to find it. There's what must have been a very exotic touch of an African (over here) who is about to dive in and do his best to find it, but it's been found. Essentially, it didn't sink very far, and this friar has found it and floats through the water almost, levitates with the reliquary and relic that he has recovered.

Once again, we have portraits over on the left and in this group of people in the foreground. We don't know whether they're from the confraternity or whether possibly Gentile Bellini put in his own family members here. That's also a possibility. This painting was painted in 1500. It's similar to Carpaccio's, but it is fuller of incident in a way because of this wonderful diving scene. The event had occurred between 1370 and 1382. The wonderful water here is really aqua-greenish water that lends itself, it gives a tone, a kind of suspended tone, meditative tone, to the whole of the painting. It really keys the painting quite beautifully.

Unquestionably, his most famous canvas is the vast *Procession in Piazza San Marco* of 1496. It is nearly 25 feet wide, and it was painted for the same Scuola that we've been looking at, and as a document, just as a picture of what it includes, it is of inestimable value since it shows the Piazza and the Basilica in precise detail as they were when he painted it. For instance, if you look at the mosaics, these are the original mosaics. Only one of them still survives; the rest have been replaced by 16th-century and 17th-century mosaics, but the gold that you see here and the glow are of the Basilica at its height. The third Basilica is the one that survived with its original decoration, and you can see the horses and you can see they too are gilds; they quite strongly show their gilding at the top.

The event that this procession chronicles, that this painting chronicles, is a procession on the Feast of Corpus Christi in 1444. It's painted half a century later, but in 1444, the procession, which took place every year on the day of Corpus Christi, is carrying the relic here underneath this canopy and carrying it through, of course, Piazza San Marco. You can see how long this procession is; they're clear down here; they've come up this point and down and continuing on. On a particular day in 1444, a miracle occurred. A merchant from Brescia had successfully invoked the aid of the relic as it passed to save the life of his son, who was dying, and his son's life was saved. I must say, they don't make much of the Brescian merchant, only really of this wonderful procession with the centerpiece below of the relic and above of the Basilica San Marco. The placing of these figures through space, though, is wonderful.

Before I let this go, though, look at the corner of the palace, the Ducal Palace over here, and this is, of course, the Campanile. Today, there's nothing on this side of it; that's been torn down, but then it had a building right up to the side of it. I thought I'd share with you a detail of the Piazza in this painting, where you get an idea of how carefully he's placed his figures, much as Perugino did in the painting that keeps gracing us here behind me, as Perugino did, placing figures in the middle distance in order to establish that space, and doing it just as effectively and just as gracefully. These people are talking their daily talk while the procession goes on around them.

Gentile Bellini was at work on another huge canvas, the *St. Mark Preaching in Alexandria* for the hall of the governing council of the Scuola di San Marco. When he fell ill and died in 1507, the Confraternity of St. Mark, for which this painting was made, was influential (obviously) precisely because it was dedicated to the patron saint of Venice. When some Venetian merchant-adventurers brought back the supposed body of the evangelist to Venice, they set in motion an extraordinary, self-sustaining phenomenon.

From the moment that the relics were in Venetian possession, they were regarded as the sacred and civic justification of the state. First, it was another act in the long-running dramatic conflict between the Moslem and Christian worlds over the status of Jerusalem, and also of Constantinople. Second, it underscored the long reach of the Venetian Republic and its dominant navy. The adoption of Mark's symbol—his zoömorphic symbol—of the lion, of course, signified power, but it also announced the pacific intentions of the Republic since Mark, after all, was an apostle, a missionary, and Bishop of Alexandria. The relics of Mark were to Venice, as I have said, what those of Peter were to Rome, and considered second only to Rome in the dignity that they conferred on the city.

The life of Mark, but especially the posthumous liberation of his uncorrupted body (as pious legend had it), was the iconographic centerpiece of Venetian art and architecture. In his will, he specified that his brother, Giovanni, finish the painting as, in fact, he did. The softly fused colors of so many of the figures are in Giovanni's style, but the most striking feature remains the fanciful "Alexandrian" architecture here in the background, which is surely owed to Gentile Bellini.

Lecture Twenty-Nine
Giovanni Bellini—The Early Years

Scope:

The career of Giovanni Bellini (c. 1430–1516), like that of his brother, seems to have begun in earnest only in his 30s, possibly because they both continued to work in their well-known father's shop rather than on their own. Extended families of artists were a particularly Venetian phenomenon. From the beginning, Giovanni became famous for his paintings of Madonnas. He also painted moving images of the *Pietá*, or *Lamentation*, in a peculiarly northern Italian half-length format. Despite repetition, his interpretation of these subjects and types rarely fails to touch us—his *Pietá* in the Brera in Milan is intensely poignant. He was Andrea Mantegna's brother-in-law, and their versions of *The Agony in the Garden* are compositionally similar but stylistically and expressively diverse. His powerful, close-up treatment of the *Entombment* was probably painted about 1474, the year before Antonello da Messina arrived in Venice for a two-year sojourn that profoundly affected the artistic development of Giovanni Bellini and of Venetian painting.

Outline

I. Both of the Bellini brothers were absorbed in the workshop of their father, Jacopo (c. 1400–c. 1470/71). Giovanni Bellini (c. 1430–1516) would eventually produce superb multi-figure altarpieces and mythologies. But from his emergence as an independent master in the 1460s and throughout his career, he was known for solemn pictures of the Madonna and Child and for very moving images of the *Pietá*.

   A. The *Madonna with the Blessing Child* (1460s) shows a mournful Madonna protectively clasping the Child with both hands. She is upright; the Child stands on the balustrade, leans to the left, and though blessing, does not look at the worshipper who receives this benediction. Rather, his eyes are focused on the unseen, the Passion implicit in the black background. The half-length composition placed behind the sill or balustrade is a composition found in Jacopo Bellini's Madonnas that is used continuously by Giovanni. In the later

Madonna of the Trees (1487), both figures are severely vertical, placed in front of a "cloth of honor," which is flanked by two delicate trees in a barely glimpsed landscape. This lyrical motif may be Giovanni's own invention.

B. Closely related compositionally is the theme of the half-length *Pietà*, in which the body of Christ is displayed by the Madonna and Saint John the Evangelist or by angels. Here, the sill may be read simultaneously as the edge of the sarcophagus and as the front of an altar, making the body of Christ a literal image of the Eucharist. This composition, with its frightful immediacy, is profoundly associated with Giovanni's art. But it owes a profound debt to Donatello's bronze relief of *The Dead Christ with Two Angels* on the High Altar in the Santo in Padua (Lecture Nine).

II. Giovanni Bellini's sister, Nicolosia, was married to Andrea Mantegna in 1453. The two artists were, therefore, in regular contact.

A. This explains the obvious similarity between Giovanni's *Agony in the Garden* (c. 1465/70) and the same subject as painted by Mantegna (Lecture Twenty-Six). This classic art historical comparison is always rewarding. The implacable harshness of Mantegna's sculptured scene is replaced by a tender vulnerability. It seems clear that Bellini was consciously creating a poetic alternative to the epic narrative of his brother-in-law's painting. The figures are smaller, the sense of spiritual isolation is enhanced, and the end of the long night of prayer is announced by one of the loveliest dawns in Renaissance art, ironically revealing the imminent capture of Jesus ("the hour is come").

B. The monumental *Entombment* (c. 1475) is also a testament to the reciprocal relationship of the brothers-in-law. Mantegna's stoic remoteness is felt here, despite the physical immediacy of the group, seen from a low viewpoint, explained by the original position of the painting as the crowning element of the large Pesaro Altarpiece, from which it was later separated.

III. At about the time Giovanni was painting the *Entombment*, there arrived in Venice an artist destined to alter the course of Venetian painting: Antonello da Messina (c. 1430–1479).

    A. Antonello's *Saint Jerome in His Study* (c. 1475) exhibits one of the notable features of his art, his knowledge of Flemish painting: in the spatial organization (a fictive stone arch opening onto the saint's study and views through windows at the rear of it), the descriptive detail and the numerous symbolic objects, and the use of the oil medium.

    B. In fact, in the 16th century, the painting was thought to be Flemish. It has sometimes been assumed that Antonello had visited Flanders, but in fact, the influence surely came from Flemish paintings and Flemish-trained painters in Naples, where Antonello spent his formative years.

    C. Antonello spent about two years in Venice. In the next lecture, we turn to the liberating influence of Antonello on Giovanni Bellini.

Works Discussed:

Giovanni Bellini:

    Madonna with the Blessing Child, c. 1460–1470, Accademia, Venice.

    Madonna of the Trees (*Madonna degli Alberetti*), 1487, Accademia, Venice.

    Pietà, c. 1465–1470, National Gallery, London.

    Pietà, c. 1465, Pinacoteca di Brera, Milan.

    The Agony in the Garden, c. 1465–1470, National Gallery, London.

    Entombment, c. 1475, Pinacoteca, Vatican Museums, Vatican State.

Donatello:

    Christ as the Man of Sorrows, 1447–1450, High Altar, Sant'Antonio, Padua.

Antonello da Messina:

    Saint Jerome in His Study, c. 1475, National Gallery, London.

Essential Reading:

Adams, chapter 13.

Hartt, chapter 15.

Supplementary Reading:

Goffen, Rona. *Giovanni Bellini*. New Haven: Yale University Press, 1989.

Questions to Consider:

1. How does Giovanni Bellini use the device of a painted sill, balustrade, or other foreground ledge in his paintings of the Madonna and Child and his paintings of the Dead Christ?

2. What are the similarities and differences between the *Agony in the Garden* painted by Bellini and that painted by Mantegna (Lecture Twenty-Six)?

Lecture Twenty-Nine—Transcript
Giovanni Bellini—The Early Years

Today I want to share the art of Giovanni Bellini with you, at least the early art of Giovanni Bellini. We looked at his brother Gentile's work at the end of the last lecture, and Gentile Bellini and his brother both seem to have been kept quite busy in their father's studio for a great many years. I haven't said much about their father, and I'm not going to begin to now, but of course he was their teacher and he was well known and he had a very active and very extensive workshop with many projects, and since both of the sons seemed to have been engaged in that shop and kept quite busy, it wasn't surprising that they didn't really begin their own independent careers until they were well into their 20s.

Giovanni Bellini was born about 1430 and died in 1516. By the time of his death, he was the dean of Venetian painters. Extended families of artists seem to be a particularly Venetian phenomenon, and both of the Bellini brothers are examples of this, of sons who kept working in the family business. Jacopo, the father, died around 1470-71, and in the years just before that, the two sons began to assert themselves as independent masters. When Giovanni Bellini did emerge as an independent painter in the 1460s, and thereafter throughout his career, he was known for solemn pictures of the Madonna and Child, and for very moving images of the Pietá. Although he would eventually produce superb multi-figure altarpieces and mythologies, these two types that I just mentioned are inextricably linked with his art and are particularly dominant in the early years of his career.

You're looking at the *Madonna with the Blessing Child*, painted in the 1460s; it's not a dated work, but was painted sometime during that first decade of his independent activity. It shows a mournful Madonna protectively clasping the Child with both hands. She is upright, her head just slightly tilted away, but basically a very vertical figure and a broad figure filling the vertical panel. The Child, which she supports, stands on the balustrade in front of her, leans to our left, and although he is blessing, his hand is in the active blessing, he does not look at us. He doesn't look at the worshiper who receives this benediction. Rather, his eyes are focused away from the painting, focused on the unseen, focused on—as so often happens in these images of the Madonna and Child—focused on the future, focused on the Passion that is implicit in this painting, in the black background. We've seen that in one other occasion at least, the black background suggesting the Passion, the death and sacrifice of Christ. But this is always a constant in images of the Madonna and Child.

The half-length composition that he uses here, placed behind a sill or balustrade of some sort, is a composition found in Jacopo Bellini's Madonnas—the father's Madonnas—that is used continuously by his son, Giovanni. The angle of the Child is slightly disturbing to me. It's not a natural pose. The lower part of the body leans to the left, our left, and is supported perhaps on the shoulder of the Madonna, whose hands very protectively clasp the body. The upper half of the body of the Child is upright, and then the head turns again at that angle to the left. There is an intentional breaking of the body, an intentional angularity and unnaturalness to the pose, which is disturbing, and the wrapping—which is rather toga-like in a sense—is also suggestive of a shroud, and again the painting is deeply mournful. These paintings of the Madonna and Child by Giovanni Bellini can absorb your eyes and your mind for a very long time.

I'm going to contrast it with a much-later Madonna, perhaps 20 years later, a Madonna now in the Accademia Gallery in Venice, the *Madonna of the Trees*, as it is known. Painted in 1487, it's actually his first dated work, and it is a very different painting, different in color, we suddenly go from that dark black background and dark colors for the Madonna and Child, to a scene that is set out of doors in front of a "cloth of honor," flanked by trees that give it its name, the two trees and with bright daylight colors. That "cloth of honor," which one often sees behind the Madonna, is an old invention found in medieval art as well as the Renaissance and later, and it's the kind of cloth that you would find behind royalty, and here it is used for the Queen of Heaven, for the Madonna.

This composition, with an outdoor Madonna and Child behind the sill again, marble in this case, with a "cloth of honor" but with a landscape opening on either side, may be Giovanni's invention. I don't know anyone who did it before then; there may be somebody, but it may be his invention. In any case, it's a very lyrical motif in his hands. Whether the two trees have symbolic allusion is not clear. I think they probably do; the tree is such a standard symbol in various ways in religious scenes, in scenes of the Crucifixion and scenes having to do with the Garden of Eden. In all sorts of ways, trees can be symbolic.

It's been suggested (without any specific point) that it alludes to something in the *Song of Songs*. I was unable to find a passage that seemed to match it. But certainly, whether they're symbolic or not, they're freshly expressive and compositionally exact. He doesn't have much space on either side of that cloth, just a narrow strip on both sides, and yet the eye goes back, is pulled back by those trees to them, even while they emphasize the verticality of the whole composition, and beyond them, you suddenly see the mountains, just the edges of the mountains at the horizon line here, a field in the near ground, and, of course, we pass that very quickly, and suddenly you're aware of the mountain range on the terra firma, the mainland near Venice again.

The whole composition is upright. She is a strong vertical, the "cloth of honor" is, including a seam in the center of it that emphasizes that, and the Child is, in this case, very erect, very upright. Again, the wonderful supporting hands; hands in Giovanni Bellini are not only expressive, but they are so extraordinarily beautiful. Look that them as they hold the Child, look at the design, if I can even put it that way, of the fingers, the angularity, the spacing, the rhythm he sets up, the way one hand nestles against the other, the way the Christ Child's hand holds his mother's fingers; it's childlike and yet, of course, it is very dignified. Even the upcurved thumb of the Madonna leading us back to the head of the Christ Child has a compositional as well as a human purpose here.

Human is the word for this because it's quite different from the first one I showed you in that we have here a new and very human majesty in his treatment of this subject. It is, by the way, painted in oil, the medium that he learned, as we will see, from Antonello da Messina in 1475-76, when that artist came to Venice, so we've moved from tempera—the medium that he used in all paintings before 1475-76 and oil—to oil, which he used either alone or in combination thereafter.

Giovanni Bellini also painted very moving images of the *Pieta* or the *Lamentation*, in a specifically northern Italian half-length format. Despite repetition, he did them many times, his interpretation of these subjects and the type—the way he presents it—rarely fails to touch us. This *Pietá*, done probably between 1465 and 1470, is in London today in the National Gallery. It's a strongly vertical composition like the Madonna and Child that we were looking at, and in it, the dead Christ is supported by angels again, and perhaps the dead Christ is on the lid of a sarcophagus. You see how his hand, the knuckles of his hand, bend as they come in contact with the surface. It may be interpreted possibly in that fashion.

This owes a noticeable debt to Donatello's bronze relief of the dead Christ on the high altar of the Santo in Padua. You'll remember that there are a great many images on the high altar there, including two images of the dead Christ, one in bronze and one in marble, and this one is quite close to this Donatello. It's just on the end of that altar, the dead Christ in bronze supported by two angels, who are wonderfully weeping here, their hands (free hands because the other hand pulls back the cloth behind the body), their free hands clasp against their face, and their mouths open in wailing, the little wings overlapping the frame. This is very moving, very beautiful, essentially symmetrical when you see it, or so you think it is essentially symmetrical, but then slightly pulled to one side—the angels too slightly differing in pose, the cloth behind them in just a slightly different pull, just a bit away from that intense verticality.

The *Pietá*, which is in the Brera Gallery in Milan today—that you're looking at now, painted about 1465, is perhaps the masterpiece of the early career of Giovanni Bellini. His *Pietá* is so poignant, so moving, so intense, that it's hard to look away from it, hard to look at and hard to look away. The theme of the half-length *Pietá*, in which the dead body of Christ is displayed to us by the Madonna and St. John the Evangelist, held for our contemplation, has a frightful quality, a frightful immediacy. It's his invention again—it's his invention. In the Crucifixion, Mary and John flank the cross. Now the Crucifixion has passed, and they flank him while holding the body, by the way, in the sarcophagus—because all three figures are standing in the sarcophagus.

Look past the front ledge and you see the back ledge here on the left-hand and on the right-hand side. This sill on the edge of the sarcophagus can still be read ambiguously, and is intended to be. It can be read simultaneously as the edge of the sarcophagus and as the front of an altar, making the body of Christ a literal image of the Eucharist. Look at their hands again. He never surpassed this. The four hands and the way that they're choreographed, and the different expressions that they have, the two dead hands of Christ, both with the wounds but not strongly emphatic on blood, just the wounds in the hands, his lifeless hand supported—held by his mother's firm, strong hand—the lower hand resting, as we saw it in the other *Pietà*, on the sarcophagus edge, next to it the hand of the Evangelist as it comes in from the side, widely spread fingers, a very different kind of expression. The whole area, just let your eye traverse the whole area of hands; it is the core of the painting.

The contrast here is extraordinary because the Mother and Child, the Mother and Son, the heads are pressed together, and one has to notice the contrast in flesh tones here as well between the pallor of Jesus and the face of the Madonna and the face of the Evangelist. She presses her face as closely as she can to his. He still wears the crown of thorns, which gives the painting an extra edge, and in contrast to that, we're given a gap on the side, a hiatus, and then the head of the Evangelist who turns away, and whose expression is overt and emotional and outward, his mouth open as he expresses his emotion away from the tight group of these two heads, the striated clouds behind the figures reiterating the horizontal theme of the sarcophagus below and also of the heads above.

The landscape hardly enters into it. It's barren; it's in the deep background. It is Golgotha I think back here, with the crosses, but one can hardly penetrate into it. You're kept in the front with these figures in the foreground. It's not hysterical, and I say that with a certain wonder because a painting like this could be hysterical. The emotion could be out of control, but he exerts immense emotional control, and the painting has a kind of silent grandeur. The Madonna and Christ, the contrast of them with St. John, the contrast of the flesh tones, the moving striated sky, everything here gives us one single powerful emotion.

I'm going to digress for just a moment to say that I frequently hear (when teaching religious subjects) from people who have not encountered them frequently, a certain level of discomfort in facing scenes of suffering, the Christ or the martyrs, and they're there all the way from medieval lives through the 17th century. You are faced with suffering, with dying, with death, and with cruelty, and yet people seem discomforted by it. They'll say, "Why did they choose to paint that?" We've been doing these lectures long enough to know why religious art was dominant and what this would have meant in terms of the faith and so forth. That we understand.

But this goes deeper because we don't question seeing death and dying on the TV news or on the shows that are based on the TV news. We don't see it directly, either; we always see allusions to it. We see people being carried off, we see car a crash, we see various things, so we don't experience that even directly; it is secondhand. This, because of the intensity of this, secondhand though it is, when looking at the *Pietá*, it is very hard not to turn your head away unless you're already so riveted to the painting. I think it's simply that in this society, in this country, we don't experience death and dying directly very often, even in our own families. People die in hospitals and so forth, and we don't have that direct connection with the fact of dying, and the fact of death, that centuries did have and that people in most parts of the world today still have. It's important to keep that in our minds when looking at these images, which are unquestionably powerful and painful.

Giovanni Bellini was Andrea Mantegna's brother-in-law. I don't think I mentioned that earlier when we talked about Mantegna. Giovanni's sister Nicolosia was married to Andrea Mantegna in 1453. Padua and Venice could hardly be closer, and the two artists were therefore naturally in regular contact. Bellini's *Agony in the Garden* of 1465-70 (probably in London in the National Gallery) is clearly similar to the Mantegna version of the same subject, which we looked at quite recently, and which I'll show you again shortly. It was Mantegna who first stated the subject; Bellini in a sense follows his compositional ideas, but stylistically and expressively is completely diverse. As a result, especially since these two are in the same museum today, in London in the National Gallery, they've become a famous art historical comparison, so let me look at the Giovanni first and then turn to the comparison.

In Giovanni Bellini's *Agony in the Garden*, it's been a long night of prayer and internal conflict because dawn is breaking. This is quite extraordinary; this is one of the loveliest, one of the earliest dawns in painting. Look at the color of the horizon; it is extraordinarily poetic, and it simply isn't found prior to this. There's a single angel in the sky, rather than the group that approaches in Mantegna's painting, a single angel almost invisible in his translucency, who holds a chalice in his hand as Christ directs his prayer upward. The weight of sleep on the Apostles, who have experienced (remember) the shock and the tension of the Last Supper just a little while ago, and they really have had enough for the day, and their sleep is so convincing, they're so remarkably taken by sleep, they don't, of course, even see, therefore, Judas leading the soldiers here in the middle ground to capture Christ.

The scene is flanked by two hill towns—not as in Mantegna, by Jerusalem on one side, but simply Italian hill towns. Here's the Mantegna that we looked at before, and it is quite wonderful to look at. The implacable harshness of the landscape, of the rockiness in Mantegna's version, in his sculptured scene, is replaced by a tender vulnerability in the Bellini. Let me show them to you together, the Bellini on the left, of course, the Mantegna on the right. You see what a wonderful contrast, and yet they are clearly related. Bellini clearly was looking at Mantegna and consciously creating a poetic alternative to the epic narrative of his brother-in-law's painting. The figures, Bellini's, are smaller, the sense of spiritual isolation is therefore enhanced, and the end of the long night of prayer, as I said, is announced by this lovely dawn, which ironically reveals the imminent capture of Jesus. The line, the Biblical text, is "the hour is come." Bellini's lyricism and his emotional resonance are what we find in that image, contrasting with the intellectual passion of Mantegna.

The *Entombment*, this monumental *Entombment*, probably painted about 1475, the date is much discussed, now in Rome in the Vatican

Museum there, this painting is also a testament to the reciprocal relationship of the brothers-in-law, for Mantegna's stoic remoteness is felt here in Bellini's painting despite the physical immediacy of Bellini's group, and it is immediate. They're pushed right toward us, cropped on three sides so that the group is right up toward us. But you must take the viewpoint into account, and you see a low viewpoint has been painted into it.

The original position of this painting was the crowning element of the large altarpiece called the Pesaro Altarpiece, for the city where the church was, and it was later separated from that altarpiece. We saw something actually quite similar to this in an earlier lecture, when we looked at the top of the Pisa Altarpiece by Masaccio and saw the *Crucifixion* and knew that it should've been seen from below instead of straight on as you do in the museum today.

This powerful, close-up treatment of the *Entombment* was probably painted just before the arrival in Venice of Antonello da Messina, a painter from the south of Italy, for a two-year sojourn, which profoundly affected the artistic development of Giovanni Bellini and of Venetian painting as a whole. Antonello da Messina, (who was born in 1430 and died in 1479) was destined to alter the course of Venetian painting. I'll hold his biography for the next lecture, but I want to conclude this lecture with a look at one of the paintings he made probably in Venice, but certainly had with him in Venice. It is the
St. Jerome in his Study of about 1475, in London in the National Gallery today. It's painted in oil, as he did throughout his career, on panel.

It's very small, much smaller than you might think. It's approximately 18x14 inches, so it's a small work, and it exhibits one of the notable features of his art: his knowledge of Flemish painting. In the spatial organization, in which we have a fictive stone arch, this has to be understood as architecture, a full-sized arch opening onto the saint's study, and then views through windows at the rear of the same study; the descriptive detail in everything within and on the edge of this, on the front edge, the descriptive detail; the numerous symbolic objects; the use of the oil medium—all of these things relate to Flemish painting and, in fact, in the early 16th century, this painting was thought to be Flemish.

Seeing the painting in the house of Antonia Pascolino in 1529, a writer who was going about looking at art works, recorded:

> The little picture representing St. Jerome reading in his study, robed as a cardinal, is ascribed by some to Antonello da Messina, but the great majority with more probability ascribe it to Jan van Eyck, or to Hans Memling, old Flemish painters, and it really shows their manner, though the face may be finished in the Italian style. The buildings are in the Flemish style; the little landscape is natural and highly finished. It is only to be seen through a window in the door of the study, and it's well in perspective. All the work as regards its finish, coloring, drawing, strength, and relief is perfect. [It's a nice bit of criticism.] A peacock, a quail and a barber's basin are represented in it. [They're all on the foreground sill.] On the desk is a little label, which seems to contain the name of the master, but by looking at it closely, one cannot distinguish any letters, as it is all a deception.

That's the end of the rather long quote, but you can see that he really looked and gave a very long look at this work, and also had to try to consider who had painted it, and the name Jan van Eyck was raised. It's sometimes been assumed that Antonello had visited Flanders, and we'll discuss this further in the next lecture on him. Further observations that I want to make, however, while we have this image, have to do (one) with its small size, and (two) with the extraordinary light. It falls from the left; you can get the first great sense of it on the foreground sill, where the peacock and the bird to the left (partridge I think, rather than quail) are here. Perhaps they're the same, and you can see the shadow of the birds as well. The light enters the large space, the large church-like space, in which this strange little action office area has been set up for the saint to do his reading and writing in his study here, little steps that go up to it.

The succession of architectural spaces, one after the other, is superb, wonderfully handled, and as the man said, the perspective is perfect. The lion, which you expect to find with this saint, is wandering back here. He's in the mid-distance in the shadow; he usually is curled up at his feet. The composition, the echoing curves for instance, and arches, the arches are obvious here on the right as well, and on the left as well, the arch of the doorway in front, they're the smaller curves just as important, the curves down here underneath the pedestal that has the staircase, the curve of the desk here as well. All of these curves lead to the larger curves within the painting and, of course, they're played against the rectilinear elements of the study itself and of the doorway.

It's a very strong and complex and yet utterly clear composition, and one in which detail is so precise, there was no one else in Italy who could paint this kind of detail; no wonder they thought it was Flemish, in Italy, there was nobody who could do this kind of small descriptive detail in a panel 18 inches high. Surely this was a showpiece, an announcement of his abilities when Antonello arrived in Venice in 1475. He may have done it there, but some historians think that it was an earlier painting, that he brought it with him as a demonstration of his talent. We'll find out about why he arrived there, but he still had to have something to show his abilities.

By the way, one reason for thinking it may have been done earlier is that the pavement, which is majolica here, is something much more common in the south of Italy than in the north. Obviously, however, the painting was in Venice in 1529 because that's when it was described by the so-called "Anonimo" who wrote that book about the paintings in Venice in that area. Antonello spent about two years in Venice. He and Giovanni Bellini were probably exact contemporaries, and in the next lecture, we will see the liberating influence of Antonello's art upon that of Giovanni Bellini.

Lecture Thirty
Antonello da Messina and Giovanni Bellini

Scope:

Born in Sicily, probably trained in Naples, Antonello da Messina (c. 1430–1479) was apparently invited to Venice by the Venetian consul in Tunis, who offered him the major commission of the painting on the high altar in the Church of San Cassiano. The resulting painting was revolutionary. Antonello took an established type, the enthroned Madonna accompanied by saints (the so-called *sacra conversazione*—"sacred conversation"—which was more common in northern Europe), and placed the group in a fictive Renaissance architectural recess that was continuous with the real architecture framing the altarpiece. The *San Cassiano Altarpiece* was dismembered, but its innovations survive in the rich legacy of emulation by other artists, especially Giovanni Bellini in his radiantly calm *Saint Giobbe Altarpiece*, unhappily no longer *in situ*.

Of even greater significance was the example Antonello gave of the artistic possibilities of the oil medium. He did not introduce it into Venice, but his richly nuanced, atmospherically translucent, coloristically vibrant painting caused many of the painters of Venice to adopt oils. Antonello is no longer thought to have visited Flanders, where oil painting originated, but to have learned it instead from Flemish artists and art in Naples, where paintings by Jan van Eyck are known to have existed. In addition, into many of his paintings, Antonello introduced extensive landscape backgrounds (another Netherlandish contribution to art history). Landscape became still more significant in Giovanni Bellini's paintings, which often depicted Venetian mainland territory. In Giovanni's *Saint Francis in Ecstasy*, the breathtaking landscape becomes the true Franciscan protagonist. Wedding the lessons of Antonello to his own generous spirit, Giovanni Bellini became one of the greatest masters of the Renaissance.

Outline

I. When Antonello was apparently enticed to Venice by the offer to paint an altarpiece for the main altar of San Cassiano, he responded by designing a painting that broke the pattern for such paintings.

A. Although the *San Cassiano Altarpiece* (c. 1475/76) was later radically cut down and only a small portion of it exists, it is accepted that Antonello's design involved unifying the painted space inhabited by the enthroned Madonna and Child and eight life-size standing saints and coordinating it with the actual frame of the altarpiece.

B. The *sacra conversazione* type, with its origins in northern European painting, was not new. There were two major precursors in Venice and the Veneto. One was Mantegna's 1459 *San Zeno Altarpiece* (Lecture Twenty-Six), in which the real frame was continued by the architecture of the painted space, but the surface of the painting was still divided into three parts in the older Byzantine and Gothic manner. The other was the 1446 Vivarini *Polyptych* (Lecture Twenty-Seven), in which a unified space was created, but a highly artificial and unlikely one with its sense of a stage and its open top.

C. Antonello's altarpiece offered something significantly new in discarding the old tripartite format and providing a continuous progression from the viewer's space through the frame's "door" into the contiguous painted space.

D. The luminosity that the oil medium made possible was masterfully utilized by Antonello to model his faces with a minimum of line and an effect of light in shadow that resembled Leonardo's *sfumato* technique. His softly voluminous figures appeal to the eye and to the tactile sense.

II. In 1475, Antonello painted two small versions of the *Crucifixion* that, although quite similar, contrast markedly in expressive intent.

A. The *Crucifixion* now in London (National Gallery) isolates the crucified Christ against the sky with a cup-like horizon below him and the arms of the cross nearly touching the sides of the frame. Below, the Madonna and Saint John the Evangelist sit on the ground, their backs also nearly touching the frame. It is a silent, iconic presentation.

B. The *Crucifixion* now in Antwerp (Royal Museum of Fine Arts) presents a more complete Calvary, with the two thieves flanking a less dominating Christ and the Madonna and John seated further into the landscape. Still, no other figures from the narrative are present; indeed, the thieves seem to have been included for their expressive potential, given that their bodies are arched outward like a drawn bow, a seemingly small detail that manages to infuse the scene with almost unbearable pain.

III. Although it is not documented that Giovanni Bellini met Antonello, it is impossible that they did not, and despite the difficulty of dating Giovanni's paintings, it is equally unlikely that his art would have developed as it did without Antonello's example. Two of Bellini's paintings from the early 1480s provide evidence of that influence.

    A. The *Transfiguration* shows an increased interest in landscape painting and broad, structural brushwork made possible by the oil medium; both of these may be traced to Antonello.

    B. The Transfiguration is an unfamiliar theme to many viewers of this and other paintings. Indeed, it is often only partially understood theologically.

        1. Jesus, together with Peter, John, and James, goes to a mountaintop to pray. The disciples witnessed Jesus "transfigured before them, and his face did shine as the sun, and his raiment was white as the light." Then, they saw "Moses and Elias [Elijah] talking with him." By invoking the Law (Moses) and the Prophets (Elijah), the Gospels confer significant authority on Jesus.

        2. Bellini played down the visionary quality of the narrative, placing his figures on a modest rise with a rocky escarpment at the near edge. The Old Testament visitants are given immense dignity but in human terms. Bellini did follow the text in giving Jesus magnificent white robes. The Gospels make it clear that the apostles saw Moses and Elias and did not turn away from the sight. Rather, it was from the voice of God ("This is my beloved Son") issuing "out of the cloud" that they fearfully "fell on their face and were sore afraid."

3. This scene, whose mystical, ecstatic potential made it popular in Byzantine art, was given a different interpretation by Giovanni. It has often been observed that he had a pantheistic response to religion, that he expressed the divine through nature. Jesus's head and hands are in the sky, as it were, and the voice, which all can hear, is from the sky, a benediction over the serene landscape.

C. Pantheism suffuses *Saint Francis in Ecstasy*, one of the most breathtaking evocations of light as a spiritually transforming force to be found in painting. It is set on the mainland, of course, because Venice itself offered no landscape vistas or features to support such a scene.

1. The saint, arms outspread, faces fully into the radiant daylight. He has already received the stigmata, and the subject is a less common one: a kind of hymn to nature, a communion with creation that is a hallmark of the story of Saint Francis. In fact, his mouth is open as if in song or prayer to "brother Sun."

2. The descriptive catalogue of nature here is astonishing and fully reflects the influence of Flemish naturalism as introduced by Antonello. The cohesive spatial development, however, surpasses anything in Antonello and the landscape in Giovanni's own *Transfiguration*.

IV. Bellini's greatest surviving altarpiece from the 1480s further documents the importance of Antonello's example, while showing his increasingly monumental aspirations.

A. While in Venice, Antonello had also painted a noble, life-size *Saint Sebastian* (1475–1476), framed by architecture and backed by a soaring sky. This beautifully poised figure, together with the *San Cassiano Altarpiece*, was immensely influential on Giovanni Bellini's *Saint Giobbe Altarpiece*.

B. Bellini's *Saint Giobbe Altarpiece* (c. 1488) continues the innovative spatial unity of Antonello's now-fragmentary painting.

1. With a fictive barrel vault leading to an apse-like chapel with a half dome, the painted space continued the architecture of the altar frame (which still exists).

Remarkably, the fictive architecture is given its true size in relation to the enthroned Madonna and six saints.

2. The subtle and varied effects of light are capped by the imitation of a Byzantine mosaic in the half dome, probably a direct reference to the interior of San Marco.

3. Two of the saints are mostly nude, and the light slides eloquently across their bodies. One is Saint Sebastian, who strongly echoes Antonello's single figure. The other is Saint Job (Giobbe). (Venetians took interesting liberties with hagiography: Job, Jeremiah, and Moses are all sainted, with churches of their own!) Both of these saints are invoked for their curative power, Sebastian for the plague and Job (because of his many sufferings) more generally. The Church of Saint Giobbe was associated with a hospital.

4. Though not without precedent, the musical angels so persuasively and charmingly rendered by Bellini were soon emulated in Venetian painting and elsewhere in Italy.

Works Discussed:

Antonello da Messina:

The Crucifixion, 1475, National Gallery, London.

The Crucifixion (*Calvary*), 1475, Koninklijk Museum Voor Schone Kunsten, Antwerpen (België).

Giovanni Bellini:

The Transfiguration, c. 1480–1485, Museo Nazionale di Capodimonte, Naples.

Saint Francis in Ecstasy, c. 1480–1485, Frick Collection, New York.

The San Giobbe (*Saint Job*) *Altarpiece*, c. 1488, Accademia, Venice.

Antonello da Messina:

San Cassiano Altarpiece, c. 1475–1476, Kunsthistorisches Museum, Vienna.

Saint Sebastian, 1475–1476, Alte Meister, Gemäldegalerie, Dresden.

Essential Reading:

Adams, chapter 13.

Hartt, chapter 15.

Supplementary Reading:

Humphrey, Peter. *The Altarpiece in Renaissance Venice.* New Haven: Yale University Press, 1993.

Rosand, David. *Painting in Cinquecento Venice: Titian, Veronese, Tintoretto.* New Haven: Yale University Press, 1982.

Questions to Consider:

1. Antonello da Messina was in Venice for less than two years. Why was he so influential on the development of Venetian painting?

2. How is the architectural setting in Bellini's *Saint Job Altarpiece* so unusual?

Lecture Thirty—Transcript
Antonello da Messina and Giovanni Bellini

In this lecture, I want to further introduce you to the art of Antonello da Messina. We looked at one of his works last time, *St. Jerome in his Study*, and we closed our discussion in that lecture of the early Giovanni Bellini with the introduction of Antonello. Today, he's here for his own sake for part of the lecture for the explicit beauty of his paintings, and also for his transforming impact on Venetian art in general, and Giovanni Bellini in particular.

It would be nice to give much more time to Antonello, but I am—because of the Venetian connection—confining myself to the works that he did in Venice and that had such a marked impact there, and they include many of his most famous works. I don't think it's an exaggeration to say that it was the wedding, the melding, of the lessons of Antonello to the generous and ardent spirit of Giovanni Bellini that made Bellini become one of the greatest masters of the Renaissance. Bellini was a great painter; that was obvious from the earlier things we've seen, but the lessons of Antonello, as we will see them, liberated him to become a greater painter, a painter who is among the finest in Italian art.

But back to Antonello, born in Sicily, we haven't discussed any painters from the south of Italy. Antonello was born in Sicily, presumably in or near Messina, from which he gets his name, but he probably trained in Naples. Antonello was born about 1430; he's the only southern Italian artist of significance during the Quattrocento. He exhibits the strong influence of Flemish painting, of Jan van Eyck and his followers, and we talked about that in looking at the *St. Jerome* in the last lecture. That model, the Flemish model, sometimes inspired Antonello's interest in descriptive detail, as it did in that painting of Jerome in his study, but even more importantly, it introduced him to the inclusion of landscape backgrounds in his paintings, and most importantly of all, to the adoption of the oil medium for his paintings. The oil medium has Flemish origins.

His encounter with Flemish art was almost certainly in Naples. There's no evidence that he ever went to northern Europe. The 19th-century literature and so forth assumed that he had, but he does not seem to have gone to northern Europe, nor did he need to because in Naples there were Flemish-trained painters, and there were many Flemish paintings including some by Jan van Eyck himself. We know that to be the case, so Antonello's training in Naples is posited in the decades between about 1445 and 1455. He traveled widely, including to Rome and to Venice, and he returned often to Messina, where he died in 1479.

Antonello was apparently invited to Venice by the Venetian consul in Tunis, Pietro Bon. Pietro Bon must have met him in Naples, and we know that he offered him a major commission for a large painting on the main altar in the church of San Cassiano in Venice, where the Bon family had strong connections. The resulting painting was revolutionary, and we will discuss it, but I want to reserve it, to hold it back until we've looked at other works by Antonello first. As I have already stressed, the example that Antonello gave to the Venetians of the artistic possibilities of the oil medium proved revolutionary for Venetian painting.

He was not the first to introduce oils into Venice, but his skillful use of the oil medium—richly nuanced, atmospherically translucent, coloristically vibrant, all the things you can do with the oil medium done so well by Antonello—caused many other Venetian painters to adopt oils in place of the older medium of tempera or in conjunction with that. The luminosity that the oil medium made possible was masterfully utilized by Antonello to model his faces with a minimum of line and with an effect of light in shadow, half-lights, light in shadow that resembled Leonardo's sfumato technique. Antonello's softly voluminous figures appealed to the eye and to the tactile sense. Oil painting originated in Flanders, modern Belgium, and Antonello certainly learned it from Flemish artists and Flemish art, the example of looking at the paintings themselves, in Naples, as I say, where paintings from that school and artists are known to have been.

I might interject to say that there is a long tradition in the 15th century and before of connections between the Netherlands, between Flanders, and the south of Europe, not only in Naples but in Spain. In fact, the connection between Spain and Naples has a lot to do with the fact that Naples was a center as well. There was trading, lots of art was commissioned or purchased by the Spanish king to go into the collections in Spain. There's a lot of connection through the decades and the centuries, so it's not surprising to find Antonello encountering Flemish art there. We make too much sometimes of how they knew Flemish painting. If we had a list of all the Flemish paintings that Italians had seen, we'd be astonished, I think.

In 1475, Antonello painted two small versions of the *Crucifixion* that are quite similar at first glance, but contrast markedly in expressive intent. The first one (in London today in the National Gallery) was painted in 1475, and in it, Antonello isolates the Crucified Christ against the sky with a cup-like horizon below him, and the arms of the cross nearly touching the sides of the frame. Below, the Madonna and St. John the Evangelist sit upon the ground, their backs also nearly touching the frame. It's a silent, iconic presentation. Look at it a little further, this cup-like horizon is one of the keys to it, it seems to me—that and the partially almost arched top. You see the top, the frame was angled in, so you had a bending in of the top of the composition, and then the cup of the horizon echoed, and there's a distant mountain, possibly distant water, it's hard to say.

Then, in the middle ground, there's a lake, again a flat circular shape with some medieval turreted buildings on it, and then we move into a greener area here in the foreground, a green background for Golgotha itself, and then the place Golgotha is marked clearly by the skulls on the ground, the skulls on the ground, the place of the skulls in front of it, yet this is not a narrative scene. Except for John and Mary, we don't have any of the other actors in this. This is not the crucifixion as a story. It is the Crucified Christ in a landscape with the Madonna and John, and they're seated in the most original way, especially the Madonna, seated with legs crossed (it seems) almost under her on the ground. I don't know outside of Antonello anyone who did this, and it has not only a sense of humility, but a tremendous sense of weariness to it. The way she sits there, it's just an emptying quality of the body, an emptied quality of the body and that cup shape of the horizon is here as well in the two bodies here, in these two figures. They also form a cup shape at the bottom of the cross. It is a striking interpretation.

The other version is today in Antwerp in the Royal Museum there, done at the same time. We don't know who commissioned these two, I don't think. This one is more complete because the two thieves on their crosses have been brought in, and yet we don't have anyone else. We don't have those who put him on the cross, we don't have the centurion, we don't have any of these figures at all, so we have a slightly more complete cast, but it's still not a narrative crucifixion in the usual sense. The Madonna again is seated in that way on the ground, but now in the picture a little more, and John kneels, and he too is into the picture a bit more, and we have not merely one, but a number of skulls on the ground marking the place as Golgotha.

The whole of the landscape appears to be much drier, more barren, less appealing in that sense, in the green sense and in the fertile sense than in the previous version. We do have this cup at the background again; this time it's the leg moved a little further back into the picture. It seems to me that he included the thieves almost solely for their expressive potential because he's placed them on the most remarkable crosses—not a cross like Jesus was crucified upon, which is a finished cross, very high, but one that is a carpentered cross, which is a true cross; whereas, the two thieves are on trees that had been fashioned into crosses. They've had their limbs lopped off and the artist makes crosses of them in—again—a very original, very imaginative fashion.

But what is most intriguing and most powerful here is that those trees on either side that the thieves are crucified on are arched outward like a drawn bow and arrow, like a drawn bow and as though to just snap those bodies into space. There is so much tension in that small detail that it infuses the scene with an almost unbearable sense of tension and of pain. The contrast between those arched, tensed bodies and the straight vertical center body is really quite remarkable. I don't know whether there's any meaning symbolically between these two contrasts, between these tree crosses and the carpentered cross or not; I haven't encountered it before.

Landscape became even more significant in Giovanni Bellini's paintings, where they often depicted the Venetian mainland territory that the Venetians called "terra firma." We know that word well enough, and terra firma was their mainland possession. Interestingly, it's not even documented that Giovanni Bellini met Antonello, but it's impossible that he did not. He could not have failed to have met this phenomenal young painter who had come to town. Despite the difficulty of dating Giovanni Bellini's paintings, it's equally unlikely that his art could have developed as it did without the intervention of Antonello's example. Two of Bellini's paintings from the early 1480s provide evidence of that influence.

One of them is the *Transfiguration*, probably painted between 1480-85, but as I say, these dates are not fixed. It's in Naples today in the Capodimonte Museum. The *Transfiguration* shows an increased interest in landscape painting to be sure for Giovanni, and broad, structural brushwork made possible by the oil medium, and both of these may be traced to Antonello and his example. The *Transfiguration* is an unfamiliar theme to many viewers. Indeed, it's often only partially understood theologically. In the *Transfiguration*, in this event, Jesus, together with Peter and John and James, goes to a mountaintop to pray. The disciples on this occasion witnessed Jesus "transfigured before them, and his face did shine as the sun, and his raiment was white as the light." Then, they saw Moses and Elias [Elijah] talking with him. "

By invoking the Law (Moses) and the Prophets (Elijah), the Gospels here confer a very significant authority upon Jesus. Bellini plays down the visionary quality of the narrative, whereas Raphael, I didn't show it to you, but a later Raphael plays up the visionary. Here it's played down. His figures are on a modest rise, not even a mountaintop as we would think of it, a modest rise with a rocky escarpment at the edge here, quite a dramatic one, even though it's just tucked in at the front. The Old Testament visitants to have come, Moses and Elijah, are given immense dignity, flanking him here, standing on either side of Jesus. They're very powerful, dignified figures, but human, very human. They're solid, and they don't look at all visionary. They look absolutely credible and real.

Bellini did follow the text in giving Jesus magnificent white robes. The Gospels make it clear when you read this event that the Apostles saw Moses and Elijah, who was called Elias frequently, and did not turn away from the sight, and yet you see that they seem to be turning away here, so what they're turning away from is the voice of

God. It was because of the voice of God saying, "This is my beloved Son," issuing "out of the cloud" that they fearfully "fell on their face and were sore afraid." This scene, whose mystical, ecstatic potential made it popular in Byzantine art, was given a very different interpretation by Giovanni. It has often been observed that he had a pantheistic response to religion, and that he expressed the divine through nature. Jesus's head here, for instance, and hands are in the sky. They're above the horizon, and the voice (which all of them hear) is from the sky, a benediction over the serene landscape.

In Giovanni's *St. Francis in Ecstasy*, the breathtaking landscape becomes the true Franciscan protagonist. Pantheism suffuses this painting. It is one of the most breathtaking evocations of light as a spiritually transforming force to be found anywhere in painting. It's set on the mainland, of course, since Venice itself offered no such landscape vistas. The saint, arms outspread, faces fully into the radiant daylight. He has already received the stigmata; one has to look close at the picture to see them, but he has received the stigmata, and the subject is therefore a less common one. Usually, we see St. Francis receiving the stigmata and in the sky a seraphim holding the Crucified Christ, a small cross or the vision of Christ from whose wounds the stigmata are transferred to Francis. We don't see that here, and so there is a kind of communion with creation, a hymn to nature in this painting that is, in fact, a hallmark of the story of St. Francis, of his life.

His mouth, in fact, is open here, as if he were in song or prayer to, as he said, "brother Sun," and yet there may be a reception of the stigmata, or may just have been here, because there are two different kinds of light in this picture: a lower light, it all comes from the left and it floods the picture, but the lower light, the more natural one, moves across, graces the landscape and the figure here; and then there's a brilliant light from the upper left-hand corner because of the way it strikes the figure of the saint, strikes the lectern in the background, strikes the rock. That more brilliant light seems to be a light of a different order, and so one light is the morning light and the other one is this brilliant supernatural light that could be argued—and has been argued—to reflect the experience of the stigmatization.

This is obviously an almost mystical approach to it, if that is the identification, but you see the animals and birds—here the crane, here the ass—are turning toward the light; they too are aware of it. This tree seems to be blown to the right by the force of that brilliant light, quivering in the light. It's an amazing descriptive catalogue of nature, not merely the crags and crevices and the rocks here, but all of the trees and plants and animals, rabbits, all sorts of objects, his wooden clogs (the saint's under the lectern at the lower right-hand side), the reading book, the Bible and the skull on top of it, but just an entire catalogue of such things back into the landscape, where we have architecture situated on the hill as well. This naturalism obviously reflects Flemish naturalism, the kind that Antonello is thought to have introduced, but the spatial development is more cohesive than anything found in Antonello, and it also—this landscape in cohesive spatial construction—surpasses that that we just saw in his own *Transfiguration*.

As I said at the outset, Antonello's arrival in Venice was apparently the result of an invitation. The Venetian consul in Tunis, who must have met Antonello in Naples, gave him the commission that I mentioned earlier for a major altarpiece in the church of San Cassiano in Venice. That and his other paintings that we've looked at were all produced during the nearly two years that he stayed in Venice, but it was the *San Cassiano Altarpiece* that revolutionized Venetian painting, which is a fact difficult to explain and to understand when one confronts the mere fragment that is left today in a museum in Vienna, in the Kunsthistorisches Museum. Instead of the altarpiece that was made, we have now three panels, three fragments from it, which have been mounted together and put on the wall in Vienna, and as beautiful as they are, they speak hardly at all to what was made originally.

Antonello responded to the challenge of the prominent placement of this picture of the high altar by designing a painting that broke the mold for such altarpieces. He started with the established type of the enthroned Madonna with saints, accompanied by saints with which we've become familiar, the so-called "sacred conversation," (the sacra conversazione). This type—this sacred conversation type—has its origins in northern European painting, but it was no longer new in Italy, but it was still being developed. It was still undergoing change, and there were two major precursors in Venice and the Veneto of this subject type that we have seen.

Let me show you the *San Cassiano Altarpiece* to the left, the fragment together with Vivarini's *Polyptych* of 1446, in which a unified space was created for the saints and the Madonna and the angels. It's all one space, but it's a highly artificial and unlikely one, with its sense of a stage here, like a little drama, and also with its open top. The whole thing has a sense of fantasy to it rather than reality. More important was Mantegna's 1459 *San Zeno Altarpiece*, in which the real frame, you see them together here, now the real frame was continued by the architecture of the painted space, and I mean all parts of the real frame. The columns—all four of them have columns painted just behind them—moving us into the space, continuing and making the frame part of the space, but in the Mantegna, it still divides the surface of the painting into three parts. It's still a strong separate tripartite painting in the older Gothic and Byzantine manner.

Should I reemphasize the reason that the development of the sacred conversation type of altarpiece was significant? Otherwise it sounds like art historical jargon. Instead of saints and Madonnas occupying isolated niches of space, belonging to another world, with no interaction with us or with their fellow saints, the innovation of the sacra conversazione placed them all together in a unified space that was a reflection—sometimes even a continuation—of the space that we stand in. The potential for interaction, even if these saints don't necessarily "converse," means that we find in these painted figures a human relationship to ourselves, that they're real to a greater degree, real human figures, however sacred, standing or sitting together in a real space. The degree of identification enhances the empathetic response of you and I to the painting. In short, this is not just an academic or artistic device; it's part of the fundamental shift in the presentation of the sacred scenes to the faithful, or simply to the viewer.

Back to the *San Cassiano Altarpiece* alone. It was later radically cut down, dismembered, savaged really, in the early 17th century, and only a small portion still exists. Based on these three fragments, which make up what you see, and copies of other fragments that were subsequently lost, and above all the evidence of other paintings that were immediately influenced by Antonello's painting, it is generally accepted that this painting in its full state was of decisive importance for Venetian art at this moment. Its innovations survive in the rich legacy of emulation by other artists. His design involved unifying the painted space inhabited by the enthroned Madonna and Child, and originally eight, not four, eight life-size standing saints, and coordinating that space and the figures with the actual frame of the altarpiece.

This pictorial solution was similar to Mantegna's painting, but without the tripartite division of the frame. Therefore, Antonello's altarpiece offered something significantly new; it discarded the old three-part format and provided a continuous progression from the viewer's space through the frame's door into the contiguous painted space. Notice I'm being redundant for a purpose; I think reiterating this may help. Notice that the viewpoint—the eye level—is that of the saint's eyes, the standing saint's eyes, and just below the knees of the seated Madonna. Extend the saints in your imagination full-length, add two more on either side, add a domed niche behind the throne and enclose the saints in an architectural space and voila, you have the reconstructed altarpiece.

Yes, it's very hard to visualize, I agree, much easier instead to look at the most famous altarpiece that was inspired by the *San Cassiano Altarpiece*, Giovanni Bellini's *St. Giobbe Altarpiece*. Giobbe—the name of the altarpiece in the church from which it came—Giobbe. The *St. Giobbe Altarpiece*, painted about 1488 perhaps, is now in the Accademia Gallery. I saved this painting and Antonello's painting—the *San Cassiano Altarpiece*, which was in progress from the time that he arrived in Venice—for this moment in order to make this essential comparison with Bellini at this point. This is Bellini's greatest surviving altarpiece from the 1480s, and it documents the influence of Antonello while showing Bellini's increasingly monumental designs.

It's such a great painting I hardly know where to begin. It's a radiantly calm painting that continues the innovative spatial unity of Antonello's now-fragmentary painting. This is, in a sense, one step from the Antonello; so let it stand for it. With a fictive barrel vault, this is all painted, all flat, with a fictive barrel vault leading to an apse-like chapel with a half-dome, the painted space continued the architecture of the altar frame (which, by the way, the frame still exists in the church), but this painting came from inside the church on the same altar with another painting in it, while the painting, leaving the frame behind, went to the museum—but we know what it looked like and looks like.

Remarkably, the fictive architecture is given its true size in relation to the enthroned Madonna and six saints; in other words, you see how big this fictive chapel is. Usually in such paintings, it was a much-reduced space to let the figures dominate. Not now, he allows the figures to be life-size and the architecture as well to be life-size. Unhappily, this painting was removed from the church in which it was and squeezed into an utterly inadequate gallery space in the Accademia. The subtle and varied effects of light in this painting are capped by the imitation of a Byzantine mosaic in the half-dome, which is certainly a direct reference to the interior of San Marco.

From left to right, let me run through the saints quickly. The saints are St. Francis, facing us with the stigmata, looking at us to establish contact, bring us into the painting; John the Baptist, just ahead here next to Francis; and then, St. Job; and then, on the other side of the altar, St. Dominic, with the prayer book; and St. Sebastian prominently; and then the bishop saint, St. Louis of Toulouse. This St. Louis of Toulouse was the 13th-century St. Louis who renounced the throne of Naples to become a Franciscan; he became Bishop of Toulouse and died at the age of 23, and he occurs in a number of Renaissance works of art. St. Sebastian and St. Job are mostly nude, and the light from the right glides across these figures, just glides eloquently across their bodies.

Venetians took interesting liberties with the hagiography: despite their Old Testament lives, both Job and Moses are sainted in Venice. They each have churches of their own. Both of these saints are invoked for their curative power, by the way—St. Job and St. Sebastian—Sebastian for the plague and Job (because of his many sufferings) more generally for illness, and the church of St. Giobbe (from which this came) was associated with a hospital, so it had a connection, a very direct one. The nobility of this painting, its unity, its powerful unified construction of surface and space, mark it as a painting of the High Renaissance, created in the same years that Leonardo was producing his own High Renaissance masterpieces in Milan. Finally, although not without precedent, the trio of musical angels so persuasively and charmingly rendered by Bellini at the foot of this altarpiece was emulated and echoed in Venetian painting and elsewhere in Italy, from the time this painting was first seen.

Perhaps it's fair to give Antonello the last word in this lecture. While in Venice, he had also painted a noble life-size *St. Sebastian*. This painting, as you see, the *St. Sebastian* is framed by architecture that is in the background and a soaring sky, a marvelous sky, and behind that, a strong perspective thrust behind the saint who dominates in the foreground, a beautifully poised figure in the foreground in wonderfully elegant pose, one that was strongly echoed in the *St. Sebastian* and Bellini's *St. Giobbe Altarpiece*, which we've just seen.

Lecture Thirty-One
Giovanni Bellini—The Late Years

Scope:

The serenity of Bellini's late work is astonishing. An example is the deceptively simple *Madonna and Child with the Magdalen and Saint Catherine*, which may show the direct influence of Leonardo da Vinci, who visited Venice in 1500. The painting holds the eye and stirs the imagination through its aura of spiritual restraint. The noble likeness of *Doge Leonardo Loredan* is apt to make the viewer think that it has never been surpassed in portraiture. Here, firmness of design is revealed by a crystalline light that seems to equate with moral and intellectual clarity. In Bellini's late Madonnas, the landscape of the *terra firma* underscores the emotion with unfailing aptness. The *San Zaccaria Altarpiece*, still in situ, is perhaps the first (1505) indisputable masterpiece of the Venetian High Renaissance. Bellini appropriated not only the architecture of the altar, but the light that falls from the western window into his painting. The resultant nobility and ineffable tranquility of his creation is beyond praise.

Near the end of his life, he completed a remarkable mythological painting for Alfonso d'Este, duke of Ferrara. *The Feast of the Gods* combines wit, sleepy sensuality, and the beauty of nature in the transformation of a lusty tale from Ovid into a poetic reverie. The painting has a deep musicality, a richness of tone, and an orchestration of form and narrative that fittingly rounds out the artist's career. It also offered a lesson and an opportunity to one of his many greatly talented students, Titian, who in an act of homage, repainted the landscape some 15 years later to better accord with his own paintings in the same room!

Outline

I. Like many long-lived artists, Giovanni Bellini developed a distinctive old-age style or, more correctly, manner. It was, in a word, serenity.

   A. His *Madonna and Child with the Magdalen and Saint Catherine* (c. 1500) is typical. The three half-length women, disposed symmetrically, are placed against an impenetrable dark ground, lit subtly from the left.

B. The mystery that emanates from the picture is reminiscent of Leonardo's art and provides the presumptive date of the picture, because Leonardo was in Venice in March of 1500.

II. Bellini painted many portraits, but one outshines them all: *Doge Leonardo Loredan* (c. 1501).

A. For some who stand in front of this painting, it is, for that moment, the *summa* of portraiture. Rectitude and reason are perfectly conjoined here. Descriptively, it is superbly painted, with every detail proclaiming its veracity and glowing with inner as well as outer light.

B. In October 1501, the doge had just been installed in the position he would occupy for almost 20 years, and this portrait must have recorded his accession.

III. Bellini's late Madonnas, presenting the Christ Child or bearing the dead Son, are now often set in front of a landscape. Although still placed immediately in front of us, even cropped at the bottom to pull them closer, these images are infused with the poetry of the landscape. Bellini is indisputably the first great Venetian master of landscape painting.

A. The *Madonna of the Meadow* (perhaps c. 1500) places the triangular group of mother and child in front of a landscape that has a prominent hill town in the background. Mary sits on the ground, a Madonna of humility (as in Raphael's *Alba Madonna*, Lecture Twenty-Three). The most notable feature of the painting, however, is the pose of the Child, unmistakably suggesting death and, therefore, foreshadowing the Passion to come. Death is also evoked by a vulture in the barren trees at the left. The expressive procession of clouds across the sky may recall Wordsworth to some minds: "trailing clouds of glory do we come, from God, who is our home."

B. The *Pietá* (c. 1505) is the inevitable sequel to the previous image. The more barren landscape and the architecture retreat into the distant landscape.

C. A *Madonna and Child* dated 1510 still uses compositional ideas that Bellini had developed 20 years earlier.

1. When this painting is compared with the *Madonna of the Trees* (1487) that we saw in Lecture Twenty-Nine, it is clear that Bellini has relaxed the format. The landscape wings flanking the Madonna and Child are not only more spacious but also more expressive.

2. On the one hand, the animated contour of the Virgin's robes ties the figures compositionally to the landscape, which is rich in human activity. On the other, these sacred personages remain resolutely separate from the world, seated in front of their "cloth of honor."

IV. Bellini's altarpieces are crowned by the *San Zaccaria Altarpiece* (1505), an enthroned Madonna with four saints that is still in situ.

   A. The church is one of the most venerable in the city, founded in the 9th century and once owning land that is the present Piazza San Marco. The altar for which Bellini painted this masterpiece is on the left wall of the broad church.

   B. The amplitude of the four saints is reinforced by the studied symmetry of the composition. Giovanni has, in a sense, cast a glance back at Byzantine symmetry, and once more (as in the *Saint Giobbe Altarpiece*), he closes the pictorial space with a half-dome Byzantine mosaic. It should be noted that the painting has been cut down at the top, qualifying the illusionistic effect.

   C. Bellini unites the architecture of the altar with the painting and unites both with the natural light that falls into the church from a window on the façade.

   D. The entire altarpiece seems to enfold space in an enveloping embrace, while projecting an inescapable aura of trance-like meditation. This is perhaps the first absolute masterpiece of the Venetian High Renaissance.

V. Bellini was a gifted teacher with talented pupils, including Giorgione and Titian, and in the last years of his life, he found himself in competition with them.

   A. His *Feast of the Gods*, dated 1514, was painted for the "Alabaster Chamber" of Alfonso d'Este, duke of Ferrara, who intended to gather in one room paintings by the finest living Italian artists. Although he was frustrated in his intentions, he nonetheless ended up with a Bellini and three Titians.

B. Bellini was assigned his subject from Ovid's *Fasti*, which involved the Olympian gods drowsing after reveling. One of the sleeping nymphs, Lotis, is coveted by Priapus, who steals in and begins to lift her skirt when the ass brays, everybody awakes, and Priapus is frustrated in his attempt.

C. The painting, one of the artist's last, is a triumph of saturated color, indeed, a demonstration of what we mean when we speak of Venetian color.

D. Although the duke was unable to secure paintings by Raphael and Fra Bartolommeo, Titian eventually painted the remaining three subjects. In order to harmonize Bellini's *Feast of the Gods* with his own works, he secured permission to alter the landscape background of the painting. Thus, the pupil literally succeeded the master, although Titian's changes should not be regarded as criticism of Bellini.

Works Discussed:

Giovanni Bellini:

Madonna and Child with the Magdalen and Saint Catherine, c. 1500, Accademia, Venice.

Doge Leonardo Loredan, c. 1501, National Gallery, London.

The Madonna of the Meadow, c. 1500, National Gallery, London.

Pietà, c. 1505, Accademia, Venice.

Madonna and Child, 1510, Pinacoteca di Brera, Milan.

(*San Zaccaria Altarpiece*, 1505, San Zaccaria, Venice.

The Feast of the Gods (altered by Titian), 1514, Widener Collection, National Gallery of Art, Washington, DC.

Essential Reading:

Adams, chapter 13.

Hartt, chapter 15.

Questions to Consider:

1. Who were Giovanni Bellini's most important pupils, and what did they learn from his work?

2. What do you think we usually mean when we speak of the *late style* of an artist, and how would you describe Bellini's late style?

Lecture Thirty-One—Transcript
Giovanni Bellini—The Late Years

Like many artists who achieve a long life, who live to an advanced age and continue to paint or make art, Giovanni Bellini developed a very distinctive old-age style; it probably would be better, more correct, to say an old-age manner. It's not so much how he paints it as the mood that he projects. That old-age manner was, in a word, serenity. The serenity of Giovanni Bellini's late work is astonishing.

You're looking at a devotional painting of the *Madonna and Child with the Magdalen and St. Catherine*, painted probably about 1500, today in the Accademia Gallery in Venice. It's typical of much of the work after 1500 by Bellini. It's deceptively simple; it shows three half-length women, disposed symmetrically and placed against a dark background—an impenetrable dark background—while they are subtly illuminated from the left side. This is a remarkably wide canvas in proportion to its height, and this leads or aids in the serenity—or of the effect of serenity—that the painting has. There is a sense of mystery in the painting as well, and that mystery that seems to emanate from it is somewhat reminiscent of Leonardo da Vinci's art and possibly provides a date for the picture because Leonardo visited Venice in March of 1500. He and Bellini would surely have met, and he may well have seen at that time art that Leonardo had with him.

The painting holds the eye and stirs the imagination through an aura of what I would describe as spiritual restraint. There is another aspect here; we've seen it once in Bellini at least, and that was in the *Pietá*, and we will see it again, and it's striking. None of the figures look at us or each other, and that sense of isolation that results from those figures not really making eye contact (it's not quite true, of course— the saint on the left looks down at the Christ Child, but there is no eye contact there) creates a sense of each of these figures in their own space in a way and in their own sanctity.

Giovanni Bellini painted many portraits, and they are fine portraits. He was an excellent portrait artist. There is one I think most people would agree outshines them all. It is the portrait of the *Doge*

Leonardo Loredan, painted in Venice at the beginning of the 16th century, in 1501, though not dated. It is in London today in the National Gallery. It is so noble, so persuasive, so hypnotic in its effect that when seen in person, it's apt to make the viewer think that this painting has never been surpassed in portraiture. In October 1501, the Doge had just been installed in the position that he would then occupy for almost 20 years, and this portrait must have recorded his accession to the ducal throne.

Descriptively, as a record of the facts of the sitter's face, it's superbly painted. Every detail proclaims its veracity. We don't have to see another portrait to compare with it. We know this is the way he looked. Rectitude and reason in a perfect balance—an ideal balance—shines from this face. Those qualities are perfectly expressed through the design, a firm design, a design completely controlled—that total design, the shapes and positioning of the shapes, not only of the head and the torso but of costume folds and facial creases. Look here, for instance, in the tunic, this curve—it's a pattern on the embroidered tunic. Look at this, and then look at the curve of the creases in his face, of the folds of his face echoing that beautifully. The patterns of the embroidery, the fall of the shadow, everything in that design is revealed to the viewer by a light. One wants to describe it by itself and say it's Bellini's light; of course, it's so crystalline, so clear, and when I say revealed I mean revealed.

The light literally makes known, discloses the sitter, the costume, the character, the purity, the clarity of that revelatory light seems to somehow equate with moral clarity, intellectual clarity. This portrait glows with inner as well as outer light, and I have to say that for some who stand in front of this painting, myself included, in front of the painting, it is for that moment the summation of the art of portraiture, and I wish I could transport each of you magically to be in front of it now.

Also in London's National Gallery—where, by the way, there is an extraordinary collection of Bellini's paintings—is this painting of, again, the turn of the century, *The Madonna of the Meadow*. I'll talk about it in a moment in detail, but in Bellini's late Madonnas, whether with the Child or with the dead Christ, the landscape of the terra firma underscores the emotion of the subject with unfailing aptness. Where the early Madonnas were sparing in their use of the landscape, or used black backgrounds (which we saw as well), these late Madonnas, presenting the Christ Child or bearing the dead Son, are now often set in front of a full, meaningful landscape. While still placed directly in front of us, even cropped at the bottom (as here) to pull them closer to us visually, these images are infused with the poetry of the landscape.

This landscape moves back from the extraordinary triangular group of the Madonna into the landscape. The triangular shape of the Madonna fills virtually the whole foreground and places the triangular group of the Mother and Child in front of a landscape that has a prominent hill town in the background. I don't know if it has been identified, but this is identifiable generically as the Veneto, the mainland belonging to Venice. This is recognizable territory to the regional viewers of this painting. In the nearer landscape, livestock is being tended. You can see at this point on both sides of the Madonna livestock tended, farming going forward, while this timeless biblical event that dominates the picture goes unnoticed in the foreground. Mary sits upon the ground, a Madonna of Humility (as in Raphael's *Alba Madonna,* lecture 23).

But the most notable feature of the figure group is the pose of the Child, unmistakably suggesting death and therefore foreshadowing the Passion to come. Death is also evoked by a vulture in the barren trees at the left. The expressive clouds that move across the sky, clouds that once they capture your eye, this trail of clouds is hypnotic, and to me, at least, they recall Wordsworth: "trailing clouds of glory do we come, from God, who is our home." There is a super reality to those clouds, which is hard to tear your eyes from; it makes it hard to tear your eyes away from them.

The *Pietà,* painted about 1505, is, as it were, the inevitable sequence of the painting we just looked at, the one predicting the death in the nativity and now the dead Christ, again, in a landscape. The landscape is more barren, and except for the symbolic enclosure of fresh green vegetation close behind, just behind the mother and son, the rest of the landscape is pushed back. It doesn't enter easily. It is backdrop, and yet it is quite prominent when you examine the three hills or rises in the back. The numerous architectural features—and there are many—retreat, to some degree, into this distant landscape, and yet this is very specific architecture.

It has been identified, I'm not going to give you chapter and verse, but the architecture has been seen as a synthesis, an imaginative bringing together, of various ecclesiastical buildings—which are recognizable—that are to be found in at least three different places— in Vicenza, in Cividale, and in Ravenna—three cities in three different directions from Venice, which not only indicates that he's inventing, as it were, in the studio, which we understand, this is not a painting of "reality," but it also demonstrates that he had either made or otherwise owned drawings of these places, of the architectural features, and was using them specifically for such landscape compositions in the backgrounds of figure compositions. If it needed stressing, and I don't think it does by now, Giovanni Bellini is indisputably the great, the first great Venetian landscape painter, even though landscape remains in the background, not in the main subject, as it would remain for some time in the history of art.

The long horizontal body of Christ in this painting would seem impossible for the Madonna to support, but just as in the preceding painting, she's seated low on the ground, and her robe spreads out to receive the body, and look at the beautiful contrasts of the colors, this brilliant saturated blue on our left and the deeper purplish-blue on the right-hand side—gorgeous colors that are also treated structurally. They're not just surface; all of this is modeled in such a way and constructed in such a way that it supports this broken body of Christ, supported on the right, his head, only by her hand under his neck, painful to look at because there is a broken and intentionally awkward quality to some of this.

The curve of his right arm leads down to this almost spasmodic right hand. The hands, again, in Bellini are always so extraordinary, and just looking at the two hands of Christ, and the two hands—one particular—the left hand of the Madonna, you see their expressiveness and their place as accents in the composition. I'm suddenly looking at her head and the way it bends down from the hill behind, as though the hill were pushing it down slightly. The whole image is a bleak image, despite the brilliant color of the Madonna's costume; it's bleak and it's pitiless.

This *Madonna and Child* a little later, 1510, it's actually dated 1510, rare in Bellini's work. It is in the Brera, the museum in Milan. It is a *Madonna and Child* that still utilizes compositional ideas that he had developed 20 years earlier. It is, however, very different in one way. Its horizontal format is unlike any of the earlier Madonnas. They were all verticals, and now he allows himself to spread it out, to relax the format, to turn it into a true triptych. One writer said that it's a sacred conversation from which the saints have departed. There's room for them, but they're not there, but he's opened it up and in their place he allows the landscape to speak more fully.

It is very interesting to compare it with the *Madonna of the Trees* in his work. If you put them side by side, the earlier *Madonna of the Trees* of 1487, it is quite clear that there's a strong similarity between the two, and yet it's as though he simply unfurled the sides of the canvas a little further to give him a horizontal composition instead of two trees that are tightly confined. As in the *Madonna of the Trees* in the right-hand side, it opens up to allow two trees with more space and with a great deal of activity in that landscape as well. The landscape wings flanking the Madonna and Child are not only more spacious they're more expressive in the later painting.

Let me turn back to the *Madonna and Child*, the whole image here, and look at it more closely. On the one hand, the animated contour of the Virgin's robes (and again, look at that blue, it's astounding, and the green of the "cloth of honor" behind her, and the white-pink or white-rose robe of the Madonna), if you look at the contour of this blue outer garment, it is not only expressive in itself, but it ties the figure compositionally to the landscape behind. It relates to the hills, to the hill that emerges on both sides from behind the "cloth of honor," and there is a kind of echo of it or prefiguration of it in the expressive and beautifully drawn contour of the costume. On the other hand, the sacred personages remain resolutely separate from the world. They're seated in front of their "cloth of honor"; they're seated immediately in front of us in that almost non-space between the green cloth and the picture surface.

The brilliant colors are distributed evenly in the foreground and in the background. The blue of the sky is very near the blue of the robe.

The green that is in the cloth can also be found in places in the landscape. The landscape supports and completes the composition. There are horizontals where they're needed. For instance, look at the line of the fields across here, the demarcation of the field, a very necessary horizontal compositionally to band the whole of the composition together, as well as to help us step back in space, the curves that echo the Madonna and her costume, the vertical trees on both sides. By the way, it's signed over here on this stone at the left, which looks somewhat like a tombstone on the left-hand side of the picture.

The world goes on about its business, again, as it did in the painting we were looking at earlier. The farmer and so forth in the background are still there. Here we have two people talking by a tree; I can't determine whether it's a man and a woman or two men, but it's an animated conversation at the left-hand side, and a horseman is to be found over on the right-hand side. There's a workman here near in the foreground, or a farmer with some animals at his feet or in front of him. Again, they're unaware of this drama of salvation, and it reminds one as a parallel to W.H. Auden's famous poem about Brueghel's painting the *Fall of Icarus*, and Icarus falls from the sky, the ship sails on, and he says, "A ship which must have seen something remarkable, a young man fall from the sky, had somewhere to go and went on about its business." I paraphrase, but that's precisely what happens here. We have a world of work and the daily things that continue and the solemn religious image in the foreground.

Bellini's altarpieces are crowned by the *San Zaccaria Altarpiece* of 1505. This is an enthroned Madonna with four saints. It is still in its place in situ in the church for which it takes its name. The Church of San Zaccaria is one of the most venerable in the city. It was founded in the ninth century, and it once owned land that extended into the present Piazza San Marco. The altar for which Bellini painted this masterpiece is on the left wall of the broad church. The amplitude of the four saints that flank in this sacred conversation that flank the Madonna and Child is reinforced by the studied symmetry of the composition. Giovanni has, in one sense, cast a glance back at Byzantine symmetry, and once more (as he did in the *St. Giobbe Altarpiece*) he closes the pictorial space with a half-dome Byzantine mosaic, again a reference perhaps to San Marco, but certainly to the Byzantine background of the city.

It should be noted that the painting has been cut down somewhat at the top, which qualifies the illusionistic effect of the architecture, but it is still a powerful continuation. St. Peter and St. Zaccaria are placed frontally on opposite sides, St. Peter on the left, St. Zaccaria here on the right in front of painted pilasters, but the pilasters in front of them are real. Those are the altar, and this is all real architecture if you follow up across the arch; this is the architecture of the arch, which comes down as it were on the altar table just behind it, and then the painted spaces behind that, but the eye is hard put in a reproduction to tell that there is any difference between the two.

I want you to look at the light, the beautiful light that falls from the left through this arcade between those two sets of pilasters, through the arcade that is defined right at this point and lights St. Peter on the proper right side of his head, floods this side of the niche with light, but leaving this properly in the shadow, and St. Zaccaria is partly shadowed as well on the right side of his face. Behind them, the female saints face the throne in pure profile, and none of the figures look at one another, again. They're isolated; I want to say isolated in air because the atmospheric feeling, the ambient air that one feels here, is so powerful, so convincing, that you see them standing in light-filled air.

The throne is quite simple. We've seen some that were very high and some that were very elaborate; this one is not too elevated. It's very architectonic in its construction. There's only one musical angel; again, there's a kind of paring down to essentials, one musical angel in the foreground, and the only figure there who looks at us is the musical angel. The viewpoint, however, is curious, the perspective, because it's ideal. It's not a logical continuation of the space you stand at in the church. The altarpiece, the bottom of it, is perhaps five feet above floor level, and then that means that the heads of those saints are another five feet off from that, but our viewpoint is directly at the young angel. You might think it's a little higher, but not much surely. Basically, I think this is about our viewpoint, and that is higher than the natural, the actual, viewpoint from the church floor, so he creates a kind of ideal space and architectural perspective.

At the top of the throne, by the way, the sculptured head at the top, it's God the Father. He makes it a sculptural or architectural object. Bellini unites the architecture of the altar with the painting, and he unites both with the natural light that falls into the church from a window on the façade to our left. The door of the church, as you look at this, is to your left. This is on the sidewall, the north wall, and to the left is the door, and it's a very high wall, and the windows there, and I have been in that church when the light actually falling from that window coincided exactly with the light painted into the painting, the angle of it and the intensity of it. It was painted for that spot and almost for that time of day.

He appropriates the architecture of the altar for his painted space, but he goes that one huge step further by painting the fall, the angle, of the actual light from the western window onto his painting, into his painting, in fact. The entire altarpiece, look at it, look at how it embraces you, the entire altarpiece seems to enfold space in an enveloping embrace, while at the same time projecting an inescapable aura of meditation, trance-like meditation. The resultant nobility, the ineffable tranquility of this painting is beyond praise, and it is perhaps the first absolute masterpiece of the Venetian High Renaissance.

The last painting that I'll show you in this lecture, the *Feast of the Gods*, is a switch, a great switch, from what we've seen in Bellini's work. The *Feast of the Gods* is signed and dated 1514; it belongs to the National Gallery in Washington, DC. Bellini was a gifted teacher with gifted pupils, including Giorgione and Titian, and in the last years of his long life he found himself in competition with his own pupils. Alfonso d'Este, the Duke of Ferrara, intended to gather in one room—that he called the Alabaster Chamber—paintings by the finest living Italian artists. Although he was frustrated in his specific intentions regarding the artists, he nonetheless ended up with a Bellini and three Titians, not too bad.

Bellini's *Feast of the Gods* was painted for this room, painted near the end of Bellini's life, when he completed this remarkable mythological painting, and it was the first to be completed for the Duke's project. The *Feast of the Gods* combines wit, sleepy sensuality, and the beauty of nature—all in the transformation of a rather lusty tale from Ovid into a poetic reverie. Bellini chose (or more correctly he was surely assigned) his subject from Ovid's *Fasti*, a subject that involved the Olympian gods drowsing after reverie (gods are so human). The story told by Ovid was intended to explain an annual sacrifice of an ass to the god Priapus.

Let me identify the figures; there's certainly enough of them, and it's one of the things that sets this apart from the other paintings, the late paintings of Bellini, is the crowd. The figures from the left, I'll just identify some, the satyr here with his back to us. Next to him but crouching down, the child in blue with a vine of grape leaves in his hair, a wreath of grape leaves in his hair, is the child Bacchus and he's drawing wine from this vat. Here is Silenus, and Silenus is accompanied by his ass, who stands here and is an important part of the story. Seated here in the lovely pink robe, green and with a helmet that's sort of tipped back (he clearly has had too much to drink), is Mercury.

Next to Mercury, behind him here (with white and orange and he is drinking) is Jupiter, and then there is a couple, at least they are perceived as a couple now, Sebel here, an earth goddess, and Neptune beside her, who has got a rather indecent gesture here, which appears to have been changed at a later date, not as originally painted by Bellini, who was a little more circumspect. Behind them is Pan, the nude figure here with his pan pipes, and then kneeling here is Ceres, the goddess of agriculture, the goddess of abundance, and she's kneeling beside Apollo, who is also drinking right here. And then there is a pair of figures over here—one is Priapus, the man who stands; the other one is Lotis. Nymphs and satyrs are also in the background of this painting, and here's the brief story.

Priapus desired Lotis. Lotis, like the others, had something to drink, was tired, lay down, and fell asleep. The other two gods, drowsy with wine, also nod off, and as they fall asleep, Priapus begins to draw back Lotis's gown, at which inopportune (or opportune, depending on the point of view) moment, the ass brayed wildly, waking everybody up. Lotis jumped up and repelled Priapus, who ran off, and the story, of course, is about excess—it's about embarrassment—Ovid says the god was laughed at by all, and it is ribald. It's hardly uplifting. This is not a moral story, though one could draw morals from it, if you chose to, but it's not meant to. It's a story that is meant to entertain and cause conversation. I should point out that Priapus is, in fact, priapic. If you look at the costume closely enough, you will see this fact is true; he is aroused, and she will be aroused by the braying of the ass any moment now.

How different this painting is from the gods that Raphael painted, from the gods that Mantegna painted, or Botticelli. These gods are rather plebeian; they're rather too much like us. They're very portrait-like by the way; a number of these heads across the foreground have very portrait-like qualities. They've never been successfully identified with members of the court, but they probably are, at least I would vote on that side. Their heads are frequently too large for their bodies, and I think that's one thing that points toward they're being actual portraits. It is almost as though Bellini had anticipated Shakespeare's *Midsummer Night's Dream*. If he had been able to be around to do the setting for that, it would have been a delight.

The painting is, as I remarked, one of Bellini's last works. It's a triumph of saturated color. Indeed, it's a demonstration of what we mean when we speak of Venetian color; just look at the range of color that is there. It is mind-boggling, and by the way, the painting not too many years ago was restored, and the colors just sang out again from underneath the previous varnish. When the Duke was unable to secure paintings by Raphael, who died, and Fra Bartolommeo, he finally engaged Titian to paint the remaining three subjects. He had the Bellini, Bellini died two years after finishing it, and Titian painted the other three, and we'll see two of them in another lecture.

In order to harmonize Bellini's *Feast of the Gods* with his own three paintings, Titian received permission to alter the landscape background of the Bellini and probably some of the details as well, exposing a breast here and there (for instance) to make it a little more like Ovid and a little less proper in the Bellini manner. Thus, the pupil Titian literally succeeded his master, but I think you should regard his changes not as a criticism of Bellini, but as an act of practical homage, bringing it together—what his changes were principally in a very different landscape background, one that looks far more like Titian's landscapes than it does like Bellini's beautiful but not so fully developed landscapes. When speaking of the *Feast of the Gods*, music seems to offer the appropriate analogy, for Bellini's painting has a deep musicality, a richness of tone, an orchestration form and narrative that fittingly rounds out his memorable career.

Lecture Thirty-Two
Giorgione

Scope:

The greatest of Giovanni Bellini's many pupils were Giorgione and Titian. The elder was Giorgione (1476/78–1510), the name by which we know Giorgio da Castelfranco, after his home town in the plain not far from Venice. He must have entered Bellini's Venice studio in the mid-1490s, when the latter's mellow, glowing late style was unfolding. Documents concerning Giorgione are few, but it is clear that the surviving works on which his later fame rested were all made in the first decade of the 16th century and most in the last six years of his brief life. Although he painted many highly esteemed frescoes with large-scale figures, they have not survived the Venetian climate and, in general, his extant work is small in size and intimate in mood. The poetry of Antonello influenced these works, and the translucent oil colors he had popularized were quickly appropriated by Giorgione, who applied them without preparatory underdrawing. His only surviving altarpiece, *The Castelfranco Madonna*, is distinguished by a classical simplicity of form and an airiness borrowed from the landscape background.

Giorgione may be best known for *The Tempest*, a haunting painting with a soldier and a nude woman and child flanking the opening into a lush, storm-menaced landscape. Musical analogies have often been made with Giorgione's art, supported by the knowledge that he was also an accomplished musician in a musically cultured city. In *The Tempest*, he has painted a sonata or *sinfonietta* comparable to one of Vivaldi's *Four Seasons* (albeit two centuries earlier). The sonorous colors of the robes worn by the so-called *Three Philosophers* (they are certainly the three Magi) and their calm self-possession is also supported by an expressive landscape, although the left side of it has been badly damaged. It is a rare viewer who is not startled from complacency by the *Old Woman*, pointing to herself and bearing a paper inscribed *col tempo* ("with time"), referring to the inevitable loss of youthful beauty. It is an unusual departure from Giorgione's poetic idealism.

Vasari summed up Giorgione's high place in Italian art at the beginning of his biography of the painter: "While Florence was winning fame through the works of Leonardo, no less glory was conferred on Venice by the talents and achievements of [Giorgione], who greatly surpassed... every other Venetian painter up to that time." He died of the plague in his early 30s, but his work was continued seamlessly by the young Titian, with whom he had collaborated on a fresco project. The continuation was so seamless, in fact, that an art historical cottage industry has busied itself ever since trying to attribute certain key paintings to one or the other of these prodigious artists, which we, too, will analyze in the subsequent lecture.

Outline

I. Giorgio da Castelfranco (1476/78–1510), known as Giorgione, entered Bellini's large workshop when the master was entering his late, expansive phase. A sadly short life confined his career mainly to one decade, but within that narrow compass is a wide range of subjects, size, expression, and approach.

    A. A small *Holy Family* (c. 1500) indicates how the poetry of Giovanni's paintings (and Antonello's, of course) stirred a responsive sensibility in the young man.

        1. The rich, saturated palette is learned from Bellini, although Giorgione's shifting, intermingled yellow and blue of the lining of the Virgin's robe is evidence of his own sensitive eye.

        2. The intimacy of this family group is the heart of Giorgione's particular lyric poetry. Even the view of the Bellini-esque landscape is scaled down to harmonize with the figures. The painting is a perfectly harmonized chord of color and form.

        3. Whether it was painted as an independent panel or was a *predella* panel of an altarpiece (such as the following) is unknown.

    B. Giorgione's only surviving altarpiece is the large *Castelfranco Madonna* (c. 1505) painted for the Cathedral of Saint Liberale in his hometown not far from Venice, from which it takes its name.

        1. The altarpiece is about 6 ½ feet tall, perhaps not large by Bellini's standards but possessing a scale that belies its measurements.

2. The Madonna and Child are greatly elevated, not on a pedestal but above an altar within the painting. This tall pyramid is flanked by Saint Liberale in armor and Saint Francis. Saint Liberale is the local patron saint, unlikely to be found elsewhere. A checkerboard pavement establishes the foreground space, and a landscape appears above a wall on either side of the Madonna, after the manner of Bellini.

3. The modeling of the Madonna's face is comparable to Leonardo's *sfumato*, if not so accomplished. Remembering Leonardo's visit to Venice in 1500, Giorgione's direct knowledge of his work is possible.

II. Soon after completing the *Castelfranco Altarpiece*, Giorgione worked on frescoes for the exterior walls of the Fondaco dei Tedeschi, the German merchant's warehouse on the Grand Canal. The folly of painting frescoes in the Venetian climate was soon proved by the nearly complete disappearance of the work.

A. The Fondaco frescoes were mainly of large single figures, and the large oil painting (originally more than 5 feet high) of *Judith*, now in the Hermitage, is somewhat similar, though it may have been painted earlier (c. 1504).

B. The subject is interpreted in a novel way. Usually Judith is shown in or near the tent where she slew Holofernes, and usually she holds the head or is placing in into a bag held by an elderly female servant. Here, she is shown as a female David, the head beneath her foot as in the sculptures by Donatello and Verrocchio, and holding a long sword by her side. The setting in an enclosed area, like a garden on a high hill with a sweeping view of the landscape, is also unprecedented for this story.

III. Giorgione's *Tempest* (c. 1505) is one of the most famous paintings in Renaissance art, one of the most evocative, and one of the most puzzling.

A. Although the palette of predominantly green and blue-green inevitably makes the painting appear to be a pastoral subject, in fact, architecture vies with landscape for dominance.

B. Two figures in the foreground landscape flank the painting: a nude woman suckling a child on the right and a soldier on the left. A stream is between them, a brick platform with two broken columns behind the soldier, stands of trees on both sides, and a bridge with buildings beyond in the center. The sky is charged with the oncoming storm that gives the painting its name.

C. The interpretation of these elements has filled many scholarly pages, and what follows is simply my preferred explanation that accounts for some of what we see. The soldier, together with the broken columns, symbolizes Fortitude or Constancy; the woman and child, Christian love (*Caritas*, or "Charity"); and the threatening storm over town and country is a symbol of Fortune or Chance. The allegorical subject must have been dictated by Gabriele Vendramin, who commissioned the painting. Such emblematic subjects were common enough in paintings and in books; what is distinctly uncommon here is the subordination of the emblematic devices to the evocative landscape.

D. Among other things, this is the first instance in Italian painting in which landscape is given the principal, not just a supporting, role.

E. It has been discovered that Giorgione made substantial changes to his composition. Our purpose is not to discuss them but to point out that Giorgione painted directly onto the support without first drawing his composition on the surface and made changes if desired. This *alla prima* technique would not have been feasible without oil paints, and it is of great importance for the artist's effects of ambient light, of a *sfumato*-like modeling of form and feature achieved directly through color, through which outline disappears in the colored mass of the surrounding atmosphere.

IV. The so-called *Three Philosophers* (c. 1508–1509) is also enigmatic and deeply poetic. Three handsomely dressed men— young, middle-aged, old—are grouped together in the right side of the painting.

A. Their varied ages and their costumes suggest that they are probably the Magi on their journey to Bethlehem. The Magi are often cast as the three ages of man, and they came from the east. It has been suggested that they are waiting for the star to guide them to Christ's birthplace, a story found in the *Golden Legend* and elsewhere.

B. But are they *just* Magi? They have no entourage, no means of transportation. The title we use is not modern: *Three Philosophers* was bestowed on them by the writer Marcantonio Michiel who saw the painting in 1525, which might suggest that the subject was always ambiguous, that Michiel did not recognize them as the Magi. However, Jacobus de Voragine in his *Golden Legend* also noted that there is a "threefold meaning of the word *magus*." He then elucidates the meanings, saying finally: "Or again, magus is the equivalent of wise man… in Greek a philosopher."

C. Thus, they are both Magi and philosophers. Philosophy is the "mother" of the seven liberal arts, of which one is geometry, the measurement of the earth. The attributes of geometry are held by the youngest man: the compass (or dividers) and T-square.

D. It may be significant that this Magus-philosopher stares toward the cave that dominates the left side of the painting, a cave that might presage the rock tomb in which the crucified Christ was buried. Thus, as one scholar suggested, "the implicit meaning is the vanity of human wisdom in the presence of death itself."

V. That sentiment is also the explicit and undeniable meaning of *The Old Woman* (c. 1508/9).

A. Here is a subject unlike any we have seen by Giorgione, an explicitly moralizing image reminiscent, for instance, of late-medieval paintings done at the time of the Black Death (Lecture One) or of northern European *vanitas* paintings, which were certainly known in Venice.

B. This beautifully painted old woman points at herself, while from between her hand and her body unfurls a paper bearing the words *col tempo*. "With the [passage of] time" you, too, will be as I am. It is surely significant that this emblematic painting was commissioned, like the emblematic *Tempest*, by Gabriele Vendramin. It is a measure of Giorgione's tact, or genius, that he did not make the woman repulsive. It does not take great imagination to see the young woman through the veil of age.

Works Discussed:

Giorgione:

The Holy Family, c. 1500, National Gallery of Art, Washington, DC.

The Castelfranco Madonna, c. 1505, Church of San Liberale, Castelfranco.

Judith, c. 1504, The Hermitage, Saint Petersburg.

The Tempest, c. 1505, Accademia, Venice.

The Three Philosophers, c. 1508–1509, Kunsthistorisches Museum, Vienna.

The Old Woman, c. 1508/9, Accademia, Venice.

Essential Reading:

Adams, chapter 17.

Hartt, chapter 19.

Supplementary Reading:

Pignatti, Terisio, and Filippo Pedrocco. *Giorgione*. New York: Rizzoli, 1999.

Settis, Salvatore. *Giorgione's Tempest: Interpreting the Hidden Subject*. Chicago: University of Chicago Press, 1990.

Questions to Consider:

1. Can you explain why Giorgione, whose art was created in only 10 years, is considered one of the most influential of Renaissance artists?

2. What do Giorgione's *Tempest* and *The Three Philosophers* have in common?

Lecture Thirty-Two—Transcript
Giorgione

The greatest of Giovanni Bellini's many pupils were Giorgione and Titian. The elder of these was Giorgio da Castelfranco, known as Giorgione, born about 1476-78, we're not sure, and died in 1510, we're unfortunately sure, a young man when he died. Giorgione is a name to conjure with in art history; he's almost mythical in a sense. He's rare, that is to say his art is rare; there's little enough of it. It is valued extremely highly, and there is something almost mystical about talking about Giorgione because of the endless disputes over what is and is not Giorgione, a subject that we may deal with a little later on.

He's known as Giorgione for short, but Castelfranco was his hometown in the plain, not too far from Venice. He must have entered Bellini's studio in Venice in the mid-1490s when Bellini's mellow, glowing, expansive old-age style was beginning to unfold. A sadly short life confined Giorgione's career mainly to one decade. But within that narrow compass is a wide range of subjects, size, expression, and approach. There are relatively few documents concerning Giorgione, but it is clear that the surviving works on which his later fame rested were all made in the first decade of the 16th century, and most of them in the last six years of his brief life. Although he painted many highly esteemed frescoes with large-scale figures, those frescoes didn't survive in the Venetian climate, something other artists found out as well.

The *Holy Family*, which you see now, is a small painting, only 18 inches wide, painted probably about 1500, and I must say that the dates here I'm suggesting are best-guess dates in most instances. But it is a small painting (now in the National Gallery) that—like most Giorgiones—has been discussed and argued about over the time that it's been known, but it is now universally accepted as a Giorgione. In general, the extant work of Giorgione is small in size and intimate in mood. The poetry of Antonello da Messina influenced these works, and the translucent oil colors that Antonello had popularized were quickly appropriated by Giorgione, who applied them without preparatory underdrawing. I'll have more to say about that.

This small *Holy Family* indicates how the poetry of Giovanni Bellini's paintings (and, of course, Antonello's as well) stirred a responsive sensibility in the young man. The rich, saturated palette is learned from Bellini, but these shifting intermingled colors, the yellow and blue in the lining of the Virgin's robe, for instance here, those are evidence of Giorgione's own sensitive eye. That kind of shifting intermingled color is his own, but look at the palette. Look at the beauty of the palette, of the pale blue, a darker more intense blue, the green-yellow, the lining, the rose-red shifting to white of her costume, of her mantle, Joseph in green and with a pale-gray lilac cloak around him.

The intimacy of this family group is the heart of Giorgione's particular lyric poetry. The intimacy is, the overworn word is "charming," it is charming, but it seems to me it goes beyond charming. The group itself is enclosed in a kind of elongated oval, particularly circumscribing the upper parts of the bodies of St. Joseph and the Virgin, with the Christ Child diagonally disposed within that oval, the heads inclined toward each other, most particularly that of St. Joseph, which is directly above the head of the Christ Child, and he looks down at him with his lips parted and looking directly at him, and this is a very big difference from the paintings of the same subject of, say, a century earlier, when St. Joseph might be off in the corner while the Madonna and Child are alone here. It's very much a family picture, and one of great beauty and touching quality.

The facial type here—the round head, the large forehead and the round face—seems to be a typical Giorgione facial type, at least in some of these early paintings. The Madonna is a slightly modified version of the same. The landscape is very lovely seen through a somewhat unlikely arcaded window it seems in what looks like a stable, after all where they were supposed to be, but suddenly you have this rather classical arch, or at least a Roman arch, and you're looking through it onto the landscape with a castle in the distance. Even this landscape which is like Bellini's, it's Belliniesque if you think of the backgrounds of the landscapes in his Madonnas and Child out of doors, it's scaled down, this landscape in the Giorgione, to match the small scale of the figures. This painting is a perfectly harmonized chord of color and form.

The question of whether it was painted as an independent panel or was a predella panel for a larger altarpiece at the bottom of the larger altarpiece, such as one we will see shortly, isn't known and can't be resolved probably, but I suspect it was an independent painting. Earlier, one might have thought any painting of this size was likely to be part of an altarpiece, a panel from the lower part or some of the part of an altarpiece, but by this time in the circle of Giorgione, around Giorgione, you find many small paintings that were painted for devotional and some for decorative purposes as well, and they were often small and intimate and were clearly made for a wide private market that existed for them.

I hesitantly let this lovely painting go to show you his only surviving altarpiece, a large altarpiece, the so-called *Castelfranco Madonna* in the cathedral at Castelfranco, painted about 1505, and Castelfranco I remind you is his hometown. The cathedral was dedicated to St. Liberale, a saint you will probably not encounter outside of Castelfranco because St. Liberale was a local saint, and the *Castelfranco Madonna*, the altarpiece rather, is about six and a half feet high, perhaps not large by Bellini's standards, but it's large, and it possesses a large scale. Its sense of size is greater than its measurements; it has a great deal of presence and projection, partly because the Madonna and Child are greatly elevated, not on a pedestal I point out, not on a pedestal but above an altar within the painting.

The throne is at the top. This is an altar below, so there's an altar and then with a large platform on the altar, almost like a back altar here, and then on top of that we have the enthroned Madonna and Child, and the device of what I have called the "cloth of honor" continues all the way down here from the altar below, and in a different form. I'm not quite sure of the color and form, but it continues above behind the Madonna as well, and her drapery, the orange-red drapery that covers her knees and her lap spreads out to cover part of the base of the upper part of this. This is unusual, this design, because it's a very tall pyramid with the Madonna completely above the other two saints. Their heads don't overlap the space in which she sits at all.

It is flanked by St. Liberale (who as I mentioned is in armor here) on the left and St. Francis on the right—easily recognizable. Liberale is the local patron saint, as I said, and you probably won't meet him anywhere else. There is a checkerboard pavement in the floor, which establishes the foreground space and gives us a perspective step into the painting, and then there is a landscape that appears above the wall on either side of the Madonna, very much after the manner of Bellini except that never in Bellini do you have this full-length figure in a larger space with the landscape flanking, always a close-up view. It's as though if you cut this across the knees of the Madonna, you'd have something very similar to a Bellini composition. Nonetheless, it is probably from Bellini that Giorgione arrived at this invention of his.

The modeling of the Madonna's face is comparable to Leonardo's sfumato. I know it's hard to tell in such a small image. It's not as accomplished as Leonardo, but it has the same kind of modeling, which is soft and continuous, and done, as it were, with atmosphere, with color, rather than with line, rather than drawing it. Remembering Leonardo's visit to Venice in 1500, which I mentioned before, Giorgione's direct knowledge of his work is possible, just as we assume that Bellini knew Leonardo's work. This altar painting is distinguished by a classical simplicity of form and an airiness that is borrowed from the landscape background. He links the two, not only by the central axis of the Madonna's throne and the altar here, linking the two parts, but also, of course, by the diagonal of St. Liberale's very long cold standard, which pulls top and bottom, foreground and background, together.

Soon after completing the Castelfranco altarpiece, Giorgione worked on frescoes for the exterior walls of the Fondaco dei Tedeschi. The Fondaco dei Tedeschi was a warehouse on the Grand Canal in Venice, used by German merchants. The walls were painted, decorated, the upper walls with frescoes by Giorgione, and the folly of painting frescoes in the Venetian climate—all that water—was soon proved by the nearly complete disappearance of the work. There is a ghost of one in the museum at the Ca'd'Oro in Venice. There's not much that has survived; we have to just take it on faith, and yet we know of their importance from their description, the descriptions by contemporaries of them. He did not continue in the fresco business after that; he worked in oil paintings.

I want to show you a painting that may be considered to be related due to the fact that it's a single large figure to the Fondaco frescoes that I just mentioned. This is a painting of *Judith*, with the head of Holofernes. We've seen the subject in a couple of different stages— Holofernes beheaded, Judith with the head. This is painted about 1504; today it's in the Hermitage in Saint Petersburg. This painting, not as large perhaps as the Fondaco frescoes (but close), this oil painting was originally about five feet high. It was cut down, especially on the sides, in the 18th century, so it changed its feeling of size, especially when you see it in a photograph. It's always surprising when you actually see this painting; it's larger than you expect from having known it only in photographs. But it is somewhat similar to the single images, the single figures that he painted in fresco.

It's interesting, however, to us also because the subject of Judith and Holofernes is here painted in a novel way. Usually, as you know, Judith is shown in or near the tent where she slew Holofernes, and usually she holds the head or is placing it into a bag held by an elderly female servant. Here, she is shown with the head beneath her foot. This is the way David is shown with the head of Goliath. She is a kind of female David here; there is no other example of this that I know of in which Judith, with the head of Holofernes, emulates, borrows from the traditional pose for David and the head of Goliath, and, of course, the two great examples we have were the two sculptures by Donatello and the later one by Verrocchio. She holds a long sword by her side, and one foot presses down on the hair or forehead of the unfortunate Holofernes, who is not in a tent; he's out in a garden. I don't know what she's doing out there.

One really wonders—this is a painting that raises all kinds of questions. Who commissioned it? Why do they want, or why did Giorgione want, to do such a different sort of interpretation? We're in a garden on a high hill with a sweeping view of the landscape, simply not part of the traditional visual way of presenting this story, and yet here we have it in this image. Even, somehow, the bare leg of Judith here is more reminiscent of the pose of the young David than it is of Judith as we usually see her. It's as though here she's still somewhat seductive. That point has passed, she has achieved her goal, but she's somewhat seductive and that's a rather odd statement. You hear me shaking my head wondering what Giorgione was about when he made this unusual painting.

Giorgione's *Tempest,* painted perhaps about 1505, is one of the most famous paintings in Renaissance art. Indeed, it's one of the most evocative and one of the most puzzling paintings in art history. There are three figures. There is a nude woman suckling a child seated at the right, under or in front of vegetation. A soldier is on the left, a kind of *landsknecht* in German, a kind of wandering knight here, not in armor but still conceived as a soldier, and they flank the opening into the landscape, a lush landscape, a storm-menaced landscape. There is a stream between them in the foreground, and running beyond. There's a brick platform with two broken columns beside and to the right of the soldier.

There are stands of trees on both sides of the picture, framing it and leading the eye back into the space. There is a bridge with buildings beyond in the center, and there is also a wall, a kind of fragmentary wall to the left-hand side, behind the soldier here, that comes in almost like a wing on a stage from the left. The buildings beyond the bridge in the center go back quite some distance in space. The sky is charged, and I mean charged with the oncoming storm that gives the painting its name. I don't know that the sense of electricity, potential lightning, and so forth had ever been caught in painting before this time. The palette is predominantly green and blue-green, and it inevitably makes this painting appear to be a pastoral subject, but in fact architecture vies with landscape for dominance in the painting and probably needs to be considered as an important part of the painting.

The interpretation of these elements has filled many scholarly pages, hundreds, perhaps thousands, and what follows here is simply (briefly) my preferred explanation that accounts for at least some of what we see in the painting. I didn't invent it, but I agree with this reading. The soldier together with the broken columns, that's an image, symbolizes Fortitude or Constancy; the woman and child, Christian love, which is also called "Caritas" or Charity; when we say faith, hope, and charity, that's a translation of Caritas, Christian love, and it is often personified by the woman suckling a child. The threatening storm over the town and the country is a symbol of Fortune or Chance. All of these meanings are often attached to the specific things that we see here. Whether you can sum all of that up into some grand statement is another question, but I think we have the basic thrust of the painting in those allegorical meanings of the figures, as well as in the drama of the landscape.

This subject—this allegorical subject—must have been dictated by the man who commissioned the painting, and we know who he was. His name was Gabriele Vendramin (who commissioned the painting), and it's such a specific subject that surely he asked for this from Giorgione. Such emblematic subjects were common enough in paintings and in books. What is distinctly uncommon here is the subordination of the emblematic devices to the evocative landscape. Among other things, this is the first instance of Italian painting in which a landscape is given the principal role—not just a supporting role, but the principal role. The fact that we call it the *Tempest* and continue to call it the *Tempest* is justified by the fact that the tempest is what we remember when we have left this painting.

It has been discovered that Giorgione made substantial changes to his composition. My purpose is not to discuss these changes, but to point out that Giorgione painted directly onto the support without first drawing his composition on the surface, and if he then wished, he made changes to the oil painting. This technique, which is called *alla prima*, simply put it down directly, alla prima, first thought as it were, and it would not have been feasible without oil paints, couldn't have been done with tempera. Oil paints permitted it, and while others—like Antonello—had used oil, Antonello had designed everything with great care, with the detail of the "Flemish school," so here we have a new use of oil, much broader than that which had been envisioned before by Italian artists.

This is of great importance in achieving the artist's effects of ambient light and of a sfumato-like modeling of form and feature achieved directly through color, through which outline disappears in the colored mass of the surrounding atmosphere. Painting as pure color has been born, one may say, one may claim here, and one can put this in contrast with the whole central Italian school, Florentine art, where painting was, in one sense, considered as sculptural, as emulating sculpture. You began with form, sculptural form; you began with form that was modeled with light and dark (*chiaroscuro*) and then you colored it. No matter how great the colorist, the painter and colorist, it began so often with that idea of a sculptural form.

Now we have a painter who begins with color. He models in color. He conceives everything; he perceives it when he looks at the world; he perceives it in chromatic masses, and he presents it in terms of pure color, and then with that as his starting point, he infuses the skeleton into it. He puts the structure into that massive color. I realize this is an analogous way of speaking, but it is a very different way than the Florentine way. Color is the key here, rather than sculptural form. Musical analogies have often been made to Giorgione's art, supported by the knowledge that he was also an accomplished musician. He was a lute player and a singer, and he was in a musically cultured city. In the *Tempest*, I might say that he's painted his own pastoral sonata, or *symphonietta*; if that's much too early in time, it anticipates musical composers of a later era.

The so-called *Three Philosophers*—a painting now in Vienna in the Kunsthistorisches Museum, the art historical museum, painted about, we assume, 1508-09—is also enigmatic, and also deeply poetic. Three handsomely dressed men—one young to the left, one middle-aged in the center, one old on the right—are grouped together on the right side of the painting. Their varied ages and their richly colored robes suggest that they are probably the three Magi on their journey to Bethlehem. The Magi are often interpreted in paintings as the three ages of man. Many times, you'll see the three Magi in procession and they're three different ages, and they're symbolic in that sense, and they came from the east—which, of course, fits these costumes that they're wearing, particularly the figure in the center.

It's been suggested that here they're waiting for the star; they've stopped on their way for the star to guide them onto Christ's birthplace. This story is found in *The Golden Legend* regarding the Magi—that they stopped and were waiting for further guidance. Their calm self-possession is supported by the expressive landscape, the beautiful landscape in the center in the distance, with a wonderful blue and then a golden glow, although the left side of the near landscape, the cave on the left, has been badly damaged in the life of this painting, but the landscape through the center into the distance is very beautiful.

But are they just Magi? They have no entourage—Magi usually come with a lot of people—no entourage, and no means of transportation. The title we use today and that the museum uses—*"Three Philosophers"*—is not a modern title. It was bestowed upon this painting by the amateur and writer Marcantonio Michiel, who saw the painting in 1525, which might suggest to us that the subject was always ambiguous and that Michiel didn't recognize them as the Magi. On the other hand, if I take you back to my favorite book these days (*The Golden Legend*), Jacobus de Voragine in his famous *Golden Legend* also noted that there is a "threefold meaning of the word *magus*." He then elucidates the meanings, saying finally: "Or again, magus is the equivalent of wise man…in Greek a philosopher." So they are both Magi and Philosophers.

Philosophy is considered the "mother" of the Seven Liberal Arts, one of which is Geometry, the measurement of the earth. The attributes of Geometry are held by the youngest man, seated here in the center. He is holding the compass (or dividers) and the T-square. It may be significant that this Magus-Philosopher, the young man, stares toward the cave that dominates the left side of the painting, a cave that might presage the rock tomb in which the crucified Christ was buried. Thus, as one scholar suggested, "the implicit meaning is the vanity of human wisdom in the presence of death itself."

That sentiment is also the explicit and undodgeable meaning of *The Old Woman*, painted probably about the same time. Here is a subject unlike any we have seen by Giorgione, an explicitly moralizing image reminiscent, for instance, of the late medieval paintings done at the time of the Black Death, or of northern European vanitas paintings—vanitas paintings, "vanity, vanity, all is vanity," gives the name to vanitas paintings, meaning paintings that encompass the brevity of life and the shallowness of temporal things. Those paintings, northern paintings of that subject, were certainly known in Venice; this was not (by any means) unknown or mysterious to Italians. This beautifully painted old woman points at herself, while from between her hand and her body unfurls a paper bearing the words "Col tempo"—"With the (passage of) time"—to fill out the meaning: "With the (passage of) time," you, too, will be as I am.

It is surely meaningful that this emblematic painting was commissioned, like the emblematic *Tempest,* by the same man— Gabriele Vendramin. It speaks of a very particular aesthetic and ethical taste. It's a measure of Giorgione's tact, or his genius, that he did not make this woman repugnant. He could have; to make the point, he could have. But he didn't, and it does not take great imagination for us to see the young woman through the veil of age in this painting, and that makes it all the more moving. It is a rare viewer who is not startled from her or his complacency by *The Old Woman*—this old woman, pointing to herself, bearing that paper inscribed "Col tempo" ("With time") referring to the inevitable loss of youthful beauty. This is a most unusual departure from Giorgione's poetic idealism.

Vasari summed up Giorgione's high place in Italian art at the beginning of his biography of the painter. He said, "While Florence was winning fame through the works of Leonardo, no less glory was conferred on Venice by the talents and achievements of [Giorgione], who greatly surpassed...every other Venetian painter up to that time." Giorgione died of the plague, another visitation of the plague, in his early 30s, but his work was continued seamlessly by the young Titian, with whom he had collaborated on a fresco project—so seamlessly, in fact, that an art historical cottage industry has busied itself ceaselessly trying to securely attribute certain key paintings to one or the other of these prodigious artists. So why shouldn't we? We too will examine the "Giorgione or Titian" controversy in the next lecture because it gives us insight into each of them.

Lecture Thirty-Three
Giorgione or Titian?

Scope:

This question has perplexed those who worry about such things—art critics and historians—perhaps more than it ought to. After all, the beauty or expressive power of the painting is what counts, is it not? Yes, but. If we don't know which works a particular artist made, we cannot, in fact, fully understand his art. Artistic style is more than visual handwriting; it is an expression of personality. To be able to think intelligently about the whole of an artist's work and to know where to draw the line between those paintings (in this case) demonstrably by the artist and the many that claim to be, anyone interested in painting needs to decide to whom to assign certain works whose dominant stylistic characteristics are shared by two or more artists. The problem is especially acute in large workshops, where a master may involve his students in the production of works commissioned from him or sold under his name. Attribution is also a problem in artistic collaborations in which painters sharing a studio absorb each other's ideas and methods or, in fact, sometimes work on the same picture, either as specialists in certain aspects (such as landscape or figures) or, as in the Giorgione-Titian problem, when one dies and the other completes his work.

The prologue was necessary to explain why we bother to revisit certain well-known paintings by Giorgione and/or Titian from around 1510. In this lecture, we will look first at the *Sleeping Venus*, a languorous nude in a landscape, then at the *Noli me tangere*, a sparse rendering of the post-Resurrection appearance of Christ to Mary Magdalen, in both cases with special attention to known changes in the composition. The *Adoration of the Shepherds* has been the cause of more acerbic argument than most such disputed paintings, including the dissolution of the business relationship between a famous art dealer and an even more famous art historian. The *Concert Champêtre* ("*Pastoral Concert*") in the Louvre has bounced back and forth between the two young masters. The standard modern catalogue of Titian believes it is by "Giorgione, largely completed by Titian"; the Louvre, its guardian, after a long period in which it allowed the painting to be a Titian, has now returned it to the more precious (because smaller) oeuvre of

Giorgione. The apparent portrait group called *The Concert* will be discussed in the light of undoubted portraits by Giorgione and Titian to prepare the way for our discussion of the early work of Titian in the next lecture.

Outline

I. We have not devoted much time to problems of attribution. This is an area of connoisseurship that is of great importance to scholars, curators, and dealers, but should it concern the average museum visitor and art lover? In the broadest sense, yes. There are documented works that we know a given artist made. There are others that we believe an artist made, because they are *like* the works we know that he made. To the degree that we—any of us—are uncertain about the latter group, we cannot fully understand the artist or the development of his work.

II. The much-visited and hotly debated topic of this lecture— Giorgione or Titian?—is probably the most significant example of the importance of attribution in Renaissance art. It stems from the fact that the two young artists studied and worked in Bellini's studio (although Giorgione may have left before Titian arrived) and worked together on occasion. Add to that the early death of Giorgione, probably leaving some unfinished works that were completed by another painter (Titian?), and the scenario is clear. It is important to know which of them *invented*, as it were, certain paintings in order to understand both their individual achievements and the flow of influence from one to the other.

    A. A recurrence of the plague in 1510 killed Giorgione. Marcantonio Michiel, whom we cited in the last lecture, reported in 1525 that the *Sleeping Venus*, "in a landscape with Cupid, is by Giorgio di Castelfranco; but the landscape and the Cupid were finished by Titian." This statement, so close to the creation of the painting, is usually (though not always) accepted as accurate, but it is still open to interpretation. For instance, "finished by Titian" need not mean invented or added by Titian, though some writers have deduced that from Michiel's words.

        1. First, two of the painting's most important characteristics—one stylistic and one expressive—must be highlighted. The elongated body of Venus, almost an elongated oval, is fitted into the curves of the landscape in the rising middle ground and the left background and the cloudscape above. The cool, un-self-conscious classicism of the sleeping nude (which owes much to these stylistic devices) distinguishes Giorgione's Quattrocento temperament from the more sensuous and coquettish nudes of Titian and the Cinquecento.

2. The cupid can no longer be judged, because its badly damaged condition caused it to be painted over in the 19th century.

3. The drapery has no precedent in Giorgione's earlier works and many echoes in Titian's later ones. Therefore, it is reasonable to suppose that it is an addition by Titian. This assumption is supported by the observation that Venus does not lie on the drapery; rather, it is in front of her.

4. The hilly landscape in the right background is most likely by Titian, because he reused it in another painting, the *Noli me tangere*, in the National Gallery, London.

B. *Noli me tangere* is the post-Resurrection appearance of Christ to Mary Magdalen, and his admonition not to touch him ("let no one touch me"). The painting (c. 1512) was once also held to have been begun by Giorgione and finished by Titian.

1. The landscape, with an almost exact quotation of the buildings on a hill in the *Sleeping Venus*, would seem to disprove that theory. It is a landscape as typical of Titian as it is atypical of Giorgione, and although Titian finished paintings by Giorgione, he did not quote from them.

2. X-rays have shown that the figure of Christ and the tree behind him were greatly altered during painting. Most experts agree that the first pose and the changes were made by the same hand. Given that the figures are dramatic in pose, the consensus is that the hand was Titian's.

III. The *Adoration of the Shepherds* (c. 1505–1510), often known as the Allendale *Nativity*, has long been a centerpiece in the

Giorgione-Titian controversy, not least because it was associated with art world stars.

A. The painting, which was then in an English collection, came into the possession of Lord Duveen, the English dealer whose principal expert on Italian paintings was the famous connoisseur and art historian Bernard Berenson.

B. Then, as now, a Giorgione is worth more than a Titian because of the extreme rarity of Giorgione's paintings. According to John Walker, former director of the National Gallery of Art in Washington, Duveen purchased the painting in the 1930s, believing it to be a Giorgione, and sold it to Samuel Kress, a collector new to Duveen, as a Giorgione. Berenson, who was on retainer to Duveen Brothers, understood that his name was being used to support the attribution, with which he did not agree, and he terminated his connection with Duveen. Although the story has been told differently, the conclusion is always the same: a rupture between dealer and art historian over an attribution. Much later, Berenson listed the painting as a Giorgione finished by Titian.

C. The Holy Family and shepherds are comparable to the *Holy Family* (also in the National Gallery in Washington) that we saw at the beginning of the last lecture. But there are portions of the landscape, specifically in the brushwork of the trees, that appear to some eyes as being clearly by a different painter. Still, despite unanswered questions, the majority opinion leans toward Giorgione.

IV. A much more famous painting, whose attribution has been even more contested, is the *Pastoral Concert* (c. 1510–1511), known more commonly as the *Concert Champêtre* or *Fête Champêtre* because it has been in the French royal collection and the Louvre since the 17th century, where its influence has been incalculable.

A. Traditionally, it has been attributed to Giorgione since the middle of the 17th century. When Manet used it as the inspiration for his *Luncheon on the Grass* in 1861, he believed it to be by Giorgione.

B. In the 20th century, Titian's name was assigned to it with increasing frequency.

C. In 1949, after pigment studies and X-rays showing design changes, it was proposed that the painting had been laid out and begun by Giorgione but completed by Titian. In other words, it was the same as the case of the *Sleeping Venus* but with the difference that Titian was considered to have done most of the actual painting, for reasons that will be discussed.

D. Still, after a long period in which the Louvre accepted it as predominantly by Titian, by the 1990s, the museum had reassigned it to Giorgione.

E. The subject matter is Arcadian, connected to poetry from Virgil to the Renaissance and suggestive of a golden age of perfect happiness for humanity. Allegorical meanings have been suggested, but little agreement exists on any more specific interpretation. In fact, literalism would be at odds with the sensuous, suggestive visual poetry of the *Pastoral Concert*. The golden age was the poetic invention of the Latin poet Ovid (*Metamorphoses*), and it captured the Renaissance imagination. This painting is one of the most evocative pictorial realizations of the first age of mankind before all the pleasures of nature—and, here, of music, as well—were lost.

V. Giorgione left a few superb portraits, and Titian is one of the finest portrait painters of the Renaissance. The portraits discussed here are, once again, a reflection of the Giorgione-Titian mystery.

   A. The *Concert* (c. 1510–1512) reflects the poetry of Giorgione and the incisive psychology of Titian.

      1. It is surely a triple portrait, but just as surely suggests some underlying meaning. The *clavicembalo* player is the most striking figure because of his incisively modeled features and active pose, turning his head sharply to look at the monk holding a *viola da gamba*, while the young man (the singer?) at the left looks at us.

      2. On one level, it alludes to the three ages of man, as did Giorgione's *Three Philosophers*. Music may allude to the passage of time, and during the Renaissance, music was considered an essential attribute of civilized man at every stage of life.

3. Like many of the above paintings, it has been attributed to Giorgione, Titian, and Giorgione-Titian (among others). Titian has been favored during the past half-century.

B. The *Portrait of a Young Man* (c. 1505) in Berlin is related in type (though not costume) to the young man in the *Concert*. Almost universally accepted as by Giorgione, it has his quiet poetry combined with a High Renaissance classicism that is less austere and remote than Giovanni Bellini's portraits and somewhat closer to those of Raphael. The parapet recalls the same device in *The Old Woman*.

C. The *Gentleman in Blue* (c. 1510–1512) is also placed behind a parapet, on which he rests his right arm in its voluminous sleeve. Though it has occasionally been attributed to Giorgione, it is almost certainly by Titian, and the initials *T V* on the parapet must signify Tiziano Vecelllio, his full name.

1. We see, once again, the enhanced psychological edge that we soon come to associate with Titian. Where Giorgione is elusive, Titian is vigorous. Both can be mysterious, but a greater drama derives from the lost profile of the *Gentleman in Blue* (the head turning from darkness into light), as well as from the bold form and color. The boldness extends to the relation of sleeve to parapet. We have seen many examples of Venetian religious paintings and portraits in which the parapet defines the space or barrier (the picture plane) between the painted world and the spectator's world: Here, they are joined by the illusionistically protruding sleeve.

2. The painting was once thought to be a portrait of Ariosto, but the features do not agree with secure portraits of the poet. It has, however, been plausibly suggested that it is a proud self-portrait. Interestingly, it served as one of the models for a self-portrait by Rembrandt, who had seen and sketched it.

Works Discussed:

Giorgione:

Sleeping Venus, c. 1508–1510, Gemäldegalerie, Dresden.

The Adoration of the Shepherds (The Allendale Nativity), c. 1505–1510, National Gallery of Art, Washington, DC.

Fête Champêtre, c. 1510–1511, Musée du Louvre, Paris.

Portrait of a Young Man, c. 1505, Gemäldegalerie, Staatliche Museen zu Berlin.

Titian:

Noli me tangere, c. 1512, National Gallery, London.

Concert, 1510–1512, Galleria Palatina, Palazzo Pitti, Florence.

Gentleman in Blue, c. 1510–1512, National Gallery, London.

Essential Reading:

Adams, chapter 17.

Hartt, chapter 19.

Questions to Consider

1. What is meant by *connoisseurship*, and what is the connection between connoisseurship and the attribution of works of art to particular artists?

2. Why has the attribution of the *Pastoral Concert* alternated between Giorgione and Titian for centuries? Who do you think painted the *Pastoral Concert*?

Lecture Thirty-Three—Transcript
Giorgione or Titian?

Good morning. In these lectures, we have not devoted much time to problems of attribution. This is an area of connoisseurship, which is of great importance to scholars, curators, and dealers, but should it concern the average museum visitor and art lover? In the broadest sense, yes. There are works we know that an artist made because they are documented. There are other works we think that artist made, because they look like the works we know he or she made. To the degree that we—any of us—are uncertain about any of that group, works we think the artist made, we cannot fully understand his art and its development.

Giorgione or Titian? This question has perplexed those who worry about such things—art critics and art historians—perhaps more than it ought to. After all, the beauty or expressive power of a painting is what counts, is it not? Yes, but. But, if we don't know which works a particular artist made, we cannot, in fact, fully understand his art. Artistic style is more than visual handwriting, it is an expression of personality. To be able to think intelligently about the whole of an artist's work, and to know where to draw the line between those paintings (in this case) demonstrably by the artist and the many that claim to be, anyone interested in painting needs to decide to whom to assign certain works whose dominant stylistic characteristics are shared by two or more artists.

The problem is especially acute in large workshops where a master may involve his students in the production of works commissioned from him or sold under his name. Or again, in artistic collaborations in which painters sharing a studio absorb each other's ideas and methods, or, in fact, sometimes work on the same picture—either as specialists in certain aspects (for example, landscape or figures) or, as in the Giorgione-Titian problem, where one artist dies and the other completes his work. The prologue was necessary to explain why we bother to revisit certain well-known paintings by Giorgione and/or Titian from around 1510. I realize that we have not even looked at Titian's art yet, only Giorgione's, but I think that comparing some of the most argued-about works by these two young painters is probably a good way to introduce Titian while distinguishing him from his colleague.

This hotly debated topic is, I suppose, the most well-known attribution problem in Renaissance art, and it stems from the fact the two young artists studied and worked in Giovanni Bellini's studio (although Giorgione may have left before Titian arrived) and worked together on occasion. Add to that the early death of Giorgione, probably leaving some unfinished works that were completed by another painter, presumably Titian, and the scenario is clear. It's important to know which of them invented, as it were, certain paintings in order both to understand their individual achievements and the flow of influence from one to the other.

Let me sketch what we will do in this lecture. We'll look first at the *Sleeping Venus,* a languorous nude in a landscape. Then we will look at the *Noli me tangere*—"do not touch me" is the translation—a sparse rendering of the post-Resurrection appearance of Christ to Mary Magdalen. In both cases, we will give special attention to known changes in the composition. The *Adoration of the Shepherds* (often called the Allendale Nativity after a former owner) has been the cause of more acerbic argument than most such disputed paintings, including the dissolution of the business relationship between a famous art dealer and an even more famous art historian. *The Concert Champêtre,* (*Pastoral Concert*) in the Louvre has bounced back and forth between the two young masters. Traditionally, it was thought to be by Giorgione since the middle of the 17th century. The standard modern catalogue of Titian states that it is by Giorgione, largely completed by Titian, and the Louvre (its guardian) after a long period in which they allowed it to be a Titian, have now returned it to the precious, because smaller, body of work by Giorgione.

Then we'll discuss *The Concert,* apparently a group portrait, whose attribution has long been argued, and finally, in conjunction with that, we'll look at two single portraits, of which one is now usually agreed to be by Giorgione and the other by Titian.

Let's begin, then, with the *Sleeping Venus,* a painting now in Dresden, painted, and these dates I will give you are obviously discussable, let us say between 1508 and 1510. I remind you that it was a recurrence of the plague in 1510 that killed Giorgione, cutting short his brilliant beginning and presenting Titian, his friend and colleague, with unexpected professional opportunities. Marcantonio Michiel, the contemporary source whom we quoted in the last lecture, reported in 1525 that the *Sleeping Venus*, "in a landscape with Cupid, is by Giorgio di Castelfranco; but the landscape and the Cupid were finished by Titian." This statement, so close to the creation of the painting, is usually (although not always) accepted as accurate, but it's still open to interpretation. For instance, "finished by Titian" does not necessarily mean that the landscape and the Cupid were designed or added by Titian, though some writers have deduced that from Michiel's words. Titian might have merely completed them.

First look at two of this painting's most important characteristics of style and of expression. The elongated body of Venus—a wonderful pose—elongated almost into an elongated flat oval, I'm speaking of the entire body, is fitted into the curves of the landscape in, for instance, the rising middle ground and in this area right here, which is a lovely harmony and harmonious comparison to the rise of her leg or to the opposite contour of her body, the lower contour of her body, and also look at the left background, and it, too, often responds to the physical anatomy of the Venus; so do the clouds in a general sense—this long, darker, sweeping area—the clouds are also comparable to the shapes below. They're harmoniously put together. Her long sloping curves on this wide, low canvas unify her with the landscape. She's a pastoral goddess, and although she's sensual, surely, I don't think she's particularly erotic. The cool, unself-conscious classicism of the sleeping nude (which owes much to these stylistic devices we were looking at) distinguishes Giorgione's Quattrocento temperament from the more erotic and coquettish nudes of Titian and the Cinquecento that was just beginning. I'm sorry, by the way, to have been so coy about the Cupid. You may have been rubbing your eyes or cleaning your glasses, the Cupid can no longer be judged since it was so badly damaged by the 19th century that it was painted out. Originally, it was at the right, just behind the left foot of Venus in here occupying this area, and it still can be seen with x-rays, what is left of it.

The drapery has no precedent in Giorgione's earlier works, and many echoes in Titian's later works. Therefore, it's reasonable to suppose that the drapery is, the drapery in front here, is an addition by Titian. This assumption is supported by the observation that Venus does not lie on the drapery; rather it is placed in front of her, just in front of her. While it would be possible, one assumes, to find the same model after Giorgione's death and have her lie down on a piece of drapery, it is a highly unlikely thing. He would have changed it instead simply by adding drapery in this area to his own taste, he, Titian, to his own taste, and it really is just laid in front of the figure of the Venus.

I want you to take a good look at the hilly landscape with architecture in the right background. This is most likely by Titian since he reused it in another painting that we will look at shortly, the *Noli me tangere* in the National Gallery in London, reused it almost precisely. It is a quote.

Here is the *Noli me tangere*, a painting usually now dated about 1512, which is to say dated after Giorgione's death, but not by everybody. The *Noli me tangere* is the post-Resurrection appearance of Christ to Mary Magdalen, and his admonition to her not to touch him—do not touch me (*noli me tangere*). "Do not touch me, I have not arisen" is the completion of that sentence. The painting was once also held to have been begun by Giorgione and finished by Titian, but the landscape, with an almost exact quotation of the buildings on a hill that we just saw in the *Sleeping Venus*, would seem to disprove that theory, at least for the landscape part of this painting, because it is the larger part of the landscape here. It's a landscape as typical of Titian, and that includes the left part of the landscape too, with this lovely evening, or perhaps morning, I shouldn't say evening, it's certainly a lovely light on the horizon. This landscape is very typical of Titian and atypical of Giorgione. Titian finished paintings by Giorgione, but he does not ever seem to have quoted from them, so we assume that to be Titian.

Then, the figures: the figures are united in a particularly organic and harmonious design, quite beautifully worked together as a unit, and a design that includes the tree behind them. They're not just in front of the tree; it continues, for instance, the line of the Magdalen's body as she kneels before Christ. X-rays have shown that the figure of Christ and the tree behind him were greatly altered during painting, and most experts agree that the first pose and the changes were made by the same hand. Thus, the artist was simultaneously composing and painting directly onto the canvas. Since the dramatic poses are of the kind we associate with Titian, very dramatic poses, the consensus is that he is also the artist of the figures, and, therefore, the entire painting.

Let's turn to another. The *Adoration of the Shepherds*, often known as the Allendale Nativity, has long been a centerpiece in this controversy of Giorgione-Titian, not least because it was associated with art world stars. The painting—now in the National Gallery in Washington and painted probably between 1505 and 1510—which was then in an English collection, came into the possession of Lord Duveen, the English dealer whose principal expert on Italian paintings was the famous connoisseur and art historian Bernard Berenson. Then, as now, a Giorgione is worth more than a Titian because of the extreme rarity of Giorgione's paintings. According to John Walker, former director of the National Gallery of Art in Washington, Duveen purchased the painting in the 1930s believing it to be a Giorgione, and he sold it to Samuel Kress, who was a collector then new to Duveen, buying from him for the first time, and he sold it to Kress as a Giorgione. Berenson, who was on retainer to Duveen Brothers, understood that his name was being used to support the attribution to Giorgione, an attribution with which he did not agree, and he terminated his connection with Duveen Brothers.

Although the story has been told differently, the conclusion is always the same: a rupture between dealer and art historian, over an attribution. To make the story much more interesting, a good deal later, Berenson, in revising his lists of artists, listed it as a Giorgione, finished by Titian.

The Holy Family and shepherds in this painting are very comparable to the Holy Family (also in the National Gallery) that we saw at the beginning of the last lecture. Let me remind you first, look at the Holy Family here, and then we'll look at them together. This very small painting on the left of just the Holy Family, the softness of the palette, the physical types, the facial types—particularly of Joseph—

are very, very similar to those that you find in the Allendale Nativity. They have the same intimacy, and it's an intimacy that we find to be particularly the trademark of the work of Giorgione.

That is very convincing, but there are some portions of the landscape, particularly in the brushwork of the trees, that appear to some eyes as being clearly by a different painter. There is a more descriptive linear quality to the brushwork in the trees here, for instance, than there is in the softness of the landscape beyond. I tend to find that same difference, but I have no solution for it, whether Titian had a hand in that or not. Despite questions that arc unanswered and I'm sure will remain an issue of discussion on this painting, the majority opinion, if you're interested, right now, leans toward Giorgione for this painting.

The *Pastoral Concert*, or *Concert Champêtre*, a much more famous painting (painted 1510-11)—its attribution is even more contested, or has been over the centuries. It is known more commonly, we call it *Pastoral Concert*, it's known more commonly in literature as the *Concert Champêtre* or the *Fête Champêtre*, simply because it has been in the French royal collection since about 1671 and then in the Louvre since that museum was created, and where its influence on the many painters who were able to see it in the museum has been immense. Traditionally, it has been attributed to Giorgione, as I remarked earlier, since the middle of the 17th century. We can't trace it back before that, but from that time it was Giorgione, and in the middle of the 19th century, when Manet used this painting as his inspiration for the *Luncheon on the Grass* (the *Le Dejeuner sur l'Herbe*) in 1861, he believed it to be by Giorgione.

But in the 20th century, Titian's name was assigned to it with increasing frequency, and after pigment studies and x-rays were made in 1949 that showed design changes, it was proposed that the painting had been laid out and begun by Giorgione but completed by Titian. In other words, as with the case of the *Sleeping Venus* but with the difference that Titian was considered to have done most of the actual painting.

Still, after a long period in which the Louvre accepted it as predominately by Titian, by the 1990s they had reassigned it to

Giorgione (to repeat, the much rarer painter). The x-rays just mentioned demonstrate that the painting was changed while in progress either by Giorgione or Titian. The standing figure on the left, surely the most striking figure in the painting, was altered from a frontal pose to the gently twisting pose that we see. Now, both Giorgione and Titian composed directly on the canvas without underdrawing. This is their innovation. But, since the pose is more complex than Giorgione's usually are, it's been argued that it was Titian who so radically and dramatically altered this figure.

The seated woman, on the other hand, on the ground, is very close to Giorgione's woman in the *Tempest*, if you recall. Let's consider the subject matter for a moment. It's Arcadian, that is, it is related to a pastoral paradise that was described in poetry from the Greek poet Theocritus to the Latin poets Virgil and Ovid, to the Renaissance, which evoked—invoked—a golden age of perfect happiness for humanity. There one finds only a blissful existence in the suspended summer afternoon of lives untouched by daily cares and needs and tragedies. That the Golden Age was understood to be a time already long past in human history infuses it with a profound nostalgia.

Certainly striking to the modern viewer is the apparent disregard of the two men for the women, and, of course, striking to the modern viewer is the nudity of the women against the clothed figures. Surely, at the very least, there is a suggestion that the men and the women belonged to different spheres of existence, although I must say that the seated woman on their plane and looking toward them, seems to partly connect with them, seems to.

Allegorical meanings have been suggested for this painting, but little agreement exists on any specific interpretation. We can, at least, point out certain aspects of the scene. The two women, although nude, are otherwise treated quite differently. The standing nude, reminiscent of classical Venuses, turns in a graceful contrapposto away from the others, ignoring them while she pours water from a crystal pitcher into a stone basin. She could be associated with the element of water: the four elements are—of course—earth, air, fire, and water.

The seated nude turns almost completely away from the viewer, as we noticed, and she holds a recorder. She may, therefore, be associated with the element of earth. Not only does she sit on the earth, but wind instruments were associated with the passions, with the animal side of mankind.

The two clothed men are in private conversation; their faces are shadowed. One holds a lute. In the Renaissance, the lute is an attribute of music, that's obvious enough, but it is also sometimes associated with Apollo, thus with poetic inspiration, the creative arts, the intellect, or sometimes with Orpheus, thus also with poetry and the ability to enchant nature. Orpheus enchanted not only the wild animals but trees and rocks as well with his playing. From these attributes and attitudes, one could attempt to deduce a more complete allegory. I'm not going to, but one could attempt to.

Because Giorgione produced at least allegorical paintings for a patron, the *Tempest* that we saw and *The Old Woman*, we know he was interested in such subtleties of meaning. On the other hand, sometimes water is water and lutes are lutes. To insist on any two specific readings seems at odds with the sensuous, suggestive, visual poetry of the *Pastoral Concert*. Whether entirely by Giorgione or mostly by Titian, this painting remains one of the most evocative paintings of the Arcadian ideal.

The Concert, which I mentioned to you, a painting again much discussed, painted 1510-12 is the dating most often given now, it's in the collection of the Pitti Palace in Florence. Giorgione left a few superb portraits, and Titian is one of the finest portrait painters of the Renaissance, and the portraits discussed here are, once again, a reflection of the Giorgione-Titian mystery. *The Concert* reflects the poetry of Giorgione and the incisive psychology of Titian. This is surely a triple portrait; it must be, even though we don't know who they are. It just as surely suggests some underlying meaning that connects the figures. The keyboard player, the clavicembalo player, is the most striking figure because of his incisively modeled features and his active pose, in which he turns his head sharply to look at the monk who holds a viola da gamba in his left hand, while the young man on the other side, probably the singer, looks at us. On one level it alludes to the *Three Ages of Man*, as did Giorgione's *Three*

Philosophers. Music may allude to the passage of time, and during the Renaissance, music was considered an essential attribute of civilized man at every stage of life.

Like many of the prior paintings, this one has been attributed to Giorgione, to Titian, to Giorgione/Titian, and to other artists who I have chosen not to drag into this affair. Titian has been favored during the past half-century in part because of the sharp, intriguing psychological interaction. Perhaps looking at the next two portraits will give you some insights into this one.

The Portrait of a Young Man, identified, as so many portraits are—it is astonishing, because so many of them are full of character and yet we don't know the sitter. I would suggest that if you ever have your portrait done, please have the artist sign it, more than once, preferably, and put your name on it so that no one will doubt who it is of and who it is by. Portraits—sorry for the digression, but portraits—clearly when you have your portrait done, most people don't assume it's going to leave the family, so everybody knows who it is of and who did it. Not so, and clearly historically not so, so make sure that information is included on the masterpiece that is made of you by a great painter.

This painting is now in Berlin, painted probably about 1505. It's related in type (though not in costume) to the young man, the singer, in *The Concert* that we just looked at, a very similar type of figure, and almost universally it is now accepted as by Giorgione, not in the past but today almost universally. It has his quiet poetry combined with a High Renaissance classicism that is less austere, less remote, than Giovanni Bellini's portraits, you remember the *Doge Loredan*, and somewhat closer to the portraits of Raphael.

The parapet in front of him recalls the same device in the portrait of *The Old Woman* by Giorgione. We don't know what the V.V. stands for in front, engraved on the parapet, although many suggestions have been made about it, but always this quietness, this recessiveness, in a sense, of this figure sitting back is very characteristic of the art of Giorgione. Let me show you the next.

This extraordinary painting of *The Man with the Blue Sleeve*, by, we tend to think today, by Titian is a painting in London in the National Gallery. Here, the gentleman in blue is also placed behind a parapet, and he rests his arm in its voluminous sleeve upon that parapet. Though it has occasionally been attributed to Giorgione, it is almost certainly by Titian, and the initials "T V" on the parapet must signify Tiziano Vecellio, his full name. I haven't given it to you before, but his full proper name is Tiziano Vecellio.

There is, once again, the enhanced psychological edge that we soon come to associate with Titian. Where Giorgione is elusive, Titian is vigorous. Both can by mysterious, but a greater drama derives from the lost profile—I mean the left side of his head in shadow, the left eye—from his lost profile of *The Gentleman in Blue* as well as from the bold form and color. The boldness extends to the relation of that sleeve to the parapet. His sleeve is voluminous and overlaps the parapet. We've seen many examples of Venetian religious paintings and portraits in which the parapet defines the space or the barrier between the painted world and the spectator's world. It's the picture plane. But, here they're joined by the protruding sleeve illusionistically, and it is tactile, and it does seem to project beyond that ledge that is, in fact, the front of the picture plane itself, therefore pushing into our space. It gives it tremendous presence, and the figure itself has a certain ominous—well, ominous is too charged, but a certain mysterious quality.

This was once thought, as so many things were, romantically to be a portrait of someone well-known, in this case the poet Ariosto, the contemporary poet, but the features don't agree with the portraits that are clearly and surely of Ariosto. It has, however, been plausibly suggested that it is a very proud self-portrait of the young Titian. Interestingly, it served as one of the models for a self-portrait by Rembrandt, who saw this painting and sketched it at auction in Amsterdam. At the same auction, by the way, he saw Raphael's great *Baldassare Castiglione*, sketched that, and the two of them meld together in his great self-portrait of that year.

I hope that this preliminary delving into the Giorgione or Titian question has proved interesting, and that it helps prepare the way for our discussion of the early work of Titian in the next lecture, at which time we will also learn more about his early life.

Thank you for your attention.

Lecture Thirty-Four
Titian—The Early Years

Scope:

Born in the foothills of the Italian Alps, Titian entered Bellini's workshop in the early 16th century, probably after Giorgione had left it. The imprint of Bellini is dominant in Titian's fresh, appealing *Gipsy Madonna* and still strong in an altarpiece now in Santa Maria della Salute, *Saint Mark Enthroned with Saints*. The altarpiece interweaves stylistic strands from Bellini, Antonello, and Giorgione. With Giorgione's tragic death from the plague, Titian (c. 1488/90–1576) had an unlooked-for opportunity to rapidly advance his career, and the rich blend of influences was soon transformed by his own burgeoning personality. As we noted in the last lecture, Titian was among the great portrait artists, and his *Young Man with Cap and Gloves* (c. 1512–1515) is an intimate, fluidly painted reverie that recalls Giorgione's work but has a breadth of form that presages Titian's mature painting.

About his famous *Sacred and Profane Love*, the first thing that must be said is that it is extraordinarily beautiful. That agreed, the allegorical subject presents complexities that have inspired scholars to insights and overreaching in equal proportion. In his *Madonna and Child with Saints George and Dorothy*, he invents a complex but focused variation on the theme using half-length figures, not behind a sill but as though in shared space with the viewer. Indeed, Titian's unflagging inventiveness is one of the marks of his particular genius.

Nothing can prepare the first-time visitor to the venerable Venetian Franciscan Church of the Frari for the impact of Titian's youthful masterpiece, *The Assumption of the Virgin*. Designed to harmonize perfectly with the Gothic apsidal chapel of the church, it is, at the same time, the supreme masterpiece of the Venetian High Renaissance, fully comparable to Raphael's frescoes in the Vatican *stanze*. It is joyous and dynamic, and the glorious reds of its principal figures resound to the far end of the nave, yet the stupendous composition achieves a monumental balance, a perpetual tension between motion and stasis, that is unforgettable.

Even as the *Assumption* was being unveiled, Titian was contemplating a new work that would hang beside *The Feast of the*

Gods, the late masterpiece by his teacher, Giovanni Bellini, recently deceased (Lecture Thirty-Two). Alphonso d'Este had approached Titian, Raphael, and Fra Bartolomeo to paint mythological fables for the duke's private study, which already contained Bellini's. Titian's three paintings for Ferrara amplify and re-orchestrate Venetian lyricism. They are somewhat larger, but more important, they contain many figures in complex interaction. The ambitious choreography is realized to perfection. These paintings—especially *Bacchus and Ariadne* and *The Andrians*—are among the most beautiful and influential achievements of the Venetian Renaissance. They mark a new stage in Titian's art. The 1520s are a pivotal decade in Italian and European history and art, and the point at which we decided to conclude this course. As with Michelangelo, the long-lived Titian must be left in mid-career, indeed, much earlier, because he had 50 years of productivity ahead of him. We will, however, have an opportunity to glance at some of his later art in our last two lectures.

Outline

I. Not long after Titian painted the *Gentleman in Blue*, he painted a masterful portrait that shows a greater maturity, the *Young Man with Cap and Gloves* (c. 1512–1515).

    A. It is a striking work that combines ideas from Bellini (the sitter faces out of the picture, does not look at the viewer) and Giorgione (the mood is deeply poetic, nostalgic), inspirited by Titian's own contribution, the vividly realized strength of character in this self-possessed young man.

    B. Coloristically, it is superb in the simple but brilliant contrasts of the black satin cloak, white shirt edged in red, rose sleeve and auburn hair, and in breadth of form, it anticipates Titian's mature style.

II. The Gipsy Madonna (c. 1510) is similar to the Madonnas of Giovanni Bellini in the composition and in the landscape. Yet there are significant differences.

    A. It is fuller, more ample, especially in the drapery that gathers around her right arm. In fact, the silver-blue drapery of her cloak is quite comparable to the drapery (which has been attributed to Titian) in front of Giorgione's *Sleeping Venus*.

B. The mood is also different from that of Bellini's Madonnas. The introspective melancholy of Bellini has been replaced by a rather placid, neutral quality.

III. *Saint Mark Enthroned with Saints* (c. 1511–1512) was originally painted for the Church of Santo Spirito in Isola, a monastery in the lagoon southwest of Venice, abandoned in the mid-17th century, at which time the painting was transferred to Santa Maria della Salute on the Grand Canal.

  A. Given that the four saints are Cosmas and Damian (doctors) and Roch and Sebastian (invoked against the plague), it seems likely that the altarpiece was occasioned by the plague and quite possible that it was Titian's personal memorial to Giorgione, his dead colleague.

  B. Saint Mark, impedestaled like a living statue, is flanked by the four saints, also statuesque and isolated. One is reminded of Giorgione's *Castelfranco Madonna*, and the figure of Saint Sebastian is a less classicizing version of Bellini's Sebastian in the *Saint Giobbe Altarpiece*.

IV. *Sacred and Profane Love* (c. 1514) is one of the key paintings of the Venetian Renaissance, very beautiful and equally enigmatic.

  A. The unusual ratio of width to height of about 2.4:1 may suggest that it was designed for a specific site, either on furniture or architecture. Titian also underscores the proportions by flanking a long, low sarcophagus with two female figures that incline slightly toward each other.

  B. The many interpretations of this scene, which at first glance seems straightforward, cannot even be broached as a list. The most widely accepted (or at least the best known) basic theory of the iconography is that of Erwin Panofsky as developed over decades.

  1. The nude woman is basically Venus (with Cupid nearby) but holding a flaming lamp. In Panofsky's neo-Platonic interpretation, she is Sacred (divine) Love.

  2. The sumptuously clothed woman is Profane (that is, secular or human) Love. This skeletal explanation leaves numerous aspects of the painting unmentioned, but it is the most that can be said with any confidence.

3. The painting has been persuasively shown to have been commissioned for the celebration of the marriage in 1514 of the distinguished Venetian official Niccolò Aurelio to Laura Bagarotto of Padua. Such nuptial paintings were frequently incorporated into the furniture of a bridal chamber, which may explain the unusual dimensions noted above.

V. The *Madonna and Child with Saints Dorothy and George* (c. 1515, Prado, Madrid) is a wonderfully composed group, the figures quite subtle in their interlocking poses.

    A. The figures are placed in a draped, tent-like interior with a vent behind Dorothy opening to the sky.

        1. The Madonna, in a lustrous red and ultramarine costume, exchanges solemn glances with the Child.

        2. The Child's hand reaches for the roses and he overlaps the ample figure of Dorothy, who in turn, overlaps the armored Saint George, whose devout gaze toward the Madonna completes the composition's unstressed triangle.

    B. The early history of this painting, which belonged to Philip II of Spain before 1593, is not known. It would be of particular interest because of the saints who attend the Madonna.

    C. Both George and Dorothy are early Christian martyrs whose very existence is dubious. Saint George is, of course, famous as the patron saint of England, but Dorothy is scarcely known.

        1. In this painting, George is such a strong and descriptively specific figure that one suspects he is a portrait, conceivably of the donor.

        2. Dorothy is identified by the basket of roses she offers the Christ Child. As she was led to martyrdom, a lawyer mocked her and asked her to send him roses or apples from Paradise after her arrival there. Roses duly arrived, and he was converted.

VI. The Franciscan Church of Santa Maria Gloriosa dei Frari, the most celebrated church in Venice after San Marco, was founded in the mid-13th century. It is one of the great Italian Gothic churches (completed c. 1443), and it houses many monuments and tombs of Venetian notables and many artistic treasures, dominant among which is *The Assumption of the Virgin* (1516–1518). The doctrine of the bodily Assumption of the Virgin was of particular importance to the Franciscans, because it was defended by Saint Bonaventure, the 13th-century Franciscan theologian.

A. Titian, not yet 30 years old, was commissioned to paint an enormous altarpiece for the Cappella Maggiore, the chancel and apse with its high altar. The importance of the commission attests to his early reputation.

   1. One hundred yards long, the church has a large enclosed choir just before the transept, but a gate on the axis permits the visitor to see the glowing *Assumption* through the choir from the end of the nave.

   2. Four stories of tall lancet Gothic windows rise from the floor to the vault of the apse, flooding the space with light. Although the stone carver who made the altar is known, it is assumed that Titian must have designed the altar, as well as the painting. This enormous structure required that four windows behind the altar be walled up before the painting, in its Renaissance frame, was set in place. Despite the contrast in style between the apse and the altar, it became an integral part of the architecture, effectually redefining it.

B. The space is towering, and Titian obviously was determined to dominate that space. To that end, he designed over-life-size figures in dynamic poses and brilliant colors.

   1. The painting was executed in a room in the adjoining monastery. This was undoubtedly necessary because of its huge size (23 feet high, or half again as tall as Bellini's *Saint Giobbe Altarpiece*), but it would also have facilitated determining the necessary scale of altarpiece and painting.

   2. The Assumption of the Virgin was traditionally painted in a static manner, with the seated Virgin carried passively up to heaven, but Titian's standing Virgin almost seems to swirl upward. The powerful torsion of her body and her upraised arms and upturned head draw her toward the extraordinary tilted airborne form of God, who caps the picture without stilling its motion. The triumphal arch of the frame is expansive even while it closes the composition.

3. The composition is almost created by color: The bright red costumes of the Madonna and two of the apostles mark the angles of an enormous pyramid. There are three tiers: the gesticulating apostles, the Madonna and angels, and God the Father, carefully interrelated by color and gesture. One is reminded of Raphael's *Disputà*, except that his work seems static in comparison with Titian's invention. It would be hard to imagine a more perfectly conceived tribute to the Frari's dedicatee—the *glorious* Saint Mary.

4. Indeed, this painting—the supreme masterpiece of the Venetian High Renaissance—is comparable in its ideal poise and dignity to Raphael's Vatican frescoes, and it even echoes some of the dramatic power of Michelangelo's Sistine figures. This is all the more remarkable because Titian had not yet been to Rome and could have known those works only through prints or drawings.

VII. When the *Assumption* was triumphantly unveiled on 19 May 1518, Titian had already been approached by Alphonso d'Este to contribute to the decoration of his Alabaster Chamber in Ferrara, for which Giovanni Bellini had so recently painted his *Feast of the Gods* (Lecture Thirty-One). Raphael and Fra Bartolommeo had been approached earlier, but Bartolommeo had died in September 1517 and Raphael had seemed in no hurry to commit to the project.

A. Titian was probably asked to take over the subject for which Fra Bartolommeo had already sketched a composition, "The Worship of Venus," because he seems to have also taken over elements from the Florentine's design. When Raphael also died, Titian assumed the responsibility for three paintings, and they occupied him until late 1522 or early 1523. We will look at two: *Bacchus and Ariadne* and *The Andrians*.

B. The last to be delivered was probably the *Bacchus and Ariadne*, but we will look at it first. It is a painting, like the other two, based on descriptions of now-lost ancient paintings by the Greek author Philostratus the Elder (in his *Imagines*). Alphonso wanted these subjects recreated for his chamber.

1. The painting has a youthful charm, a certain combination of grace and willful awkwardness that suggests first love. The splendid color of the painting (the result of a strenuously debated restoration 40 years ago) harmonizes this love song.

2. A teenage Bacchus leaps impetuously from a chariot drawn by cheetahs as Venus turns away in surprise. The train of attendants following Bacchus includes two wonderfully contrasting figures: a bearded satyr struggling to rid himself of a serpent (certainly inspired by the *Laocöon*, of which Titian would have seen copies) and an utterly charming child faun dragging a calf's head.

C. *The Andrians* (probably the second to be finished) is one of the most memorably choreographed paintings of the Renaissance, and it had enormous influence on other painters, including Rubens, who copied it.

1. There is much drinking, much amorous behavior abetted by the drinking, and some sleep, induced by the drinking. The last category includes a sleeping old man on the hill at top right (perhaps a god of the place) and the robust nude at the lower right, who is based on the already famous classical image of the sleeping Ariadne.

2. The visual poetry is stunning. Choose, if you can, from among the nude faun pouring wine into a *kylix* at the left center, the inebriated fellow balancing a crystal pitcher of wine aloft against the sky, or the dancing couple who only have eyes for each other.

D. The paintings for the Alabaster Chamber begin a new phase in Titian's career, introducing him as among the greatest poets in paint of any era, with a complete command of all that painting can do to produce sheer seductive beauty for the eyes. The historically imposed limitations of this course mean that we must leave him with 50 years of painting to come, although we will glance at one or two of his later achievements in our summary.

Works Discussed:

Titian:

Young Man with Cap and Gloves, c. 1512–1515, National Gallery, London.

Gipsy Madonna, c. 1510, Kunsthistorisches Museum, Vienna.

Saint Mark Enthroned with Saints, c. 1511–1512, Santa Maria della Salute, Venice.

Sacred and Profane Love, c. 1514–1515, Galleria Borghese, Rome.

La Virgen con el Niño, Santa Dorotea y San Jorge (*The Madonna and Child with Saints Dorothy and George*), c. 1515, Museo del Prado, Madrid.

Assumption of the Virgin, 1516 –1518, Santa Maria Gloriosa dei Frari, Venice.

Bacchus and Ariadne, c. 1522, National Gallery, London.

The Andrians, 1518–1525, Museo del Prado, Madrid.

Essential Reading:

Adams, chapter 17.

Hartt, chapter 19.

Supplementary Reading:

Pedrocco, Filippo. *Titian*. New York: Scala/Riverside, 1993.

Rosand, David. *Painting in Cinquecento Venice: Titian, Veronese, Tintoretto*. New Haven: Yale University Press, 1982.

Questions to Consider:

1. What might be the connection of Titian's early *Saint Mark Enthroned with Four Saints* to an outbreak of the plague in Venice?

2. How would you describe the importance of Titian's *Assumption*, in the Church of the Frari, to the development of Venetian painting?

Lecture Thirty-Four—Transcript
Titian—The Early Years

Good morning. In the last lecture we spoke at length of Titian and the characteristics of his paintings in comparison with the paintings of Giorgione. We said nothing at that time of Titian's life other than his training with Giovanni Bellini. So, a brief bio.

First, his name is properly Tiziano Vecellio, and he was born in Pieve di Cadore, north of Venice and closer to the Austrian Tyrol than to Venice. His attachment to his birthplace never waned throughout his long life. He returned constantly when he had an opportunity to visit his hometown.

He was born about 1488-90, and he lived until 1576—long enough a life, but he used to be given ten extra years before it was pretty much ascertained about 1488-90. In English speaking countries, he has always been called Titian. It's an anglicized form, obviously, from the Latin form of his name, which is Titianus, just as we derived the English Raphael from the Latin form of his name.

When Titian was nine he went with his brother, or a brother, to Venice to be apprenticed to a mosaicist, a master of mosaic art. Certainly, though he changed from mosaic art to painting, the color of mosaics wasn't a bad beginning for a young artist.

He then studied painting with Gentile Bellini before finding him old-fashioned, according to a friend, and entering the studio of Giovanni Bellini. By 1508, when he was working with Giorgione on the frescos for the Fondaco dei Tedeschi—those lost frescos—Titian was an independent master.

As we noted in the last lecture, Titian was the great—among the greatest—portrait artist. The painting you are looking at, the splendid *Young Man with Cap and Gloves* of about 1512-15, now in the National Gallery in London, is proof enough of that. Not long after

Titian painted *The Gentleman in Blue*, which may be a self-portrait; he painted this masterful portrait that shows a greater maturity yet. *The Young Man with Cap and Gloves* is an intimate, fluidly painted reverie that recalls Giorgione's work but has a breadth of form that looks ahead to Titian's mature painting. It's a striking work that combines ideas from Giovanni Bellini (the sitter faces out of the picture, does not look at the viewer) and from Giorgione (the mood is deeply poetic, very nostalgic), and yet it's inspirited, if I can put it that way, by Titian's own contribution, the vividly realized strength of character in this self-possessed young man.

Coloristically, it's superb in the simple but brilliant contrasts of his black satin cloak (anyone who can paint black like that is a great colorist), his white shirt edged in red, his rose-colored sleeve, and his auburn hair—all of this just a beautiful coloristic ensemble, and in breadth of form, as I say, it anticipates his mature style. Look for a moment at the background, which is fairly clear in this image, there is a wall behind him at the right, and at the left is a kind of column or pier that has on it a sculpture and what looks like a coat of arms and so forth. Nonetheless, we have (if it is a coat of arms of this young man) never identified the sitter here. Look also at the sill, which I didn't mention yet, the sill on which he rests his hand that holds the glove, almost like two hands on that light-gray sill, which divides our space, and he doesn't project beyond it. He pushes, as it were, the picture plane, but unlike *The Man with the Blue Sleeve* from the last lecture, he doesn't push into our space in an illusionistic way. It's a haunting painting in many ways—extraordinarily handsome both in subject and in painting.

The so-called *Gipsy Madonna* was painted about 1510. It's now in Vienna in the Kunsthistorisches Museum, the art history museum. The *Gipsy Madonna* takes her name, I think, from the costume in part and also from the multi-colored hanging that is partly behind her in the center and off to the right. The composition is very similar to the Madonnas of Giovanni Bellini, in the composition both of the Madonna and Child in this triangular form, with the Child here standing on a partial sill or ledge of some sort, and also because it opens to the landscape on one side. Bellini almost invariably opens his landscape onto both sides equally, but here it is asymmetrical. There are other significant differences between this and the

Madonnas of Bellini. Titian's Madonna is fuller, more ample in form, especially in the drapery that gathers around her right arm. This is just a wonderful, wonderful area here of massing up of different colored draperies at this area, which gives great volume and great force to that area, and the color—particularly here of the silver-blue drapery of her cloak—is quite comparable to the drapery in front of Giorgione's *Sleeping Venus*, drapery that we attributed to Titian.

The mood here is also different from that of Bellini's Madonnas. The introspective melancholy of Giovanni Bellini has been replaced by a rather placid quality, almost neutral. Her eyes are downcast and it's quiet, but it doesn't have that deeper introspection that we saw in Giovanni Bellini. It is a very beautiful painting with an exquisitely beautiful landscape in the background.

Bellini's influence is also still strong in an altarpiece of *St. Mark Enthroned with Saints*, with other saints. The figure of St. Sebastian, for example, in this, to the right, the nude figure, is a less classicizing version of Bellini's St. Sebastian in his *St. Giobbe Altarpiece*. But Giorgione's style played a role here too, and one might be reminded of Giorgione's *Castelfranco Madonna* in the placement of St. Mark. You remember in the *Castelfranco Madonna*, the Madonna was very high, a throne on top of an altar, and here we have St. Mark elevated on a pedestal like a living statue, and he is flanked by the other saints who are also statuesque, and to some degree isolated. Nowhere outside of Venice and its dominions would you expect to find an image of St. Mark elevated in the manner that the Madonna is usually elevated in, but nothing was too good for the patron saint of Venice, and here he holds forth as though he were alone on that pedestal.

This painting, probably painted about 1511-12, was originally painted for the church of Santo Spirito in Isola (Isola means island) and that was a monastery, Santo Spirito, in the Lagoon southwest of Venice. Now, plague victims were buried, often in mass graves, outside of cities, and in Venice that meant on other islands of the Lagoon. Since the four saints here are Cosmas and Damian on the left (who are doctors), and St. Roch and St. Sebastian on the right (who are both invoked against the plague), it seems likely that the altarpiece was occasioned by the plague and quite possible that it also served as Titian's personal memorial to his dead colleague, Giorgione, who died in the plague. Now, it would have been commissioned by someone else, but that would not prohibit Titian from putting in his own, as it were, private commemorative note to Giorgione. I might note that when Santo Spirito, the church in the Lagoon, was abandoned in the mid-17th century, this painting was transferred to a church on the Grand Canal, the famous church of Santa Maria della Salute, which was a church newly built to commemorate deliverance from yet a more recent plague, and there may well have been a knowledge of the plague relationship, as it were, of this earlier altarpiece when it was moved.

About his famous *Sacred and Profane Love*, which you see now, painted probably about 1514-15, and today in the Borghese Gallery in Rome, about this painting, the first thing, and maybe the last, that must be said is that it is extraordinarily beautiful. It is just breathtakingly beautiful. That agreed, the allegorical subject presents complexities that have inspired scholars to insights and overreaching in equal proportion. *Sacred and Profane Love* is one of the key paintings of the Venetian Renaissance, very beautiful and equally enigmatic. The unusual ratio of width to height of about 2.4:1 may suggest that it was designed for a specific site, either on furniture or on architecture, the paneling of a room.

Titian also underscores the proportions of the canvas by flanking this long, low sarcophagus with two female figures (seated at either end of it) who incline slightly toward each other—all of that emphasizes the width and, of course, the nude figure rises nearly the full height of the panel. Then, you've got the marvelous horizon behind it— literally, the horizontals of the sky emphasize the same low-lying quality of the composition.

The many interpretations of this painting cannot even be broached as a list, a painting that I suppose at first glance is straightforward; we have a nude lady and a clothed lady but what is it about? But, even a list of the interpretations that have been suggested are beyond the scope of this lecture. It has, as I say, inspired a great many words. The most widely accepted (or at least the best known) basic theory of the iconography—of the meaning—is that of the great scholar Erwin

Panofsky, as developed in essays by him over decades. He kept coming back to this painting, but I am only giving you the most obvious parts of it: the nude woman is basically Venus; Cupid is nearby in the middle there of the sarcophagus; leaning into the sarcophagus is apparently a kind of spring or well; and Venus, however, holds a flaming lamp, not her usual attribute here.

In Penofsky's interpretation, which is an interpretation derived from Neoplatonic ideas, and we touched on these apropos of Michelangelo in particular, in Penofsky's Neoplatonic interpretation, she—the nude with the lamp—represents Sacred (Divine) Love. The sumptuously clothed woman is Profane Love (by which is meant secular or human). This is the most skeletal explanation imaginable, leaving numerous aspects of the painting unmentioned, and yet it is the most that can be said with any confidence that you won't get into an argument with someone. It is just about as far as you can go in the interpretation of what we see. I might add, however, if you look at the lower part of the sarcophagus near the clothed woman, you see quite clearly a horse. The horse is very close in pose to one or two of the life-sized bronze horses on San Marco, on the front of San Marco, and I think clearly inspired in pose by them. He just borrows them and uses it here as a relief.

The painting has been persuasively demonstrated to have been commissioned for the celebration of a wedding, of the marriage in 1514 of a distinguished Venetian official whose name is Niccolò Aurelio to a woman from Padua named Laura Bagarotto. Now, such nuptial paintings as this were frequently incorporated into the furniture of a bridal chamber, which may, obviously I think does, explain the unusual dimensions of the painting.

I show you a painting that demonstrates Titian's unflagging inventiveness because I think that continuous inventiveness over a long, long life of painting is one of the marks of his particular genius. Here we are in a painting of the *Madonna and Child with Saints Dorothy and George*, painted probably about 1515, and he invents a complex but focused variation on the very familiar theme to us now of the Madonna and saints, using half-length figures, though not behind a sill or other barrier; it's as though they were in a shared space with the viewer, not cut off by a low wall or sill.

It's a wonderfully composed group, which is why I particularly wanted you to see it, quite subtle in the interlocking poses of the figures. They're placed in a draped, tent-like interior with a vent behind St. Dorothy opening to the sky. The Madonna, in a lustrous red and ultramarine costume, exchanges solemn glances with the Christ Child. The Child's hand reaches for the roses in Dorothy's basket that she carries in her right hand, and he, the Child, overlaps in that gesture, overlaps her ample figure that, in turn, her figure overlaps that of the armored St. George, whose devout gaze toward the Madonna completes the composition's unstressed triangle. They do lean in, the Madonna and St. George, and there is a slight triangulation continued by the curtain on the left, and a wonderful interlocking and overlapping composition.

The early history of this painting, which once belonged to King Philip II of Spain before 1593, is not known. It would be of particular interest because of the saints who attend the Madonna. Both George and Dorothy are early Christian martyrs whose very existence is dubious. Don't let that bother you, by the way—real or not—they inspired some great art.

St. George is, of course, famous as the patron saint of England, but Dorothy is scarcely known. In this painting, St. George is such a strong and descriptively specific figure that one suspects that he's a portrait, conceivably of the donor, whose name would have, therefore, probably been George.

Dorothy is identified by the basket of roses that she offers the Christ Child. The story is that as she was led to martyrdom, a lawyer mocked her and asked her to send him roses or apples from Paradise after she got there. Well, roses duly arrived, and he was converted to Christianity.

The Franciscan Church of Santa Maria Gloriosa dei Frari, the most celebrated church in Venice after San Marco, was founded in the mid-13th century. It is one of the great Italian Gothic churches (completed about 1443) and it houses many monuments and tombs of Venetian notables and many artistic treasures, dominant among which is *The Assumption of the Virgin*, painted between 1516 and

1518 by Titian. The doctrine of the bodily assumption of the Virgin was of particular importance to the Franciscans because it was defended by St. Bonaventure, the 13th-century Franciscan theologian.

Titian, not yet 30 years old, was commissioned to paint an enormous altarpiece for the Cappella Maggiore (the major chapel), the chancel and apse of the church, with its high altar. The importance of the commission attests to his early reputation.

One hundred yards long, the church has a large enclosed choir before you reach the transept. You see that choir, with its wooden walls or its marble walls, but a gate on the axis permits us, as visitors, to see *The Assumption* through the choir from the end of the nave at the far end, right through it, and framed by it, as it were, in this photograph. That is the entire picture, but far down in the apse. Nothing can prepare the first-time visitor to the venerable Venetian Franciscan church of the Frari for the impact of Titian's youthful masterpiece.

Painted in the adjoining monastery, it was designed to harmonize perfectly with the Gothic apsidal apse of the church, the apsidal chapel, and we are looking at it now, this great soaring four-story Gothic arch of the apse, and in front of it, on a Renaissance altar, *The Assumption* by Titian. That the painting was executed in a room in the adjoining monastery was undoubtedly necessary, necessitated by its huge size—it is 23 feet high, half again as tall as Bellini's *St. Giobbe Altarpiece*, but it would also have facilitated determining the necessary scale of the altarpiece and the painting with the architecture, with four stories of tall lancet Gothic windows rising from the floor to the vault of the apse, flooding the space with light. Although the stonecarver of the Renaissance altar—in which the painting is—is known, it is assumed that Titian designed the altar as well as the painting. This enormous structure required that four windows behind the altar be walled up before the painting in its Renaissance frame could be set in place.

Despite the contrast in style between the apse and the altar, it became an integral part of the architecture, effectually redefining it. The space is towering, and Titian obviously was determined to dominate that space. To that end, he designed over-life-sized figures in dynamic poses and brilliant colors. It is a three-tiered composition that offered an entirely new approach to the Assumption of the Virgin, to this subject. The lowest level holds the empty tomb, which is almost completely obscured by the agitated Apostles—who shrink back, or strain forward, or look up in awe, or reach out in farewell toward the Virgin. The Virgin dominates the second tier, accompanied and sustained by a wonderful glory of angels beneath and beside her, and God the Father—attended principally by one large angel—closes the composition at the top.

I want you to observe a few things. For instance, the curve of the clouds on which she stands is completed by the arched top of the frame—so, that it's one complete circle. The energized silhouette of the Apostles' heads and hands just follow this line—what a wonderful line, like a very dramatic musical score melody going across that area.

Look at the outstretched arm of the Apostle in red, this full-length Apostle with his back to us. Together with the little angel's leg that comes down here, it connects the bottom tier with the middle tier, and also echoes the position of the Madonna's upstretched arms, a position that is almost completely new—Mantegna had done something slightly similar, but basically this is Titian's invention. She is not praying. The Assumption of the Virgin was traditionally painted in a very static manner, with the seated Virgin—hands folded in prayer—carried passively up to heaven, but Titian's standing Virgin almost seems to swirl upward. The powerful torsion of her body and her upraised arms and her upturned head—tilted airborne toward the tilted airborne form of God—is astonishing. The fact that this form, this figure of God the Father, is not just horizontal across the top but is on a diagonal, almost as though banking, gives the picture a top—it caps it, without stopping the motion. There's still a sense that this motion will continue, literally, to heaven. The triumphal arch of the frame is expansive even while it closes the picture like a dome, like the dome of heaven, in fact.

The composition is almost created through color: the intense red costumes of the Madonna and two of the Apostles, here below, mark the angles of a wonderful, enormous pyramid here. There are three tiers, three separate levels: the gesticulating Apostles, the Madonna and angels, and God the Father, carefully interrelated by color and gesture. One is reminded of Raphael's *Disputà*, except that Raphael's work seems static in comparison with Titian's invention. It would be hard to imagine a more perfectly conceived tribute to the Frari's dedicatee—she's not just St. Mary in this church, she is Santa Maria Gloriousa—the glorious St. Mary. This painting is the supreme masterpiece of the Venetian High Renaissance, fully comparable in its ideal poise and dignity to Raphael's Vatican frescoes in the Stanze. It even echoes some of the power of Michelangelo's Sistine figures, and that is remarkable because Titian hadn't been to Rome yet, and could only have known those works through prints or through drawings.

The Assumption is joyous; it is dynamic; the glorious reds of its principal figures resound to the end of the nave, and yet the stupendous composition achieves a monumental balance, a perpetual tension between motion and stasis that is unforgettable. When this painting was triumphantly unveiled on 19 May 1518, Titian had already been approached by Alphonso d'Este, the Duke of Ferrara, to contribute to the decoration of his Alabaster Chamber in Ferrara, for which Giovanni Bellini had, as we've seen, so recently painted his *Feast of the Gods*.

Raphael and Fra Bartolommeo had also been approached by the Duke, as I mentioned in an earlier lecture, but Fra Bartolommeo had died in September 1517, and Raphael had seemed in no hurry to commit to the project, and then he died, so Titian assumed their commissions as well. They occupied him until late 1522 or early 1523. His three great paintings for Ferrara amplify and reorchistrate Venetian lyricism as invented by Bellini and Giorgione. Titian's most important innovation in these mythologies was that they contained many figures in complex interaction. The ambitious choreography of these actors is realized to perfection. We'll look at two of these paintings: the *Bacchus and Ariadne*, which you see now, and then *The Andrians*, which I think are among the most beautiful and influential achievements of the Venetian Renaissance, and they mark a new stage in Titian's art.

Bacchus and Ariadne, now in London in the National Gallery, was the last to be delivered, probably, but we'll look at it first. It's a painting like the other two Titians for this spot, the Alabaster

Chamber, based upon the descriptions of now-lost ancient paintings by the Greek author Philostratus the Elder—the descriptions were by him in his "Imagines." Alphonso wanted these subjects recreated for his collection.

Here we see Ariadne on the left, wandering disconsolately on the shore of Naxos, having been abandoned by Theseus, who has sailed off. Bacchus arrives suddenly and noisily, you might say, with his extraordinary entourage. It is love at first sight—at least it is for Bacchus. Ariadne's crown, she was the daughter of King Minos of Crete, and Bacchus has already caused her crown to be thrown into the heavens, and it is a constellation up in the upper left-hand corner, the constellation of Ariadne. This is a mythological moment. By the way, he had to do exactly what Botticelli had had to do when faced with doing the birth of Venus. There wasn't anything except a description of such a subject. One had not been painted in modern times. So, Botticelli had had to find something to base it on, and as you may recall, he tried using the Baptism of Christ to form his compositional basis.

Well, here, we had the same thing, and Titian, I think, has probably had his mind on the arrival of the angel Gabriel to the Virgin Mary—a young, divine figure suddenly arrives and the young woman is startled and slightly frightened by his arrival and pulls back. It's a teenage Bacchus that we have here leaping impetuously from a chariot drawn by cheetahs; you see them here between the two of them—by cheetahs, as Ariadne turns away in surprise, although looking at him with interest. The train of attendants following Bacchus includes two wonderfully contrasting figures: this bearded satyr here, who is struggling to rid himself of a serpent (well, this was certainly inspired by the *Laocöon*, of which Titian would have seen copies)—there's a wonderful contrast with this struggling figure and the utterly charming child faun, who is dragging a calf's head behind him. A French writer at the earlier part of the 20th century spoke of that little figure and called him *petit délicieux faune* (this delicious little faun), and it's exactly the right adjective for him.

The painting has a youthful charm, a certain combination of grace and youthful awkwardness that suggests first love. The splendid color of the painting harmonizes this love song. The singing color, incidentally, reemerged after a strenuously debated restoration more than 40 years ago in London. *The Times of London* was flooded with letters for months about the propriety of restoring the painting. The British care about such things, or at least they did then.

The Andrians (probably the second of Titian's trio to be finished for the Alabaster Chamber) is one of the most memorably choreographed paintings of the Renaissance, and it had enormous influence upon other painters, including Rubens—who copied it. Choreographed is the right word, for much of the composition in *The Andrians* is danced by the characters. The Andrians were inhabitants of the Aegean Island of Andros, and they became drunk from the river of wine that flowed there, I can well imagine, and Andros was therefore, in antiquity, the center of the cult of Dionysus, or Bacchus, and in this picture there is much drinking, much amorous behavior abetted by the drinking, and some sleep, induced by the drinking. The last category includes a sleeping old man on the hill at top right who is probably considered a god of the place, a god of the locale, and then the robust female nude at the lower right who is based upon the already famous classical image of the sleeping Ariadne in the Vatican, famous ancient statue. She, however, was much more clothed than Titian's version of the same figure.

The visual poetry is stunning. I ask you to choose, if you can, from among the nude faun (here to the left) pouring wine into a kylix held by this woman at the center, and this wonderful act of pouring the wine and the circle that is completed of the arms; the inebriated fellow who is balancing a crystal pitcher of wine aloft against the sky, one of the most beautiful inventions imaginable here, and it's spectacularly painted, and how very difficult to paint as well; or the dancing couple (here to the right) who only have eyes for each other. It is charm—one charm upon another, just utterly poetic.

The paintings for the Alabaster Chamber begin a new phase in Titian's career, introducing him as among the greatest poets in paint of any era, with a complete command of all that painting can do to produce sheer seductive beauty for the eyes. The historically imposed limitations of our course means that we must leave Titian with 50 years of painting still to come, just as we had to omit the second half of Michelangelo's career. We will, however, have an opportunity to glance at some of their later art—both Michelangelo and Titian—in our last two lectures, in which we will attempt a bit of summary and a look at what lay ahead.

Thank you for your attention.

Lecture Thirty-Five
A Culture in Crisis

Scope:

Because summation is even more difficult than introduction, we propose to begin this lecture by simply comparing several works of art to remind us of the distance we have traversed from the Early to the High Renaissance. In the history of art, both artists and students are (to borrow an analogy from Plutarch) like oarsmen, "who look astern while they row the boat ahead." Then, with Michelangelo as the measure of the change that came over Italian art in the 1520s, we will enumerate the key political and religious events that strongly affected the cultural climate, not only in Italy but throughout Europe. When Michelangelo's *Pietá* (1498–1499) in Saint Peter's is compared with his *Tomb of Giuliano de'Medici* (c. 1526–1533), one quickly perceives that the unified, concentrated grief of the former has been displaced by an unfocused and profound malaise.

What had happened in the intervening years to account for this change? Powerful Italian city-states, including Florence, Rome (the Papal States), and Venice, often warred with one another, and the resultant instability invited military intervention. The pope also led an alliance that briefly deprived Venice of its mainland territories, and he encouraged the sale of indulgences (forgiveness of sins) to help raise money for the rebuilding of Saint Peter's. This practice, continued by his successor, Leo X, was a huge step toward the Protestant Reformation. In the mid-1520s, the ill-considered machinations of Pope Clement VII precipitated an attack (1526) on Saint Peter's and the Vatican by the Roman Colonna party, and Emperor Charles V seized this opportunity to invade the city. In May 1527, his unpaid mercenary troops commenced the horrifying seven-month sack of Rome, which essentially rendered the papal city desolate and nearly impotent for half a century.

Michelangelo next painted the immense altar wall of the Sistine Chapel with *The Last Judgment* (1535–1541). Nothing could be a greater contrast to his ceiling frescoes of 30 years before. The weight of the artist's pessimism is felt in every detail, and the whole, even after restoration revealed its brighter colors, is oppressive and terrifying. Painters of the subject usually stress damnation (it is an alluring pictorial subject), but Michelangelo paints salvation with equal cheerlessness.

It was not only in the art of Michelangelo that the psychological damage was evident. Paintings by Rosso Fiorentino (before the sack) and Pontormo (afterward) offer their own evidence that the High Renaissance had ended. In most artistic centers, it was replaced with mannerism, an inexact but usable style name. Mannerism asserted that justification could be found in ancient art for any style one wished to adopt or develop. For the mannerists, it was Hellenistic art with its expressive exaggerations and distortions. Mannerism became the dominant style until near the end of the 16th century.

Outline

I. The last two lectures together are devoted to a retrospective glance at the territory covered in this course, a summary of the political, sociological, and theological events of the early 16th century that altered Italy and the rest of Europe and a sketch of the artistic developments that issued from that much-changed culture. We begin with a backward glance.

   A. It is instructive and fascinating to compare Masaccio's *Trinity* (c. 1428) with Raphael's *School of Athens* (1510–1511).

      1. In the *Trinity*, Masaccio first established the principle of linear perspective as a means of creating the illusion of a consistent three-dimensional space on a flat surface. As we saw, he did not hesitate to take liberties with the system, to depart from it for practical or expressive reasons. The theological mystery of the Trinity is his subject.

      2. In the *School of Athens*, Raphael uses the same principle to create a much deeper and wider space, populated with a multitude of figures. His subject is more abstruse and general, concerned with philosophy as discussed by Renaissance humanists. Visually, one could imagine placing the *Trinity* fresco within the central arcade of the *School of Athens*. It is as if Raphael added wings to Masaccio's concept.

B. The altarpiece with Madonna and saints gathered in a single space (a *sacra conversazione*) was a significant innovation of Renaissance painting. The development is clear in the comparison of Domenico Veneziano's *Saint Lucy Altarpiece* (c. 1445) and Giovanni Bellini's *Saint Zaccaria Altarpiece* (1505).

   1. Domenico's smaller-than-life-size figures are placed in a shallow space that does not disrupt the two-dimensional flow across the surface. The pastel hues and even the nuanced fall of light tend to unite the elements as surface pattern. The arcade, considered as surface design, also separates the figures into cells, at least to some degree.

   2. Bellini's life-size figures inhabit a space that is not merely larger but continuous. Its depth is created by greater contrasts of light and dark expressed through strong color, which simultaneously produces a feeling of an enveloping atmosphere. This compelling space also incorporates the real space and the real light of the altar and the church. Although Bellini's saints do not interact any more than do Domenico's, and make even less eye contact with the viewer, they carry much more conviction as real figures in a real space.

C. Now we will compare two works by Michelangelo, one that we have studied, the *Pietá* (1498–1499), and one that we have not, the *Tomb of Giuliano de' Medici* (c. 1526–1533).

   1. The *Pietá* in Saint Peter's is, among other things, an expression of the ideal High Renaissance compositional design of a stable pyramid. The artist managed to establish this form despite the problem of positioning the large body of Christ on the lap of his mother. The sculpture also encapsulates deep grief in a restrained, even lyrical way.

   2. The *Tomb of Giuliano de' Medici*, part of the Medici Tombs in the so-called New Sacristy of San Lorenzo, also presents a pyramidal composition, albeit in different spatial planes. The duke's statue sits in a niche with the tomb below. The tomb is surmounted by two enormous allegorical statues, one of Night (the female nude) and one of Day (the male nude).

<ol type="a">
<li>a. It is an unstable pyramid for several reasons: the two spatial planes, the uncertain poses of the allegories, and the curved sarcophagus from which the nudes appear likely to slip. Instead of a broad architectonic base, we have a shifting foundation.</li>
<li>b. The psychological expression of the nudes is also disquieting. Night is shown in a pose not conducive to sleep (and that would be remembered by Rodin when he designed The Thinker), and the body of Day is likewise twisted and emerging from sleep with difficulty and hesitancy.</li>
</ol>

II. The explanation for this profound stylistic and expressive shift is at once historically complex and fundamentally simple to perceive. From the 1490s to the 1520s, Italy had experienced a series of destabilizing events.

A. Many of the city-states were often at war with one another, in a shifting series of alliances. Florence, the Papal States, Milan, Venice—all were involved in these debilitating actions. In addition to their respective military powers, they used what diplomatic weapons they had: bribery, promises of territory, dynastic marriages, excommunication (a pope could excommunicate whole cities, and did).

B. These inter-peninsular struggles obviously invited foreign intervention, especially from France and the Holy Roman Empire. When Ludovico Sforza, duke of Milan, invited Charles VIII of France to invade Italy in 1494, to counterbalance the threat of Naples (under imperial control), it was a fateful turn in Italian Renaissance history. When the duke tried to expel the French, he could not and died in a French prison.

C. The French also expelled the Medici from Florence in 1494 and remained until 1512, when the papal armies of Pope Julius II drove them from Italy (and returned the Medici from exile). Julius II also fought to regain territory for the Papal States, mainly at the expense of Venice, achieving this briefly through the League of Cambrai.

D. At the same time, in his zeal to rebuild Saint Peter's from the ground up, the pope raised money through the sale of indulgences (forgiveness of sins), a practice that continued under his successor, the Medici Pope Leo X. It led more or less directly to Martin Luther's famous 95 Theses, posted in Wittenberg in 1517. This and the 1521 excommunication of Luther at the Diet of Worms were foundation stones in the Protestant Reformation that shook the Roman Church.

E. At this point, another Medici, Clement VII, came to the throne. A weak pope who failed to grasp the threat of the Reformation, he lost the English Church by mishandling Henry VIII's annulment, allied himself with the French, and argued with the emperor. These actions precipitated an unprecedented attack on the Vatican by a cabal of Roman nobles around the ancient Colonna family and gave Emperor Charles V the opportunity to invade Rome.

F. What followed was, in a sense, a matter of chance. The emperor's mercenary troops—some 20,000 Germans, Spaniards, and Italian irregulars—went unpaid and turned on the city. The sack of Rome in 1527 was horrific. Massacres and physical destruction left the city desolate. Much art was destroyed, as well. The city nearly ceased to be habitable, and the pre-sack population of some 100,000 dwindled. It was more than half a century before the city, during the papacy of Sixtus V, began to recover and rebuild.

III. We continue with a look ahead. To fully comprehend the sea change that came over art following the sack of Rome we need only to look at the next great creation of Michelangelo—the *Last Judgment* (1535–1541), frescoed on the altar wall of the Sistine Chapel. We shall look at it in direct contrast to the ceiling of three decades before.

A. The Sistine ceiling (1508–1512), for all of its variety and the changes that occurred during its creation, is a measured, unified, harmonious, and *humane* composition. It is an expression of the High Renaissance in its confidence, optimism, and heroic expression of both the human and the divine.

B. The *Last Judgment* is an oppressive juggernaut—a very great juggernaut. But even since superb conservation has restored it, like the ceiling, to a startling palette that few suspected, its huge forms, relentless rhythms, and oppressive weight appall the viewer. Its greatness is not in question, but the achievement is of a sort diametrically opposed to the Sistine ceiling.

1. The forms and their expressive content are those of despair, pessimism, and the near certainty of damnation. Michelangelo's vocabulary is still that of the human body, but his *Last Judgment* suggests that it will be a titanic struggle for anyone to get into heaven. This is the unleavened pessimism of Jeremiah, magnified a hundredfold.

2. Compare two figures only: Adam from the *Creation of Adam* and the enormous figure, with one eye staring in stark horror while the other is covered with his hand as demons drag him down to hell. Compare them: the utter innocence—blankness—of the yet-to-be-fully-created Adam and the haunted expression of one who knows his awful fate. One artist imagined and painted both these men, but an artist who, one feels, had lost hope in redemption in the interim.

3. That artist may be seen in the central portion of this terrifying fresco, in the figure of Saint Bartholomew just below and to the right of Christ. This saint was martyred by being flayed alive. In Christian neo-Platonic thought, the sloughing off of the human skin was a release of the soul from the corporeal prison. Here, Bartholomew holds the knife of his martyrdom in his right hand and his skin in his left. The face on the skin is the face of Michelangelo.

IV. But it was not only Michelangelo who made visible the profound trauma of the period. In most of the artistic centers of Italy, a new style arose that radically replaced that of Renaissance humanism. It is, in English, called *mannerism*, a title that seems appropriate but is nonetheless misleading. Appropriate because the style features distortions of drawing, space, and color that are the antithesis of the norms of the Renaissance—thus, the English word *mannered* seems to fit—but misleading because its derivation is quite different.

A. Mannerism derives from the Italian *maniera*, which is shorthand for *maniera della antiqua*—"manner of the antique." That is to say, that the artists who practiced and codified mannerism found their sources and their justification in ancient art, in their case, the art of late Hellenistic Greece (c. 100 B.C.–c. 100 A.D.). That style was dynamic, expressive, frequently departing from the norms of proportion and composition known in the classical period of Greek art of the 5th century B.C. In other words, one could (and can) find a model and justification for almost any style in the long history of ancient Greek art.

B. Mannerism had already emerged by the time Raphael died. His pupils and, it seems, Raphael himself had already begun to subvert the principles of the Renaissance in the designs for the last *stanze* in the Vatican. The new anti-classical style was essentially in place before the 1527 sack of Rome, a response to the massive social disorder.

C. Among the leading practitioners of the first phase of mannerism was Rosso Fiorentino (1495–1540), a Florentine (as his name attests) who visited Rome to see the Sistine ceiling for himself and borrowed many of its figurative inventions. His art immediately makes apparent the other aspect of mannerism, its extraordinary content. Extreme emotion and violent action, psychological expressions of neurosis or psychosis that seem strikingly modern in the post-Freud era, are all to be found somewhere in mannerist art, and Rosso's great *Descent from the Cross* (1521) in Volterra is one of the most remarkable. Spidery, angular, anguished, with a great void at its center, it is deeply moving but utterly anti-humanistic.

D. In the immediate post-sack period, Jacopo Pontormo (1494–1557), the exact contemporary of Rosso, finished an *Entombment* (1528; in Santa Felicitá, in Florence just across the Ponte Vecchio) that equals Rosso's masterpiece but in an utterly different vocabulary. Weightless, balloon-like figures somehow support Christ while walking or crouching on tip-toes. The painting seems about to dissolve in puffs of pink-white smoke. It is not even clear whether it is an entombment or a deposition, because neither tomb nor cross is evident.

E. In the next and final lecture, we will conclude the course with a look at the changed art of post-sack northern Italy, specifically in Parma and Venice. As had been the case during the Quattrocento and early Cinquecento, the artistic situation there developed in strikingly idiosyncratic ways.

Works Discussed:

Masaccio:

The Trinity, c. 1428, Santa Maria Novella, Florence,

Raphael:

The School of Athens, Stanza della Segnatura, 1510–1511, Vatican Palace, Vatican State.

Domenico Veneziano:

Saint Lucy Altarpiece, c. 1445, Galleria degli Uffizi, Florence.

Giovanni Bellini:

San Zaccaria Altarpiece, 1505, San Zaccaria, Venice.

Michelangelo:

Pietà, 1498–1499, Saint Peter's, Rome.

Tomb of Giuliano de' Medici, 1526–1533, San Lorenzo, Florence.

Sistine ceiling and detail Creation of Adam, 1508–1512, Sistine Chapel, Vatican Palace, Vatican State.

The Last Judgment, 1535–1541, Sistine Chapel, Vatican Palace, Vatican State.

Rosso Fiorentino:

Deposition (The Descent from the Cross), 1521, Pinacoteca, Volterra.

Jacopo Pontormo:

Entombment, 1528, Capponi Chapel, Santa Felicita, Florence.

Essential Reading:

Adams, chapter 18.

Hartt, chapters 18, 20.

Supplementary Reading:

Chastel, André. The Sack of Rome, 1527. Trans. by Beth Archer. Princeton: Princeton University Press, 1983.

Franklin, David. *Painting in Renaissance Florence, 1500–1550*. New Haven: Yale University Press, 2001.

Partridge, Loren, et al. *Michelangelo: The Last Judgment, A Glorious Restoration*. New York: Harry N. Abrams, 2000.

Questions to Consider:

1. What were the major sociopolitical crises of the 16th century and what was their effect on the Renaissance?

2. Contrast Michelangelo's Sistine ceiling and his *Last Judgment* in the same chapel, and explain that contrast.

Lecture Thirty-Five—Transcript
A Culture in Crisis

Good afternoon. The last two lectures together are devoted to a retrospective glance at the territory covered in this course, a summary of the political, sociological, and theological events of the early 16th century that altered Italy and the rest of Europe, and a sketch of the artistic developments that issued from that much-changed culture. We will begin with a backward glance. Because I find summation even more difficult than introduction, I want to begin this penultimate lecture by simply comparing several works of art to remind us of the distance we've traversed from the Early to the High Renaissance.

Looking back—in order to understand how we've reached our current position—is a necessary method. To borrow a simile from Plutarch, both artists and students of art are like oarsmen, "who look astern while they row the boat ahead."

First, it's instructive, and I hope fascinating, to compare Masaccio's *Trinity* with Raphael's *School of Athens*. We'll look first at the *Trinity*. I remind you that it was painted in 1428, a fresco in the Church of Santa Maria Novella in Florence. In the *Trinity*, Masaccio first established the principle of linear perspective as a means of creating the illusion of a consistent three-dimensional space on a flat surface. As we saw, he did not hesitate to take liberties with the system, or depart from it, for practical or expressive reasons. The theological mystery of the *Trinity* is his subject. As you look at it for just one more minute, I remind you that while he has a clear perspective system created by the lines in the vault of the receding vault, and his figures step back in space, nonetheless his figure of God the Father departs from that system. The feet of the Father are on a shelf at the back, but the figure floats forward to join the crucified Christ in the front plane. It is that kind of expressive departure from the system, in this case in the service of his subject, of his theological subject.

Raphael, in the *School of Athens*, used the same principle of perspective, of spatial perspective, to create a much deeper and much wider space, populated with a multitude of figures. His subject is less focused and more general, concerned with philosophy as discussed by Renaissance humanists in a very generalized fashion here, but he has given us a tremendously deep space, far deeper than was attempted by Masaccio, and we go back through these barrel vaults to a very distant space, which at the same time these receding arches get smaller and smaller in the surface of the composition, and they frame these central two figures in the fresco. But this is a tremendous expansion of Masaccio's *Trinity* in a way. Let me show them to you together. You could imagine placing the *Trinity* fresco within the central arcade of the *School of Athens*. It would probably fit, too, in terms of the actual size, but I'm thinking of it in another sense. It is as though Raphael had added wings to Masaccio's concept. It is, instead of a single barrel vault, a system of vaulting and a much broader, wider, and more thoroughgoing spatial construct that Raphael has created here.

We have already spent a lot of time talking about the altarpieces with Madonnas and Saints (the so-called sacra conversazione) gathered together in a single space. The sacra conversazione (the sacred conversation) was a significant innovation of Renaissance painting, and we've talked a good deal about it. I just wanted to make the development clear in one more, in one final as it were, comparison of Domenico Veneziano's *St. Lucy Altarpiece* of about 1445, and in a moment, Giovanni Bellini's *St. Zaccaria Altarpiece*, painted 60 years later.

Domenico Veneziano in his altarpiece gives us smaller than life-size figures. They're placed in a shallow space that does not disrupt the two-dimensional flow across the surface. They still read very much as a frieze, a lineup of figures, across the surface. The pastel hues and even the nuanced fall of light tend to unite all the elements as surface pattern. The arcade, the tripartite arcade, considered as surface design, also tends to separate the figures into cells, at least to some degree, to separate them one from another.

In the painting we've seen much more recently, Bellini's *St. Zaccaria Altarpiece* of 1505, the life-size figures inhabit a space that's not merely larger but continuous—continuous inside from one fictive space to another, from the actual frame of the altarpiece itself into the painted architecture within, and, to some degree, a continuous space with that in which we stand. Its depth in this picture is created by greater contrasts of light and dark expressed through strong color, very different than what we saw in Domenico Veneziano, and this simultaneously produces a feeling of an enveloping atmosphere. This compelling space also, as I say, incorporates the real space of the church and the real light of the altar that falls upon the altar and that falls from the church window. Let me show you these together as well.

A great difference between these two related subjects, but a great difference in treatment. Although Bellini's saints don't interact with each other any more than do Domenico's, in fact, perhaps even less, and make even less eye contact with the viewer (after all, in Domenico Veneziano's, John the Baptist looks right at us, and here we have only the small angel in the Bellini who makes any eye contact), Bellini's figures carry much more conviction as real figures in a real space. There's also a difference in relative physical presence. Domenico's saints in this comparison are demure, almost recessive in their twilight space. Giovanni's saints are monumental, even though they are solemnly posed and very quiet, magisterial. They take possession of their space. It's the difference between Early Renaissance of the Quattrocento and the High Renaissance that gradually superseded it in the Cinquecento in the 16th century.

Next, with Michelangelo as the measure of the change that came over Italian art in the 1520s, we will enumerate the key political and religious events that strongly affected the cultural climate, not only in Italy but throughout Europe—that sounds like an awfully big thing to try to do in a short time; however, we'll give you a sketch.

When Michelangelo's *Pietá*—the 1498-99 famous *Pietá* in St. Peter's—is compared with Michelangelo's later *Tomb of Giuliano de' Medici*, about 1526-33, one quickly perceives that the unified, concentrated grief of the former has been displaced by an unfocused and profound malaise. To demonstrate, first, the *Pietá*.

Among other things, this magnificent sculpture is an expression of the ideal High Renaissance compositional design of a stable pyramid. The artist managed to establish this form despite the problem of positioning the large body of Christ on the lap of his Mother. The sculpture also encapsulates deep grief in a restrained, even lyrical way. One could spend a long time analyzing the composition of this piece, but always coming back to its unity and to its profound feeling.

Now, we have not looked at the Medici Tombs in the so-called New Sacristy of San Lorenzo in Florence. The *Tomb of Giuliano de' Medici* is one of the two tombs in that space, and he worked on this between 1526 and 1533. Here, also, we have a pyramidal composition, but a very different one. For one thing, it is in different spatial planes. The two reclining figures in the foreground are close to us. The duke's statue sits back in a niche, the tomb forward below. The tomb is surmounted by two enormous allegorical statues, one of "Night" (that is the female nude on the left) and one of "Day" (the male nude on the right-hand side). Unlike in his *Pietá*, the tomb is an unstable pyramid, not a stable pyramid. It's unstable for several reasons: first of all, the two spatial planes that I pointed out; secondly, the uncertain poses, shall we say, of the allegorical figures (they find themselves in odd and difficult-to-sustain positions); and the curved sarcophagus on which the nudes recline, and from which they appear all too likely to slip. They're too big for it; they overlap the ends of the sarcophagus; they are not settled there. Instead of an architectonic base, we have a shifting foundation.

The psychological expression of the nudes is also disquieting. "Night" is shown in a pose not conducive to sleep (and which would be remembered, by the way, by Rodin in 1880, when he designed the famous *Thinker*). Next time you see it, *The Thinker*, just look at the right arm of *The Thinker* crossed over to the left leg, and you'll see that he was looking long and hard at Michelangelo as he always did. The body of "Day," on the other side, is likewise twisted and, shall we say, emerging from sleep with hesitancy and difficulty.

Let me show you the two together. You could hardly imagine a more profound difference between these two works that are only a quarter century apart. The explanation for this profound stylistic and expressive shift is at once historically complex and fundamentally simple to perceive. From the 1490s to the 1520s, Italy had experienced a series of destabilizing events.

Many of the city-states were often at war with one another, in a shifting series of alliances. Florence, the Papal States, Milan, Venice, all were involved in these actions that were debilitating to the stability of the peninsula. In addition to their respective military powers, they used what diplomatic weapons they had: bribery, promises of territory, dynastic marriages, excommunication was a good one (a pope could excommunicate entire cities, and he did). These inter-peninsular struggles obviously invited foreign intervention, especially from France and from the Holy Roman Empire. When Ludovico Sforza, Duke of Milan, invited Charles VIII of France to invade Italy in 1494, he did it because he wanted to counterbalance the threat of Naples (under Imperial control)—the Holy Roman Empire controlled the south—and when he invited that intervention from France, it was a fateful turn in Italian Renaissance history because when he tried to expel the French he couldn't, and he died in a French prison.

The French also expelled the Medici from Florence in 1494, and the French remained in Italy until 1512, when the Papal Armies of Pope Julius II drove them from Italy (and returned the Medici from exile). Julius II also fought to regain territory for the Papal States, mainly at the expense of Venice, which was briefly deprived of its mainland territories by the papacy–led league called the League of Cambrai. At the same time, in his zeal to rebuild St. Peter's from the ground up, the pope raised money though the sale of indulgences (forgiveness of sins), a practice that continued under his successor, the Medici Pope Leo X. That led more or less directly to Martin Luther's famous 95 theses, posted in Wittenberg in 1517. This and the 1521 excommunication of Luther at the Diet of Worms were foundation stones in the Protestant Reformation, which shook the Roman church.

At this point, another Medici became pope; he was Clement VII. He was a weak pope. He failed to grasp the threat of the Reformation, and he lost the English church by mishandling Henry VIII's annulment. He allied himself with the French, and he argued with the Emperor—two bad ideas. All this precipitated an unprecedented attack on the Vatican itself by a cabal of Roman nobles gathered around the ancient Colonna family, and that gave Emperor Charles V the opportunity to invade Rome. What followed was, in a sense, a matter of chance. The Emperor's mercenary troops—some 20,000 Germans, Spaniards, and Italian irregulars—were unpaid and turned upon the city, the city of Rome. The Sack of Rome in 1527 was horrific. Massacres and physical destruction left the city desolate. Much art was destroyed as well, of course. The city nearly ceased to be habitable, and the pre-Sack population of about 100,000 persons dwindled. It was more than half a century before the city of Rome, during the papacy of Sixtus V, began to recover and rebuild.

Let's continue with a look ahead. To fully comprehend the sea change that came over art following the Sack of Rome, we need only to look at the next great creation of Michelangelo—*The Last Judgment*, frescoed on the altar wall of the Sistine Chapel between 1535 and 1541. We shall look at it in direct contrast to the Sistine Ceiling of three decades earlier. Here is the Ceiling (1508-12). For all of its variety and all of the changes that we saw that occurred during the creation of the Sistine Ceiling, it is a measured, unified, harmonious, and humane composition. It is an expression of the High Renaissance in its confidence, its optimism, and its heroic expression of both the human and the divine. *The Last Judgment* was painted by Michelangelo, as I said, between 1535 and 1541. It is, of course, the immense altar wall of the Sistine Chapel. There had been two frescoes from the 1482 fresco cycle there. They had to be destroyed to make way for this.

Nothing could be a greater contrast to the Sistine Ceiling than this in the same chapel. *The Last Judgment* is an oppressive juggernaut. It is a very great juggernaut. The depth of the artist's pessimism is felt in every detail and in the whole, and even after restoration revealed a brighter palette that very few people expected, its huge forms, its relentless rhythms, the unendurable weight of its figures and of the whole, appall the viewer. Painters of this subject, of the last judgment (and they've been doing it from the Middle Ages onward) usually stress damnation—damnation is an alluring pictorial subject in literary, as well. Milton knew that. It always comes off better than salvation somehow. But Michelangelo paints salvation with as much cheerlessness as he paints damnation.

The greatness of *The Last Judgment*, of this fresco, is not in question, but you must realize that it is an achievement diametrically opposed to the achievement of the Sistine Ceiling. Form and content are unanimously expressed, the near certainty of damnation. Michelangelo's vocabulary is still that of the human body, his entire vocabulary is the human body, but his *Last Judgment* suggests that it's going to be a titanic struggle for anyone to get into heaven. This is the unleavened pessimism of Jeremiah, magnified a hundredfold. Look for a moment at it, just stop and look for a moment at it, and realize that this side—the left as we look at it—is the side of the saved, and realize that these figures are being hauled up literally by ropes and by a strong arm up. They're not rising up in salvation; they're being, when they get there, they're being heaved out of the earth here below (and with great effort) up to the elect above. On this side, the damned really don't look that much different than do the blessed on the other side. Just to locate you, remember here at the very top we have, and we saw this when we finished the Sistine Chapel, here we have Jonah the great prophet representing the Resurrection, looking upward at the scene of the Ceiling, of the creation of the world, in a sense, the separation of light and dark, and then *The Last Judgment*, and here the altar below. What an extraordinary vertical iconographic thrust this has.

Let me compare two figures only: Adam from the Creation of Adam on the Sistine Ceiling, together with one of the damned in this painting. Here is Adam. The utter innocence—blankness—of the face, of the—we could put it this way—of the yet to be fully created Adam. He is a potential life waiting to be infused with the life force. Compare it with one of the damned on the altar wall—this enormous figure, with one eye staring in stark horror while the other is covered with his hand as demons drag him down to hell, a life lived and a soul lost and all the muscular life within his mammoth body cannot prevail over the force of death and damnation. Let me show you them together.

They are both an expression through the human body to totally different ends—the innocence of the blameless and the haunted expression of one who knows his awful fate. One artist imagined and painted these emotional extremes and every emotion in between. It is hard to disagree with Vasari's verdict when he wrote that

Michelangelo portrayed all the emotions that mankind can experience. Michelangelo's figures reveal thoughts and emotions that only he has known how to express. It's hard to disagree with that.

There is one other figure where the artist himself may be seen on the Ceiling. It's in the central portion of this terrifying fresco, just below Christ and to the right of Christ, and it's St. Bartholomew. Here he is, St. Bartholomew, holding a knife in his right hand. This saint was martyred by being flayed alive. Now, in Christian Neoplatonic thought— and that joining a conjunction of Christian thought—and Neoplatonic thought drove Michelangelo, the sloughing off of the human skin was a release of the soul from the corporal prison. Here, Bartholomew holds the knife of his martyrdom in his right hand, and his skin in his left. The face on the skin is the face of Michelangelo. It was not only in the art of Michelangelo that the psychological damage inflicted by the events of the age was evident. In most of the artistic centers of Italy, a new style arose that radically replaced that of Renaissance Humanism. It is, in English, called "Mannerism," a title that seems appropriate but is nonetheless misleading.

It is appropriate because the style includes distortions of drawings, space, and color that are the antithesis of the norms of the Renaissance, and the English word "mannered" seems to fit the result. But it's misleading because its derivation is quite different. Mannerism derives from the Italian word *Maniera*, which is shorthand for a phrase *maniera della antica*—manner of the antique. Which is to say, the artists who practiced and codified Mannerism found their justification, and sometimes their sources, in ancient art, in their case, however, in late Hellenistic art, the art of the Greek Diaspora typified by the *Laocöon*, which we have seen earlier. That style was dynamic and expressive, and it frequently departed from the norms of proportion and composition that had been known in the Classical period of Greek art of the 5th century B.C. In other words, one could (and can) find a model and a justification for almost any style in the long history of ancient Greek art. Mannerism had already emerged by the time Raphael had died. His pupils and, it seems, Raphael himself had already begun to subvert the principles of the Renaissance in the designs for the last rooms, the last stanzae, in the Vatican. The new anti-classical style, a response to the massive social disorder, was essentially already in place before the 1527 Sack of Rome.

Evidence that the High Renaissance had ended is found in paintings by Rosso Fiorentino before the Sack of Rome and in paintings by Jacopo Pontormo afterwards. Rosso Fiorentino was among the leading practioners of the first phase of Mannerism. He was Florentine, as his name attests. He was born in 1495 and died in 1540. He visited Rome to see the Sistine Ceiling for himself, and he borrowed many of its figurative inventions. His art immediately makes apparent the other aspect of Mannerism, its content. Extreme emotion and violent action, psychological expressions of neurosis or psychosis that seem strikingly modern in the post-Freud era, are all to be found somewhere in Mannerist art, and Rosso's great *Deposition* (or, if you prefer, *Descent) from the Cross* (1521) in Volterra (which is some 40 miles southwest of Florence) is one of the most remarkable. Look at it a moment—spidery, angular, anguished, with an incredible void at its center. Look at all this—this is all left empty. Between the knees of Christ and the Magdalen at the bottom, and St. John to the right, and the figures grouped to the left, is emptiness. The center, where you depend upon the balance, the anchoring element, has been abandoned, and everything is built up around it. The figures are angular in many cases, kind of spidery in the way they are designed; look at the one at the top of the cross, probably Nicodemus here, a long beard, angular arms, and an angularity that continues on down.

The figure that is perhaps the most extraordinary is this great figure of John the Evangelist who looks like he has been carved from wood somehow; with this yellow—light-yellow—robe over green and his head in his hands, he is an enormous and yet unweighty figure—he is an unanchored figure. This is a deeply moving painting, but it is utterly anti-humanistic.

Pontormo, whose full name is Jacopo Pontormo, was born in 1494 and lived until 1557, an artist in the immediate post-Sack period, and he produced this *Entombment* in 1528 just after the Sack in Florence, in the Church of Santa Felicita, which is just across the Ponte Vecchio from the center, from the center of the city with the Palazzo Vecchio and with the Uffizi, and so forth. This painting is just as memorable as Rosso's masterpiece that we just saw, but it is created in an utterly different vocabulary. It's weightless, but in a different way. These are balloon-like figures that somehow support Christ while walking or crouching on tiptoes—look at the bottom here, and everything seems to be inflated with helium here. The painting seems about to dissolve in puffs of pink-white smoke and pink-white draperies. It's not even clear whether this is an Entombment or a Deposition because there is not a tomb and there's not a cross. So, it's not even clear what the precise subject is except that it presents the dead body of Christ—an astonishing pair of paintings to represent all by themselves the great change in style that Mannerism represented when the 1520s came to fruition.

In our next lecture, which unhappily is our final lecture, we will conclude with a look at the changed art of post-Sack northern Italy, specifically in Parma and Venice, and as had been the case during the Quattrocento and the early Cinquecento, the artistic situation in the north developed in strikingly idiosyncratic ways, and so we shall treat it separately.

Thank you for your attention.

Lecture Thirty-Six
The Renaissance Reformed

Scope:

In the northern city of Parma, some remarkable artists appeared in the early 16th century. Parmigianino (1503–1540) painted several works in the mannerist style, none more striking than the *Madonna of the Long Neck*. He was influenced by Correggio (1494–1534), whose innovative art included remarkable illusionistic dome paintings. His influence on Baroque illusionism was immense.

Venice, however, presents a different circumstance. Because the Renaissance arrived late there and because its political institutions and its independence remained intact throughout the entire period, it proved less susceptible to the turmoil of the century and artistically more able to continue the expansive, optimistic, lyrical style that had marked it thus far. Titian, in particular, seemed to answer to no impulse but his own, and his opulent chromatic painting developed according to its own law. A moving religious artist, a great portraitist, he is also, as we have already seen, a dazzling painter of mythological paintings. One famous example is the *Rape of Europa*, a sensual work of his old age. Paolo Veronese (c. 1528–1588) was his closest successor, but his greatest genius was for large decorative paintings, such as the *Wedding at Cana*. Of the great trio of Venetians of the later 16th century, only Tintoretto (1518–1594) showed the influence of central Italian mannerism to any degree, and he often used it to attain intense mystical expressiveness.

The religious schism and tensions generated by the Protestant Reformation and the Catholic Counter-Reformation were vividly reflected in the contrasting artistic styles of the years between 1520 and the end of the century. A long glance back at the Renaissance achievement helps illuminate the artistic situation toward 1600. Thus, a final look at three masterpieces, three vastly different interpretations of the same subject, the Last Supper, measures once again the ground traversed. Castagno's version of 1447, Leonardo's of about 1498, and Tintoretto's startling vision of about 1594. With Tintoretto's *Last Supper*, the humanism of the Renaissance, whether calm or impassioned, has been replaced with an urgent, mystical vision.

Outline

I. Parma was absorbed briefly into the Papal States from 1512–1515, then again from 1521–1545, and this led to a brief but important cultural revival.

   A. The mannerist style, which we saw in the last lecture in paintings by Rosso Fiorentino and Pontormo, was also strongly manifest in Parmigianino, the nickname of Francesco Mazzola (1503–1540). This short-lived artist had gone to Rome when he was 20, absorbed the lessons of the Sistine ceiling and of antiquity, when he was unfortunately captured during the sack of Rome. He escaped and, by 1530, had returned to Parma.

      1. His *Madonna of the Long Neck* (c. 1536–1540) is perhaps the most famous of his extraordinarily distorted but elegant inventions. The elongations (not only of the neck!) in these bodies is matched for artifice by the utter collapse of logical space.

      2. There was also a religious literary conceit at play here. In some medieval hymns to the Virgin, her neck is compared to a white column (it may derive from the Song of Solomon—"Thy neck is as a tower of ivory"), and this in turn, is apposite to the idea that the Virgin stands for the Church. By the way, it is worth noting that echoes of the *Laocöon*, which Parmigianino had copied, are detectable in this utterly unrelated subject.

   B. Before his Roman sojourn, Parmigianino had worked on frescoes in the recently built Church of San Giovanni Evangelista, where his older contemporary Correggio (Antonio Allegri, 1494–1534) was frescoing the cupola with *The Vision of Saint John* (1520–1524).

      1. Correggio's emergence as a great painter has never been adequately explained, because he did not come from the studio of a noted artist or from a major artistic center, but for this particular work, his departure point was Mantegna's illusionistic oculus in the *Camera degli Sposi* in nearby Mantua (1471–1474; Lecture Twenty-Six).

2. Mantegna's illusionism depended on the apparent opening in the architecture of the ceiling and the view of the sky. He then deployed his figures around the circumference of the oculus in various witty poses, strongly foreshortened, to further startle and delight the viewer.

3. Correggio relied less on architecture and more on figures. Apostles and angels seated on clouds form the concentric circles that seem to rise into space where, rapidly ascending in the center of the cupola, Christ is seen in a radically foreshortened position. The evangelist of the title is crouched almost unseen at the rim of the cupola with his eagle, looking up in astonishment. This remarkable fresco, and that in the dome of the cathedral that immediately followed, were the inspiration for many of the great dome frescoes of the 17th century.

II. A different artistic situation pertained in Venice. First, the Renaissance had arrived late in Venice. Second, the republic was an unusually stable institution amid the turbulent shifts of power that characterized the rest of Italy. Third, its political independence translated into a remarkable degree of artistic independence in which outside trends, whether abrupt or gradual, were assimilated more gradually. Titian, especially, continued in the optimistic, lyrical, and expansive vein of his earlier work.

A. This does not mean that Titian was unaffected by the work of artists outside of Venice. Michelangelo, for instance, had a notable impact on him, but even before that, he showed interest in the asymmetrical and centrifugal compositions that became more common after 1520.

1. His *Madonna of the Pesaro Family* (1519–1526) followed his own impossible achievement for the same church, the Frari. Set in a prominent location in the north aisle, the large painting contrasted in several ways with the *Assumption* in the apse. It is asymmetrical, with the Madonna and Child enthroned at the right side at the top of a rising diagonal, while Saint Peter dominates the middle of the canvas.

a. The reason for the displacement of the Madonna is found in the group at the right. In 1502, Jacopo Pesaro had defeated the Turks at the Battle of Santa Maura. Here, Jacopo kneels in the left foreground, with a Moorish prisoner behind him, and his victory offering, as it were, is presented to Saint Peter, who represents the Church. Peter, whose keys are on the step below him, is associated with a soaring column behind him and the Madonna and Child, with another.

b. The remarkable thing about the columns is that they soar out of the confines of the picture, swelling the effect of space. This dynamic and open-ended composition, invented by Titian, was much-used by Venetian High Renaissance painters and became an essential element in Baroque art of the next century.

2. When he was almost 75, Titian painted one of the most sensual, sumptuous, coloristically triumphant paintings of any era, *The Rape of Europa* (1562). Painted for Philip II of Spain, it eventually found its way to the Boston collection of Isabella Stewart Gardner.

a. According to Ovid (*Metamorphoses* and *Fasti*), Jupiter desired Europa, daughter of the king of Tyre; taking the form of a white bull, he joined her and her attendants by the seashore. Captivated by the bull's docile nature, Europa climbed on its back and was thereupon taken out to sea.

b. Titian revels in the richly erotic story, treating it as a light-hearted fantasy. Nearly 7 feet wide, it is composed on a long, low diagonal from the cupid on a dolphin's back at lower left to the head of the bull-Jupiter turning toward us at the right edge. They seem about to exit the scene. Titian painted it with an astounding technique and command of color that are indescribable and breathtaking.

B. Paolo Veronese (c. 1528–1588) is Titian's closest stylistic counterpart who, though 40 years younger, worked in the older master's shadow for much of his career. Veronese was a great decorative painter, creating elegant illusionistic scenes on the walls of villas on the Venetian mainland and vast canvases for the huge refectory walls of Venetian churches.

1. For the monks' refectory in the monastery of the Palladian Church of San Giorgio Maggiore, he created a joyful masterpiece, *The Wedding at Cana* (1562–1568).

   a. The painting has plenty of serious religious significance, but it is impossible to ignore the theatrical sweep of the scene, its color and activity. At the lower center is a quartet of musicians, artists all, for he has painted Titian on the bass, Jacopo Bassano on the flute, Tintoretto on violin, and himself, in white, on the viola.

   b. The Benedictine monks must have thoroughly enjoyed meals in the refectory at San Giorgio. But not everyone approved of the liberties that Veronese took with such subjects. In the refectory of Ss. Giovanni e Paolo, he painted a *Last Supper*, much more sober, that contained extraneous figures; this bothered Counter-Reformation Church authorities.

   c. The Inquisition, given new papal authority in 1542, had the job of investigating departures from doctrine, including in art. In 1573, Veronese was called to account for his unscriptural additions, and in brief, he said that the painting "is large and, it seemed to me, it could hold many figures." Ordered to make changes, he made one: He changed the title from the *Last Supper* to the *Feast in the House of Levi*.

2. Veronese's *summa*, the painting which was surely his most prestigious commission, is *The Apotheosis of Venice* (1583), a 30-foot oil painting mounted on the ceiling of the Great Council Hall of the Doge's Palace.

   a. In one important respect, it is a perfect product of the Venetian High Renaissance as exemplified by Titian's *Assumption* 65 years before: It is symmetrical and enclosed, and its serene nobility is not all that far removed from either Titian or Raphael.

   b. But there is something we have not seen, although it had already been introduced elsewhere by Titian.

The illusionism is strong, creating a vision of reality above us. But it is unlike Correggio's cupola in Parma with its extreme foreshortening. It is a compromise illusionism that works perfectly from only one viewpoint on the floor, which corresponds to the approximately 45-degree angle of vision painted into the picture. It was the favored Venetian illusionistic treatment of ceilings, and in the Baroque, it would become the preferred alternative to Correggio's more extreme drama.

C. Of the great trio of Venetian painters in the second half of the century, only Jacopo Tintoretto (1518–1594) fully embraced the stylistic language of mannerism. He used it brilliantly in the service of violent emotional drama and mystical expression.

1. A famous example is *Carrying the Body of Saint Mark* (1562–1565), one of the paintings (formerly in the Scuola di San Marco) depicting the crucial moments in the recovery and return of Mark's body, a drama that had already been the founding myth of Venice for seven centuries.

2. Once more, asymmetry is at the heart of the design, and spatial manipulation at the emotional core. It is a wind tunnel of space, seemingly created by the storm that God has sent to enable the "liberation" of the (fully preserved) body of Mark. The Venetian merchants display the body even as it is removed, while all the Alexandrians in the courtyard flee into the arcade as if they were sucked into it.

III. We have seen the radical changes in Italian art of the last three-quarters of the 16th century. To a large degree, they reflected the schism of the Reformation and Counter-Reformation and the tremendous tensions of that epochal struggle. Students of art, no less than artists, are in the position of Plutarch's oarsmen: We are looking backward while rowing forward. The distance traversed is clear enough in a reprise of two masterpieces and the introduction of a third, all paintings of the same subject, each markedly different from the other. The subject is the Last Supper.

A. In 1447, Andrea del Castagno painted his *Last Supper* on the wall of the refectory of the convent of Sant'Apollonia in Florence (Lecture Eight). His startling achievement was to open the wall into another room, a convincing box of space, at the back of which sat Christ and the apostles at a long table, Judas isolated on the near side. Expressively, he hit upon the wonderful device of the dramatically veined marble slab that formed the backdrop for Jesus, Peter, and Judas. The fictive space and architecture are the true protagonists of the fresco. The overall effect is static and solemn.

B. Half a century later, Leonardo da Vinci re-imagined the sacred event and its setting in the refectory of Santa Maria delle Grazie in Milan (Lecture Nineteen). His apostles became dramatic actors of a kind not seen before in this sacramental subject. All, including Judas, were integrated into the drama, which was staged in a room both deep and shallow, established by a perspective scheme that simultaneously collapsed it and thrust the figures at the viewer. The overall effect is of surging drama held in check by the serene transforming center, Christ as celebrant and subject of the Mass.

C. At the end of the 16th century and the end of his life, Tintoretto painted a *Last Supper* (1592–1594) destined not for a refectory but the presbytery of San Giorgio Maggiore, where it is still in situ to the right of the high altar. The subject was central to the church's dedication to the doctrine of transubstantiation.

    1. The event takes place in a dark and dimly seen room, lit by the spiritual light that seeps into the room from a hanging lamp, from cloud-like angels, and in the center, emanating from Christ himself.

2. The table, in a literally revolutionary change, thrusts back into the space. It is no longer the altar table of the Mass but, like the agitated apostles, a full participant in the mystical event. We saw this violent rush into space in Tintoretto's *The Carrying of the Body of Saint Mark*, but here, it is also a considered part of its placement. The church has a double-sided altar, with the back altar facing the monks' choir. It is only there, among the monks daily celebrating Mass, that the perspective plunge of Tintoretto's *Last Supper* makes visual and spiritual sense.

3. The institution of the Mass is, thus, directed principally at the monastic audience. In this respect, it is important to notice that Christ is, in fact, the celebrant of the Mass, giving communion to an apostle. Among the agitated apostles at the near end of the table, one can find a direct quotation from Leonardo's *Last Supper*, but the emotion is not in response to the revelation of imminent betrayal; rather, it is to the mystical event of transubstantiation. To make theological ritual (rather than narrative climax) the engine of high drama is an interpretation of the Last Supper unimaginable before the needs and dictates of the Counter-Reformation appeared on the historical scene.

Works Discussed:

Parmigianino:

Madonna of the Long Neck, c. 1536–1540, Galleria degli Uffizi, Florence.

Correggio:

The Vision of Saint John, 1520–1524, Church of San Giovanni Evangelista, Parma.

Titian:

Madonna of the Pesaro Family, 1519–1526, Church of Santa Maria Gloriosa dei Frari, Venice.

Rape of Europa, 1562, Isabella Stewart Gardner Museum, Boston.

Veronese:

The Wedding at Cana, c. 1562–1568, Musée du Louvre, Paris.

The Apotheosis of Venice, 1583, Doge's Palace, Venice.

Tintoretto:

The Carrying of the Body of Saint Mark, c. 1562–1565, Accademia, Venice.

The Last Supper, 1592–1594, Church of San Giorgio Maggiore, Venice.

Andrea del Castagno:

The Last Supper, 1447, Convent of Sant'Apollonia, Florence.

Leonardo da Vinci:

The Last Supper, c. 1495–1498, Church of Santa Maria delle Grazie, Milan.

Essential Reading:

Adams, chapters 17–18.

Hartt, chapters 18–19.

Supplementary Reading:

Rosand, David. *Painting in Cinquecento Venice: Titian, Veronese, Tintoretto*. New Haven: Yale University Press, 1982.

Questions to Consider:

1. Can you list some of the stylistic characteristics of mannerism and some of the artists who practiced it? What is the derivation of the term?

2. We have concluded the course with a comparison of three versions of *The Last Supper* painted between 1447 and 1594. Many other comparisons could have been made. Can you suggest comparisons of several versions of other subjects painted or sculpted during the Quattrocento and Cinquecento that would also be instructive?

Lecture Thirty-Six—Transcript
The Renaissance Reformed

Good afternoon. We have not spoken of the city of Parma before because there was no reason to do so artistically. The northern Italian city of Parma was absorbed briefly into the Papal States from 1512 to 1515, and then again from 1521 to 1545. This led to a brief but important cultural revival. In Parma, at this time, some remarkable artists appeared.

The Mannerist style, which we saw in the last lecture in paintings by Rosso Fiorentino and Pontormo, was also strongly manifest in Parmigianino, the nickname of Francesco Mazzola, who was born in 1503 and died in 1540. This short-lived artist had gone to Rome when he was 20, absorbed the lessons of the Sistine Ceiling and of antiquity, when he was unfortunately captured during the Sack of Rome. He escaped and by 1530 had returned to Parma.

He painted several works in the Mannerist style, none more striking than his *Madonna of the Long Neck*, now in the Uffizi Gallery in Florence, painted between 1536 and 1540. This is perhaps the most famous of his extraordinarily distorted but elegant inventions. The elongations, and not only of the neck I might point out, the elongations in these bodies is matched in artificiality by the utter collapse of logical space. Let me point out that space for a moment here. It is from the foreground (where the Madonna is) to the background (where this tall, tall row of columns is) and a prophet, apparently here at the bottom—look at how small that prophet is, and yet there is no measurable space from the foreground to the background. You just leap there in one gigantic and very disconcerting leap from this huge foreground figure to this tiny background figure and beyond him to the columns, which, as I say, are not one, but one can see (if you look closely) they are in a row. The painting was not finished, so at the top, in this area, this is an unfinished part of the painting.

Incidentally, there was also a religious literary conceit at play here. In some medieval hymns to the Virgin, her neck is compared to a white column (it may derive from the "Song of Solomon,"—"Thy neck is as a tower of ivory"), and this in turn, this idea, is apposite to the idea that the Virgin stands for the Church. By the way, it's worth noting I think, a little odd but worth noting, that there are echoes of the *Laocöon*, which we know he copied in Rome, detectable in this utterly unrelated subject. The position of the Madonna's leg echoes that of the Laocöon's himself, and this long-legged angel, a bare-legged angel at the left, relates to one of the sons, and the billowing cloak on the right-hand side takes the place of the other son in the *Laocöon*. I think if you check it out you'll find a remarkable similarity.

Before he went to Rome, before his Roman sojourn, Parmigianino had worked on frescos in the recently built Church of San Giovanni Evangelista in Parma, where his older contemporary, Correggio (born in 1494 and died in 1534), was frescoing the cupola with *The Vision of St. John* between 1520 and 1524.

Correggio's vision of St. John is one of two remarkable ceiling paintings that he did in the city of Parma. His emergence as a great painter has never been adequately explained. He didn't come from the studio of a noted artist or from a major artistic center, but for this particular work, this dome painting, his point of departure was probably Mantegna's illusionistic oculus, which you will recall from the *Camera degli Sposi* in nearby Mantua. Let me show you a comparison of the two. You remember in the early 1470s, when you're looking at the image on the left now, we have Mantegna's wonderful illusionistic opening to the sky, his illusionism—Mantegna's illusionism was dependent on the apparent opening of the ceiling up to a view of the sky, and then he deployed his figures around that opening—standing near it, leaning over it, in a variety of witty poses, strongly foreshortened, to further delight and startle the viewer.

Correggio, the image on the right, relied less on architecture and more on figures. Apostles and angels seated on clouds—and there are a fair number of them here—form concentric circles that seem to rise into space where, rapidly ascending in the center of the cupola, Christ is seen in a radically foreshortened position, from the bottoms and lower parts of his legs on up. Let me return to the whole image of the Correggio. The Evangelist—this is called *The Vision of St.*

John—the Evangelist of the title is crouched almost unseen at the rim of the cupola. I'm not even sure that in this image we will find him, but I think he's right here. In any event, he just peeks up over the edge, almost invisibly in most photographs, and he's crouched there with his eagle, and he looks up in astonishment, just as we do, at the receding figure of the ascending Christ. This remarkable fresco, and that in the dome of the Cathedral that was done immediately after, and which is next door to this church, appeared not merely to open up to the sky but to be blown into it, as though the ceiling were blown out—the dome is gone and the sky is there. It is not something casual or gentle but something very dramatic and, as I say, explosive. This was the inspiration for many of the illusionistic dome frescoes of the following century, of the 17th century.

Since we have just completed our extended look at Venice, it is easy to recall the different artistic situation that pertained there when compared to Florence and Rome. The Renaissance had arrived late in Venice, and the Republic was an unusually stable institution, so it proved less susceptible to the turmoil of the century, less affected by the turbulent shifts of power that characterized the rest of Italy. Its political independence translated into a remarkable degree of artistic independence in which outside trends were assimilated, but assimilated gradually. Thus, it was mostly able to continue the expansive, optimistic, lyrical style that had marked Venetian art thus far.

Titian, in particular, seemed to answer to no impulse but his own, and his opulent chromatic painting developed according to its own law. This does not mean that Titian was unaffected by the work of artists outside of Venice. Michelangelo, for example, had a notable impact upon Titian, but even before that Titian showed interest in the asymmetrical and centrifugal compositions that became more common after 1520.

His *Madonna of the Pesaro Family*, which you see here, painted between 1519 and 1526, in the church of the Frari, followed his own impossible achievement in that church, his achievement of *The Assumption*, which we saw in an earlier lecture. Set in a prominent location in the north aisle, this very large painting—about 16 feet high—contrasted in several ways with *The Assumption* in the apse of the church. It is asymmetrical, first and foremost, with the Madonna and Child enthroned at the right side at the top of a rising diagonal, while St. Peter dominates the center of the canvas. Here is the diagonal movement up, Madonna here, St. Peter here, and members of the Pesaro family below. The displacement of the Madonna from her traditional central position is so striking that it needs to be explained.

This painting, in the church, is located near the tomb, very near the tomb, of Jacopo Pesaro, who in 1502 had defeated the Turks at the Battle of Santa Maura. Now, although he was a Venetian aristocrat, he was serving as Commander of the Navy of the Pope, the Borgia Pope Alexander VI, when he had this victory. Therefore, behind Jacopo, who kneels here in the left foreground in adoration of the Madonna and of St. Peter, behind him there is a Moorish prisoner, and then there is a banner that has not the Pesaro arms but the arms of the Borgia family, of the papal family. He, Jacopo Pesaro, offers his victory to St. Peter, who represents the Catholic Church and therefore takes center stage. Peter—whose keys (his attributes), by the way, are on the steps just below him—is associated, as it were, visually with a huge column behind him, while the Madonna and Child are matched with another enormous column, and despite the cap of clouds with small angels, the remarkable thing about these columns is that they thrust upward, through those clouds and beyond the confines of the picture, swelling the effect of space in this picture. It's dynamic and it's open-ended. It is not contained (even as *The Assumption* was contained) at the top—this one is not. The architectural elements go out of it. It is an invention of Titian's, and it became much used by Venetian High Renaissance painters, and it was an essential element in Baroque art of the next century.

It should be mentioned, by the way, I shouldn't ignore the other Pesaro family members in the lower right-hand corner. These are all male members of the family—some of them children, some of them adults—and they kneel and are recommended to the Madonna here by St. Francis, who gestures toward them and looks toward the Madonna. This is, remember, a Franciscan church.

A moving religious artist, a great portraitist, Titian is also, as we have already seen, a dazzling painter of mythological paintings. One famous example is *The Rape of Europa*, painted in 1562, a sensual work of his old age. When he was almost 75, Titian painted this—one of the most luscious, sumptuous, coloristically triumphant paintings not only of the Venetian Renaissance era, but of any era. It was painted for Philip II of Spain, and it eventually, amazingly, found its way to Boston, to the collection of Isabella Stewart Gardner, in whose museum it still remains, the greatest Titian in an American collection.

The story, according to Ovid—found both in his *Metamorphoses* and in the *Fasti*—Jupiter desired Europa. Europa was the daughter of the King of Tyre, and so he took, he always taking the form of something other than himself, so he took the form of a white bull, and he joined Europa and her attendants by the seashore. She was captivated, as her handmaidens were, by the docile nature of the bull, and so, eventually—after decking him with garlands and so forth—she climbed onto the back of the bull and was thereupon taken out to sea. The title, by the way, *The Rape of Europa*, the word "rape" that is used very often in both literature and art of this time means "abduction," and it has to be understood in that rather less modern way, though it certainly has its sexual element, but it is an abduction by the god in disguise.

Titian revels in this richly erotic story. He treats it as a light-hearted fantasy, really. This painting is about seven feet wide, and it is composed on this long, low diagonal that runs from the cupid at the lower left, up through the figures and toward the head of the bull. The bull is Jupiter, of course, and you see his head turns toward us, toward the viewer, at the right edge of the canvas. They seem about to exit the scene—again, this open-ended quality, this asymmetry, this feeling that the painting moves beyond its boundaries.

It's painted with an astounding technique, simply so free and inventive, and his command of color is so indescribable, so breathtaking. There's a cute little mimicry going on here. As Jupiter carries the figure of Europa on his back, so the little cupid down here rides on the back of a fish. It's a kind of visual echo in small, and he treats it, as I say, quite light-heartedly. Here are the handmaidens of

Europa, back on the shore hopelessly watching her being carried away. One could spend—go to Boston and see this—one could spend hours with it.

Paolo Veronese, Titian's closest stylistic counterpart (though he was 40 years younger than Titian), worked most of his career in the shadow of Titian, of the aged Titian. Veronese was a great decorative painter. He created elegant illusionistic scenes on the walls of villas on the Venetian mainland and vast canvases for the huge refectory walls of Venetian churches. This is *The Wedding at Cana*, now in the Louvre; it was taken by Napoleon, and unlike many of the things that were returned after Napoleon's fall, this remained in Paris. Painted between 1562 and 1568, it is 33 feet wide. It covers the end of one of the largest galleries in the Louvre.

This was painted for the monks' refectory in the monastery of the Palladian church of San Giorgio Maggiore, on the island of St. Giorgio, a great church, and in its refectory of the monastery this is a great and joyful masterpiece. The setting is thoroughly theatrical, literally so, since the stage is constructed with a terrace and stairs at the side, like stage designs in contemporary theatres in Venice. Christ is here—he's in the center, but one wonders at first. He's here very still, very calm, very solemn, in the center of the composition, together with his mother, at the center of this wedding banquet, but he seems almost, to me, out of place amid the celebration of about a hundred guests, more than in most other images of the marriage at Cana. He doesn't seem to take credit, by the way, for the miracle of turning water into wine, which goes on in the lower right-hand corner here—lots of water, lots of wine—and presided over, it seems, by this splendidly costumed, rather elegant, foppish Venetian gentleman who stands right here.

The painting has—or it could claim to have—plenty of serious religious significance, but, frankly, it's impossible to ignore the theatrical sweep of the scene, its glorious color, its activity. One writer nicely said, "It has a grandiose choral effect, and music is often apropos in discussing the art of Veronese." In fact, in the center of this, the lower center, right here, you find a quartet of musicians, and I show them to you now. A quartet of musicians, artists all, for he has painted Titian at the right, wonderful in this red costume, the old man on the viola da gamba; Jacopo Bassano plays the flute; behind, Tintoretto is playing a violin here; and Veronese himself (in this wonderful white costume) has the viola da braccio. So, they are shown here as musicians. It's a wonderful cross-cultural or cross-artistic reference that he makes. The Benedictine monks, can you imagine how thoroughly they must have enjoyed their meals in the refectory at San Giorgio? Quite different from other Last Suppers we have seen.

But not everyone approved of the liberties that Veronese took with such subjects. In the refectory for San Giovanni e Paolo, the church outside of which Verrocchio's great equestrian monument is, Veronese painted (in 1573) a *Last Supper* that is much more sober than this painting, and nonetheless it contained extraneous figures that didn't belong in the Last Supper, and that bothered the Counter-Reformation Church authorities. The Inquisition had been given new papal authority in 1542, and it had the job of investigating departures from doctrine, including in paintings. In 1573, after Veronese painted that particular Last Supper, he was called to account by the Inquisition. He had to appear and answer their questions about his unscriptural additions, and in brief—and it is in brief because the whole thing is recorded, and you may read it all—but in brief, he said the painting "is large and, it seemed to me, it could hold many figures," and then at one point he added, "we painters are all a little mad." Ordered, nonetheless, to make changes in it, he made one. He changed the title from the "Last Supper" to the "Feast in the House of Levi," where all those figures that he had painted would not be out of place.

Veronese's summa, if you will, the painting that surely was his most prestigious commission, is *The Apotheosis of Venice*, a painting of 1583. This is a 30-foot oil painting mounted on the ceiling of the Great Council Hall of the Doge's Palace. It's not a fresco. They'd given up on fresco in the climate, so it's an oil painting that is mounted on the ceiling. *The Apotheosis of Venice*, in one important respect, it is a perfect product of the Venetian High Renaissance as exemplified by Titian's *Assumption* 65 years before: it is symmetrical and enclosed, and its serene nobility is not all that far removed from either Titian or, for that matter, Raphael. But, there's something here that we've never seen before, although it had already been introduced by Titian in paintings we haven't seen, the illusionism in this scene is very strong. It creates a vision of reality above us, but it's not like the extreme foreshortening in Correggio's cupola in Parma, where we saw almost the lower part of the legs of the figure of Christ looking very sharply upward.

Instead, Veronese used a compromise illusionism that worked perfectly from only one viewpoint on the floor, although it's adjusted so you can move back and forth without having the composition collapse completely, but basically it is a 45-degree angle, more or less, that is painted into the picture. You can see that here, and you have to be just at that point on the floor for everything to fall perfectly into place. This modified illusion, illusionism, was the favored Venetian illusionistic treatment for ceilings, and it also carried on into the 17th century. It became, in the Baroque, an alternative to the more extreme, dramatic foreshortening in Correggio's illusionism.

Before I let it go, I should point out where Venice is because this is, of course, an apotheosis of a figure who is personified. Here is Venice—a female figure representing Venice—being crowned, enthroned, here on the clouds, these great columns going up on either side, and at the very bottom, flanking—as it were—the opening to this space, you have these great rearing horses and a dog, and men controlling them all.

I'll point out one further thing quickly, and that is these columns. I haven't had a chance to point out these twisted columns. They occur a lot in the 16th century and more in the 17th century, and they are properly called not just "twisted" or "serpentine," they are properly called "Solomonic columns" because they refer to the Temple of Solomon and to columns that theoretically came from that Temple, which were given to the Constantinian Basilica of St. Peter's and still exist. Whenever you see them, it has a Solomonic attribute to it, and therefore it suggests the authority that comes from such a great distance, from such great references as the Temple of Solomon.

Of the great trio of Venetian painters in the second half of the century, only Jacopo Tintoretto, who was born in 1518 and died in 1594, fully embraced the stylistic language of Mannerism. He used it brilliantly in the service of violent, emotional drama and mystical expression. Here is his *Carrying the Body of St. Mark*, painted between 1562 and 1565; it's a famous painting, one of a series, formerly in the Scuola di San Marco, therefore all about the history of the saint, depicting the crucial moments in the recovery and return of Mark's body from Alexandria, that drama that had been the founding myth of Venice now for seven centuries.

Once more, asymmetry is at the heart of this design. The main group of figures is off to the right, throwing the whole weight to that side, and this is countered by the spatial manipulation, this great rush of space, like a wind tunnel that rushes back in space and that imparts an immense emotional charge to the painting. It's a wind tunnel that seems to be created, you see, in the sky, a storm sent by God, to enable the "liberation," the freeing, of the (by the way, fully preserved) body of St. Mark.

As Tintoretto arranges this composition, the Venetian merchants who removed the body displayed the body to us, to the viewer, to the worshipper, even as it's removed, and, by the way, all of the Alexandrians in the courtyard when this occurs flee into the arcade to the left. They are very ghost-like. They are all as white and gray as the architecture is, and it's as though they were sucked into this space by some vortex on the left-hand side. It is a painting of incredible drama.

We have now seen briefly the radical changes in Italian art of the last three-quarters of the 16th century. To a large degree, those changes reflected the schism of the Reformation and the Counter-Reformation and the tremendous tensions of that epochal confrontation. To help illuminate the artistic situation around 1600, let's first look back. Look with me at three masterpieces—two of them known to you, and one that will be new—three vastly different interpretations of the same subject, the Last Supper.

You remember Castagno's *Last Supper* of 1447 in Sant'Apollonia in Florence. When he painted this *Last Supper* on the convent wall, the refectory wall of the convent of Sant'Apollonia, his startling achievement was to open the wall into, as it were, another room, to give a convincing box of space beyond the refectory itself, at the back of which sat Christ and the Apostles at a long table, with Judas isolated on the near side. Expressively, Castagno hit upon the wonderful device of the dramatically veined marble slab, which formed the backdrop for Jesus, Peter, and Judas. The fictive space and the architecture are the true protagonists of this scene. The overall effect is static and solemn.

Half a century later, Leonardo da Vinci reimagined the sacred event and its setting in the refectory of Santa Maria delle Grazie in Milan. His Apostles became dramatic actors of a kind never seen before in this sacramental subject. All of them, including Judas, were integrated into the drama, which was staged in a room both deep and shallow, simultaneously deep and shallow, established by a perspective scheme that collapsed the space and at the same time thrust the figures in the painting toward the viewer. The overall effect is one of surging drama—both sides, for instance, activity of the Apostles on both sides, like little waves moving toward the center—and then held in check by the serene transforming center, the figure of Christ as celebrant and subject of the Mass, both celebrant and subject, both priest and subject of the Mass, and this gap that is placed between the groups on either side of him allows everything to stop, as it were, at that point, and everything to be contained, all of that energy, all of that rush.

At the end of the 16th century and the end of his life, Tintoretto pained a *Last Supper* also, destined not for a refectory, by the way, but for the presbytery of San Giorgio Maggiore, which already had a *Last Supper* in the refectory, which we've just looked at, by Veronese. Where this painting, in the presbytery, flanks the high altar on the right—there's a painting by him to the left and another to the right, and they are displayed at a slight, let's call it a 45-degree angle, so that they are visible, of course, to the congregation, but visible from elsewhere as well.

The subject here is central, of course, to the doctrine of Transubstantiation because the church, this church, had a particular dedication to the doctrine of Transubstantiation of the miracle that the Mass represents. The event takes place in a dark and dimly seen room, lit by the spiritual light that seeps into the room from a hanging lamp above, from the cloud-like angels here to the right and elsewhere—and in the center, the light emanating from Christ himself. The table, in a literally revolutionary change, thrusts back into the space—not across the space as every other *Last Supper* you've seen and will see, which is across the space, but no, back, strongly back, into the space. It's no longer the altar table of the Mass but, like the agitated Apostles, it's a participant in the mystical event. The table is an active participant. We saw this violent rush into space in his *Carrying of the Body of St. Mark*, but here the space design is also connected to the placement of this painting.

The church has a double-sided main altar. The front faces the congregation while the back altar faces the monks' choir and, of course, was in use many times throughout the day. The viewpoint in this painting that initiates this plunge into space is the viewpoint from the monks' choir. Imagine, in other words, that you are behind the high altar looking at the reverse side where there is another altar, and you are aligned with the beginning of that spatial rush from the left, whereas if you are out among the congregants, you are not directly aligned with it. You see the picture but you're not in, as it were, the perspective chain and the perspective continuum. It's only from the monks' choir, where the monks are celebrating Mass, that the perspective plunge of Tintoretto's *Last Supper* makes visual and spiritual sense. The Institution of the Mass is thus directed principally at the monastic audience. In this respect, it's important to notice that Christ—here at the back—is, in fact, the celebrant of the Mass. He is giving communion to an Apostle. Among the agitated Apostles at the near end of the table, you can find a direct quotation from Leonardo da Vinci's *Last Supper*, but the emotion of the Apostles in Tintoretto's interpretation is not in response to the revelation of imminent betrayal but rather to the mystical event of Transubstantiation.

To make theological ritual (rather than narrative climax) the engine of high drama is an interpretation of the Last Supper unimaginable before the needs and dictates of the Counter-Reformation appeared on the historical scene. We have come a very long way indeed in the painted interpretation of a single, central, Christian subject.

Well, art history—like all history—is a continuum, and in our attempts now at summary, we find ourselves well into another period in the history of art, one with its own genius, its own fascination, its own beauty. On the other hand, you are well aware that our introduction to Italian Renaissance art has been just that, an introduction, which I hope will develop into a long, deep, and cherished relationship. And as I have so often before, I thank you for your very kind attention.

Timeline

313 A.D. .... Roman Emperor Constantine issues the Edict of Milan, granting official freedom of worship to Christians.

c. 337 .... The construction of Saint Peter's Basilica in Rome is complete.

476 .... Western Roman Empire falls to the Goths, leaving a power vacuum in Italy and throughout Europe that was filled partially by the Roman Catholic Church.

800 .... Charlemagne crowned first Holy Roman Emperor, creating the appearance of a united Western Europe, with the pope as the spiritual leader and the emperor as the temporal leader.

829 .... According to Venetian legend, the relics of Saint Mark the Evangelist are brought from Alexandria to Venice, bestowing great religious significance on the young city, whose main patron saint he becomes, replacing Saint Theodore.

1204 .... Crusaders and Venetians sack Constantinople, carrying off many artistic treasures to Venice.

1206 .... Saint Dominic founds the Dominican Order.

1209 .... Saint Francis founds the Franciscan Order.

1299–1310 .... The Palazzo Vecchio, city hall of Florence, is constructed.

1305 .... Giotto frescoes the Scrovegni (Arena) Chapel in Padua with scenes from the life of the Virgin and the life of Christ, a cycle that becomes a touchstone for later artists, particularly in the Renaissance.

1309–1378 .... Papacy moves from Rome to Avignon.

1310–1340 .... Original construction of the Doge's Palace, Venice; fires resulted in several later reconstructions, culminating in the rebuilding in the 1580s.

1321 .... Dante completes his *Divine Comedy*, a landmark in the Italian language and world literature.

1348 .... The Black Death devastates Florence and Siena, and the material and spiritual trauma that ensues radically changes the course of art.

1353 .... Boccaccio publishes the *Decameron*, a collection of 100 tales "told" by men and women in a rural retreat to avoid the plague.

1354–1357 .... Orcagna paints the Strozzi Altarpiece, a stylistic regression to the hieratic Byzantine style, reflecting the traumatic effect of the plague on the spiritual tenor of the age.

c. 1400....................... Rise of the International Gothic, a late medieval style, which flourishes for several decades, even while the new forms of the Renaissance develop.

1401 .... Competition for the North Doors of the Florentine Baptistery won by Ghiberti whose doors, finished in 1424, led to the commission for a second set of doors.

c. 1415....................... Donatello completes his heroic marble sculpture of *Saint George* for an exterior niche on Orsanmichele, the Florentine guildhall and church. His conception of the heroic warrior typifies the new Renaissance humanism.

1420–1436 .... Construction of the dome of the Florence Cathedral, designed by Brunelleschi, whose fame was as much for the engineering feat as for the architectural beauty.

1424–1427 .... Fresco cycle of the Brancacci Chapel begun by Masolino and continued by Masaccio, whose achievement was the first great landmark of Italian Renaissance painting.

1428 .... Masaccio paints the fresco of *The Trinity* in Santa Maria Novella in Florence, a work in which linear, or one-point, perspective is for the first time the governing principle. It is assumed that he learned the method from the architect Brunelleschi.

1425–1452 .... Lorenzo Ghiberti designs and completes the *Gates of Paradise*, his second set of doors for the Baptistery.

1434 .... Cosimo de' Medici returns from exile to become de facto ruler of the nominal republic of Florence. His rule was generally benevolent and progressive, and the Medici remained in control for 60 years.

1435 .... Leon Battista Alberti publishes *On Painting*, a treatise that includes the first description of the method of linear perspective.

c. 1443–1450............. Donatello creates the *Gattamelata* in Padua, the first life-size bronze equestrian monument since antiquity.

1453 .... Fall of Constantinople to the Turks.

c. 1453–1454............. Piero della Francesca paints the fresco cycle of *The Legend of the True Cross* in the Church of San Francesco at Arezzo.

1465–1474 .... Mantegna paints the *Camera Picta* in the Gonzaga ducal palace in Mantova.

c. 1466....................... Construction begun on the new ducal palace at Urbino, designed by Luciano Laurana.

1469 .... Lorenzo de' Medici, called "the Magnificent," grandson of Cosimo, becomes ruler of Florence and one of the greatest cultural patrons of the Renaissance. He dies in 1472.

1475–1476 .... Antonello da Messina documented as working in Venice.

1475	Hugo van der Goes paints the *Portinari Altarpiece* for a Florentine church, and the novelty of its Flemish realism alters Florentine art.
1478	The Pazzi conspiracy (in which Pope Sixtus IV was complicit) results in the assassination of Giuliano de' Medici in the Duomo; Lorenzo de' Medici escapes; members of the Pazzi family are executed.
1478–1482	Botticelli paints for a Medici patron the beautiful and mysterious *Primavera* ("*Spring*"), which apparently reflects the elaborate neo-Platonic philosophy then popular among Renaissance humanists.
1481–1482	Fresco decoration of the walls of the new Sistine Chapel, ordered by Sixtus IV, introduces the Florentine Renaissance style into Rome. Works by Perugino, Botticelli, and Signorelli are included in the decorations.
1492	Voyage of Columbus to the New World.
1494	Invasion of Italy by Charles VIII of France, at the invitation of the duke of Milan, results in the subjugation of Florence and the exile of the Medici.
1495–1498	Leonardo da Vinci paints *The Last Supper*, the exemplar of the High Renaissance style, for the refectory of the ducal church of Santa Maria delle Grazie in Milan. Deteriorating practically from the day it was finished, it nonetheless revolutionized the history of art.
1497	The Dominican friar Savonarola, who had preached against the perceived sins of the Medici and of Florentine society generally, is excommunicated and, the following year, is burned at the stake in Florence.

1503–1504 .... Leonardo and Michelangelo commissioned to paint two huge paintings for the new council hall of the Palazzo Vecchio. Neither work was ever completely finished, and though both are lost, they were among the most influential designs of the period.

1505 .... Giovanni Bellini paints his serene masterpiece of the Venetian High Renaissance style, the *San Zaccaria Altarpiece*.

1506 .... The discovery in Rome of the Hellenistic sculpture *Laocoön*, a famous sculpture of the 1st century B.C., provided a dramatic source for Michelangelo and other Renaissance artists.

1506–1514 .... On the request of Pope Julius II, Bramante designs the plan for a new basilica of Saint Peter's, to replace the thousand-year-old Constantinian church.

1508 .... The League of Cambrai, under control of Pope Julius II, temporarily relieves Venice of its mainland territories.

1508–1511 .... Michelangelo, with assistants, paints the ceiling of the Sistine Chapel which, along with Raphael's Vatican *Stanzae*, forms the apogee of High Renaissance painting in Rome.

1510–1514 .... Raphael paints the *Stanzae*, the rooms of the papal apartments in the Vatican.

1512 .... Julius II expels the French from Italy and restores the Medici to power in Florence.

c. 1515–1516............. Michelangelo carves the figure of *Moses* for the tomb of Julius II, the largest sculpture commission of his career but destined to dwindle to a shadow of the original design.

1517 .... Martin Luther posts his 95 Theses in Wittenberg, beginning the Reformation.

c. 1517–1520............. A new style, mannerism, begins to develop within the matrix of the High Renaissance. It can be seen in the last works of Raphael in the Vatican, in the stylistic changes of Michelangelo's art, and in the work of younger artists. Confirmed by the political and religious crises of the 1520s, it becomes the principal style of central Italian art by the 1530s.

1518 .... Titian's *Assumption* unveiled in the Church of the Frari, Venice.

1519–1534 .... Michelangelo designs and executes the sculpture and architecture for the Medici Chapel in San Lorenzo, Florence.

1521 .... Martin Luther excommunicated at the Diet of Worms.

1527 .... Sack of Rome by the mercenary troops of Emperor Charles V devastates the city, leaving it depopulated and powerless for 50 years. This event signals closing of the Renaissance era.

1535–1541 .... Michelangelo frescoes the huge altar wall of the Sistine Chapel with a *Last Judgment*.

1545–1563 .... The theological Council of Trent meets intermittently in response to the Protestant Reformation. In this Counter-Reformation, abuses are corrected and doctrine is clarified. The tribunal of the Inquisition (extant since 1233 to suppress heresy) becomes the enforcement arm of the Roman Catholic Church in this struggle.

1550 .... Giorgio Vasari publishes the first edition of *The Lives of the Artists*, the earliest encyclopedic biographical-historical account of Italian art and artists from Giotto to Vasari's own day.

1564 .... With the death of Michelangelo, the long period of central Italian artistic dominance comes to an end, and with Tintoretto's death in 1594, the great age of Venetian art similarly concludes.

Glossary

Note: Many of these terms are Italian in origin, though widely used today in English.

Aerial perspective: The effect of deep space in a landscape painting, created by diminution of scale and softened contour line and by giving a bluish-green tint to the distant hills and other objects. This technique gave an equivalent of the optical effect perceived by our eyes when looking at the landscape, which results from water and dust particles suspended in the atmosphere. Also called *atmospheric perspective.*

Apse: Semicircular or polygonal recess at the end of the long axis (nave) or a chapel or the choir of a Christian church.

Basilica: Any church that has a longitudinal nave, flanked by side aisles, terminating in an apse. Originally an ancient Roman public building with the same ground plan.

Campanile (Italian): The bell tower of a church.

Cantoria (Italian): Choir gallery or balcony.

Cartoon: Full-size preparatory drawing from which a design is transferred to a surface for painting. From the Italian *cartone* ("cardboard").

Cathedral: A church where a bishop has his diocese and official seat (from *cathedra*, "throne").

Chancel: The part of the church reserved for the clergy, most often at the east end of the nave, beyond the crossing (transept).

Chiaroscuro (Italian): "Light-dark," refers to the dramatic or theatrical contrast of light and dark in painting.

Cinquecento (Italian): "Five hundred," short for *mille cinquecento*, or one thousand, five hundred, and refers to the 1500s, what is called in English the 16th century.

Condottiere (Italian): Mercenary general.

Contrapposto (Italian): "Set against," refers to the method of introducing movement into the human body in sculpture or painting by placing the weight principally on one leg with the other leg relaxed, which causes the body to assume an asymmetrical posture with a modified S-curve.

Diptych: Religious image consisting of two equal paintings, usually on panel, often hinged to be opened and closed.

Doge (Venetian or Genoese dialect): "Duke," signifying the head of state.

Donor: The person who commissioned a work of art and whose portrait, along with portraits of other family members, may sometimes be included in the composition.

Duomo (Italian): Cathedral.

Eucharist: The sacrament of the Lord's Supper, celebrated in the Mass. Also the bread and wine used in the rite.

Fresco (Italian): Literally, "fresh." The technique of painting in wet plaster on a wall. If the color becomes part of the plaster wall, it is "true fresco" (*buon fresco*). If it is painted onto the dry surface, it is "dry fresco" (*fresco a secco*). The latter technique is used with expensive pigments or for finishing details.

Linear perspective: The system of creating the illusion of three-dimensional space on a flat surface that was first known in ancient Rome and was re-developed in the early 15th century in Florence. The architect Filippo Brunelleschi is generally credited with the invention.

Mass: The celebration of the Eucharist, in reference to the sacrifice of Christ. The central rite of the Christian liturgy.

Nave: Central aisle of a (basilican) church, extending from the entrance to the chancel.

Neo-Platonism: A system that attempted to reconcile the ancient philosophy of Plato and Plotinus with the teachings of Christianity. Developed in Alexandria and other Greek centers in the 3rd century A.D. and revived in the Italian Renaissance.

Oil: Describes the medium in which pigments are suspended in a drying medium, such as linseed or walnut oil. Because they are not rapid drying (as tempera), they can be applied freely over a wide area, and because they are translucent rather than opaque, they create effects of depth and luminosity. When dry, they are solid films. The

Renaissance development of the oil medium can be traced to the Netherlands in the early 15th century, and it became the dominant medium from the 16th century onward.

Orthogonals: Diagonal lines drawn or painted on a two-dimensional surface that illusionistically extend into space, appearing to converge at a single point (the vanishing point) and giving the effect of a measurable three-dimensional space in linear perspective. Also used in relief sculpture.

Perspective: See **linear perspective** and **aerial perspective**.

Pietà (Italian): "Pity." The name given to a representation of the dead Christ supported by the Virgin Mary, sometimes with angels or saints.

Polyptych: An altarpiece or other devotional picture or relief sculpture, made up of multiple panels. Typically a central panel flanked by wings and surmounted by gables or other forms and sometimes placed on a base (*predella*).

Predella (Italian): The base or pedestal of a large altarpiece, often decorated with small paintings relating to the figures above.

Putto (pl. *putti*; Italian): Small nude boys, sometimes winged, seen in both religious and secular Renaissance painting and sculpture.

Quatrefoil (French): A decorative shape similar to a four-leaf clover combined with a diamond, common in Gothic art as a field for relief sculpture or painting.

Quattrocento (Italian): Literally "four hundred," short for *mille quattrocento*, or one thousand, four hundred, and referring to the 1400s, what is called the 15th century in English.

Refectory: Dining hall in a convent or monastery.

Rilievo schiacciato (Italian): Flattened or very low relief sculpture.

Sacra conversazione (Italian): Literally, a "sacred conversation." A group of saints that accompanies the Madonna and Child (or, occasionally, a central saint) in a painted or sculptured altarpiece, all of whom appear to occupy the same illusionistic space, in which they might "converse" or interact with one another.

Scuola (pl. *scuole*; Italian): "School." In art history, the term specifically refers to a company or confraternity of Venetian citizens with a religious affiliation. Organized for charitable purposes, they were also important patrons of art. In other cities, they were simply called companies or confraternities.

Sfumato (Italian): Literally, "smoky." The method of painting subtle gradations of light and dark, especially in modeling the human figure, developed by Leonardo da Vinci.

Tempera: Water-based painting medium in which ground colors are usually suspended in egg yolk. The principal medium before the *Cinquecento*, it is characterized by a gleaming surface, decorative flatness, and durability. Often used in conjunction with oil paints.

Tondo (Italian): A circular painting or relief, referred to as a *roundel* in English.

Transept: The short axis, or cross arm, of a basilican church. It intersects the nave just before the chancel. The ground plan of such a church is cross-shaped.

Trecento (Italian): Literally, "three hundred," short for *mille trecento*, or one thousand, three hundred, and referring to the 1300s, what is called the 14th century in English.

Triptych: An altarpiece or other devotional image made up of three painted or carved panels. The wings usually are smaller than the center panel and are sometimes are hinged for closing.

Tympanum: Either the triangular space created by the intersection of a vault with a wall or a similar pointed or semicircular arched shape above a window. It may be decorated with sculpture or painting.

Biographical Notes

Alberti, Leon Battista (1404–1472). Important Florentine architect and theorist whose lasting fame derives from his book *On Painting*, in which the principles of perspective were articulated for the first time, and from his *Ten Books on Architecture*, the first publication on the subject since Roman times.

Angelico, Fra (Giovanni da Fiesole)(c. 1400–1455). Florentine painter whose career was mostly spent in the service of the Dominican Order, especially in the decoration of the Convent of San Marco.

Antonello da Messina (c. 1430–1479). From Messina, studied and worked in Naples before going to Venice for two years, where he produced paintings that greatly affected the direction of Venetian art by their influence on Giovanni Bellini, Giorgione, and Titian. Especially important was his use of the oil medium, learned from Flemish painters, which then became the favored medium of Venetian painters.

Bellini, Gentile (c. 1429–1507). A major Venetian artist who painted narrative cycles and other large paintings in which contemporary Venice was vividly rendered. He also redecorated the Doge's Palace in 1474 (destroyed by fire in 1577). Painted for the sultan in Constantinople, where he traveled with a diplomatic mission in 1479–1481. Older brother of Giovanni Bellini, see below.

Bellini, Giovanni (c. 1430–1516). The first great master of the Venetian Renaissance, a major painter of Madonnas and large altarpieces that span the period from the Early to the High Renaissance. Among the first to introduce landscape as an important expressive element of his paintings.

Berruguete, Pedro (c. 1450–1503/4). Spanish painter who worked for King Ferdinand and Queen Isabella and painted in Toledo and Avila. Worked for Federigo da Montefeltro in Urbino, completing a series of famous men begun by Justus of Ghent.

Boccaccio, Giovanni (1313–1375). Humanist, poet, and author of the *Decameron*, a collection of 100 stories whose backdrop was the Black Death. These tales established the vernacular Italian prose style.

Botticelli, Sandro (1445–1510). Student of Filippo Lippi who became one of the most original painters of the last quarter of the Quattrocento. A lyrical style joined to innovative religious and allegorical subject matter resulted in famous works, such as the *Birth of Venus* and *Primavera* ("*Spring*"), both created for the Medici family, who often patronized his art.

Brunelleschi, Filippo (1377–1446). Seminal architect and engineer of the Italian Renaissance, he was widely famous for designing the dome of the Duomo in Florence. Usually credited as the inventor of linear perspective, he was also a sculptor.

Carpaccio, Vittore (c. 1465–c. 1526). Venetian portraitist and painter of narrative cycles decorating the halls of confraternities, he excelled in the depiction of contemporary Venice.

Castagno, Andrea del (c. 1419–1457). A specialist in fresco, he concentrated on the illusion of three-dimensionality in the figures in his paintings. He worked primarily in Florence.

Castiglione, Baldassare (1478–1529). Author of *The Book of the Courtier* (1528), a vivid description of the manners and ideals of a humanist court (Urbino) and the intellectual and cultural life of the Renaissance aristocracy. Himself an aristocrat, he later served as Mantuan ambassador to Rome and as Papal Nuncio to Spain.

Correggio (Antonio Allegri) (1494–1534). Centered in Parma, he took spatial illusionism to a new level of daring in his dome frescoes in the cathedral and the Church of Saint John the Evangelist there. He also had a soft, fluid brushwork in his easel paintings (especially of nudes) that anticipated the 18th-century Rococo style.

Dante Alighieri (1265–1321). Dante is the author of the *Divine Comedy*, one of the enduring masterpieces of world literature. This long theological poem, written in the vernacular rather than Latin, was the most influential work in establishing Italian as the written language of Italy. A Florentine, he spent most of his life as a political exile.

Domenico Veneziano (c. 1410–1461). A Venetian artist who moved to Florence, bringing a new style characterized by a delicate, light-filled palette. Probably the teacher of Piero della Francesca.

Donatello (Donato di Niccolò Bardi) (1386–1466). The greatest sculptor of the early Renaissance, he worked in Florence and in Padua. He was equally adept in carving stone and wood and in modeling and casting bronze figures. He was among the first to introduce linear perspective (in relief sculpture) and the first since antiquity to create a life-size bronze equestrian statue.

Duccio di Buoninsegna (active c. 1278–1318). Sienese painter, contemporary with Giotto, famous for his extensive altarpiece for the Siena Cathedral, *The Majesty* (*Maestà*).

Federigo (or Federico) da Montefeltro (1422–1482). Duke of Urbino and one of the most famous patrons of Renaissance culture. A mercenary soldier (*condottiere*) by profession, he made the small principality of Urbino into a jewel of Quattrocento civilization.

Francesco di Giorgio Martini (1439–1501/2). A versatile Sienese artist gifted in sculpture, painting, and architecture. He also worked for the duke of Urbino.

Gentile da Fabriano (c. 1385–1427). Painter who continued in the International Gothic style through the first quarter of the 15th century. He worked in Venice, Florence, Siena, and Rome.

Ghiberti, Lorenzo (c. 1381–1455). Celebrated sculptor whose greatest achievements were two sets of bronze doors for the Florentine Baptistery, including the so-called "Gates of Paradise."

Ghirlandaio, Domenico (1449–1494). Florentine fresco specialist who operated one of the most sought-after large workshops of the late 15th century. His narrative scenes are packed with details of contemporary life and with portraits of notable Florentines.

Giorgione (Giorgio da Castelfranco) (c. 1476/78–1510). Exceptional Venetian artist who studied with Giovanni Bellini and worked with Titian. He is considered one of the central revolutionary painters of the Venetian Renaissance. His extensive inclusion of landscape in his paintings, his masterful use of oil paints, and his characteristic softness of touch, together with his ambiguous subject matter and the rarity of his surviving paintings, have made him one of the most-discussed and admired artists of the Renaissance.

Giotto di Bondone (1266/67–1337). One of the greatest Italian painters of any period, his frescoes in the Scrovegni (Arena) Chapel in Padua became a pilgrimage spot for subsequent artists. He is often described as a proto-Renaissance painter, because his emphasis on substantial figures of solemn and significant bearing and his early use of perspective recession anticipate the Quattrocento by more than a century.

Goes, Hugo van der (c. 1440–1482). A Flemish painter from Ghent who was commissioned by Tommaso Portinari, a Medici banking agent in the Netherlands, to paint a huge altarpiece for a family chapel in Florence, where it had a measurable impact on Florentine painters.

Gozzoli, Benozzo (1420–1497). A painter who worked in Fra Angelico's shop in Florence and in the Vatican and with Ghiberti on the second set of doors for the Baptistery. He is best known for his frescoes in the chapel of the Medici Palace.

Justus of Ghent (1430–c. 1480). Flemish painter active in Antwerp and Ghent, he went to Rome, then to Urbino by 1472. There, he painted a series of famous men and a notable altarpiece of the *Communion of the Apostles* for the Church of Corpus Domini.

Laurana, Luciano (c. 1420/25–1479). Architect from Dalmatia, he worked in Mantua and Pesaro before he was chosen by Federigo da Montefeltro to be the architect of the ducal palace in Urbino (1465–c. 1472). His courtyard there is widely regarded as one of the finest architectural achievements of the Renaissance.

Leonardo da Vinci (1452–1519). The embodiment of the Renaissance man, Leonardo was a universal genius in painting, sculpture, architecture, drawing, and the sciences of his day. He trained in Verrocchio's workshop. In addition to Florence, he later worked for a long period in Milan for the Sforza family, as well as in Rome. He spent his last years in France at the court of Francis I.

Lippi, Filippino (1457/8–1504). Son of Filippo Lippi, he studied with his father and with Botticelli. He completed the fresco cycle in the Brancacci Chapel. He worked in both Rome and Florence.

Lippi, Fra Filippo (c. 1406–1469). A Florentine Carmelite monk and painter, he left the monastery, married, and continued to paint religious subjects. His lyrical style was much favored by the Medici family.

Mantegna, Andrea (c. 1430/31–1506). Master painter in Padua and Mantua, his art has a sculptural quality, combined with rich color and a spirit of pathos. Deeply influenced by the remains of Roman art that he studied carefully, he was also an innovator in spatial illusionism in painting. He was a major influence on Venetian Renaissance painting through his brother-in-law, Giovanni Bellini.

Masaccio (Tommaso di ser Giovanni) (1401–1428). The most important and famous early Renaissance painter in Italy, his fame centers on the Brancacci Chapel in Santa Maria del Carmine in Florence. His frescoes in both the Brancacci Chapel and Santa Maria Novella present a new sense of solidity in his figures and a greater understanding of scale and perspective than that of any of his contemporaries.

Masolino da Panicale (1383–1440 or 1447). Masolino was the artist who began work in the Brancacci Chapel before being joined by Masaccio. He left that project to work in Hungary for two years, followed by four more years in Rome. His art essentially continues the International Gothic style.

Michelangelo Buonarotti (1475–1564). One of history's greatest and most famous artists, he was a sculptor, architect, and painter whose work was so overpowering in its effect that his influence was inescapable during his own lifetime and has never abated. His training was in Florence, and his career was divided between that city and Rome, where his imprint on the architecture and decoration of Saint Peter's and the Vatican is permanent.

Monaco, Lorenzo (c. 1370–c. 1425). A Sienese painter of the International Gothic style, he also worked in Florence. For a time he was a Carmelite monk, hence his name.

Orcagna, Andrea (c. 1308–1368). Fourteenth-century Florentine painter, sculptor, and architect, whose mature career coincided with the catastrophic plague that ravaged Italy and Europe. His art consequently was regressive and medieval in its severe hieratic style.

Paolo Veneziano (active 1333–1358). An important Trecento Venetian artist who painted in the older Byzantine style throughout his life, specializing in ornate altarpieces.

Parmigianino (Francesco Mazzola) (1503–1540). Born in Parma, where he was influenced by Correggio, he was a fluent draftsman, printmaker, and painter. He was imprisoned during the sack of Rome. His mature style was mannerism, characterized by the stylized elongation of forms.

Perugino (Pietro Vanucci) (1446–1523). As his name implies, he was from the central Italian hill town of Perugia. He was the head of a large and influential workshop. An esteemed Quattrocento painter, he worked in the Vatican in 1482 and 1508. Perugino was the teacher of Raphael.

Petrarch (Francesco Petrarca) (1304–1374). Petrarch was an extremely important and influential Italian humanist and poet, who along with Dante, wrote in Italian, as well as Latin.

Piero della Francesca (c. 1420–1492). Now considered one of the greatest of Renaissance painters, he was primarily associated with smaller urban centers, such as Urbino and Arezzo, where he created the fresco cycle *The Legend of the True Cross*. He was also a theorist and skilled mathematician.

Pisanello, Antonio (c. 1395–1455/6). Pisanello was the most important Renaissance sculptor of medals. He was also an important painter in tempera and fresco in the International Gothic style.

Pollaiuolo, Antonio (1433–1498). Significant sculptor, painter, and engraver, who (with his younger brother, Piero) headed a large workshop in Florence. Pollaiuolo was also an early innovator in printmaking and exquisite small bronze sculpture.

Pontormo (Jacopo Carucci) (1494–1556). A 16th-century Florentine painter of frescoes, portraits, and religious subjects on canvas. He worked in a mannerist idiom characterized by ambiguous expressions, illogical space, and strangely weightless forms.

Raphael (Raffaello Sanzio or Santi) (1483–1520). The illustrious Renaissance painter born in Urbino who studied first with his father, then with Perugino. He worked in Florence from 1504 to 1508 and later in Rome until his widely mourned premature death. A major portrait artist who also was renowned for his many graceful images of the Madonna, his larger masterpieces were the frescoes decorating the papal apartments in the Vatican that were painted for Popes Julius II and Leo X. His historical importance and fame has continued throughout the subsequent 500 years.

Robbia, Luca della (1400–1482). Luca was the most important artist of a large family of sculptors associated with the invention and use of glazed terracotta. He was one of the most important of the first generation of Renaissance artists in Florence, famous for his *Cantoria*, or choir gallery, executed for the Duomo.

Rossellino, Antonio (1427–c. 1479). A major Florentine sculptor who was the pupil of his brother, Bernardo. Rossellino created many important portrait busts, as well as his masterpiece, the Tomb of the Cardinal of Portugal in San Miniato al Monte, Florence.

Rosso Fiorentino (Giovanni Battista di Jacopo) (1495–1540). Rosso was a Florentine painter who was deeply affected by the sack of Rome. He developed a personal version of the mannerist style, which he later introduced into France, where he worked for Francis I at Fontainebleau from 1530.

Sansovino, Jacopo (Jacopo Tatti) (1486–1570). Florentine architect and sculptor, worked in Rome and Florence. From 1529, he was the official architect of Venice, where he introduced the classical Renaissance style. He designed the state library in Venice that now bears his name.

Savonarola, Girolamo (1452–1498). Savonarola was a charismatic Florentine religious reformer and Dominican monk. His popular preaching in Florence against the vanity and materialism of the upper classes and the corruption of the clergy coincided with the expulsion of the Medici. He also urged the invasion of Italy by Charles VIII of France. In 1497, he was excommunicated, and the following May, he was burned at the stake in Florence.

Signorelli, Luca (c. 1441–1523). Luca was a painter of powerfully modeled nude figures, especially in the San Brixio Chapel in the Cathedral at Orvieto, that later influenced Michelangelo.

Tintoretto, Jacopo (Jacopo Robusti) (1518–1594). The dyer's son was a Venetian painter of religious altarpieces and large decorative cycles, most prominent among them the complete decorations of the two-story Scuola Grande di San Rocco. He was the major Venetian artist to respond to the elements of central Italian mannerist style.

Titian (Tiziano Vecellio) (c. 1488/90–1576). The long-lived Titian was the greatest Venetian High Renaissance painter. The unsurpassed richness of his color and his sensuous and monumental figures defined Venetian painting, and his influence has reverberated through the history of art from Rubens to Delacroix to Renoir.

Uccello, Paolo (1397–1475). Painter and designer of stained glass. Notable for his emphasis on linear perspective, his paintings often sacrifice everything else to perspective effects.

Vasari, Giorgio (1511–1574). Famous biographer of Italian artists, as well as an architect and painter. He was a close friend and disciple of Michelangelo.

Veronese, Paolo (Paolo Cagliari) (c. 1528–1588). In the 16th century, Veronese worked in Venice as the greatest decorator of palaces, mainland villas, and monastery refectories. He was famous for his depiction of richly colored, sumptuous costumes and his immense, illusionistic settings. He worked extensively in the ducal palace in Venice, as well as on numerous other wall and ceiling frescoes. He was also an important painter of altarpieces.

Verrocchio, Andrea del (c. 1435–1488). Florentine sculptor, goldsmith, painter. Although Verrocchio was active mainly in Florence, he was famous throughout Italy. Versatile and gifted, he designed the *Colleoni* statue in Venice, the second great bronze equestrian statue of the Renaissance, after Donatello's *Gattamelata*. He was also the teacher of Leonardo.

Vivarini, Antonio (c. 1418–c. 1476/84). One of the last major Italian painters in the Gothic style, he often worked with his little-known brother-in-law, Giovanni d'Alemagna. He and his brother, Bartolomeo, ran a large workshop in Venice.

Bibliography

Note: An asterisk before an entry in this bibliography indicates that the book is out of print.

Essential Reading:

Adams, Laurie Schneider. *Italian Renaissance Art*. Boulder, CO: Westview Press, 2001. A recommended survey text. Well organized, with good reproductions.

Alberti, Leon Battista. *On Painting*. Trans. and with an introduction by John R. Spencer. New Haven: Yale University Press, 1956. Inexpensive translation of a seminal source.

————. *On Painting*. Ed. by Martin Kemp, trans. by Cecil Grayson. New York: Viking Penguin, 1991. Translated from the 1435 Latin text rather than the 1436 Italian text; some consider this version superior. Also inexpensive.

Carr, Dawson W., and Mark Leonard. *Looking at Paintings: A Guide to Technical Terms*. London: J. Paul Getty Museum in association with the British Museum Press, 1992. An excellent guide to materials, techniques, and terminology.

Edelstein, Debra, ed. *Pronunciation Dictionary of Artists' Names*. 3rd rev. ed. Boston: Bulfinch Press (with the Art Institute of Chicago), 1993. The only comprehensive, reliable guide.

Gilbert, Creighton E. *Italian Art, 1400–1500*. Englewood Cliffs, NJ: Prentice-Hall, 1980. A volume in the essential series *Sources and Documents in the History of Art*, it presents the Quattrocento in the words of contemporary artists, patrons, clergy, and writers.

Hall, James. *Dictionary of Subjects and Symbols in Art*. Rev. ed. Boulder, CO: Westview Press, 1974. Indispensable. Should be at hand whenever studying mythological, historical, or religious themes in art.

Hartt, Frederick, and David G. Wilkins. *History of Italian Renaissance Art*. 5th ed. New York: Harry N. Abrams, 2003. Long the classic survey text on the period and regularly updated. Lively reading, authoritative. Considerably longer and more comprehensive than Adams (above).

Holt, Elizabeth G. *A Documentary History of Art*, vol. I, *The Middle Ages and Renaissance*. Princeton, NJ: University of Princeton Press,

1982. Together with vol. II, this is an indispensable compendium of source material on the period.

————. *A Documentary History of Art*, vol. II, *Michelangelo and the Mannerists, the Baroque, and the Eighteenth Century*. Princeton, NJ: University of Princeton Press, 1982. See above.

Klein, Robert, and Henri Zerner. *Italian Art, 1500–1600*. Englewood Cliffs, NJ: Prentice-Hall, 1966. Invaluable volume in the series *Sources and Documents in the History of Art*.

Murray, Peter, and Linda Murray. *Dictionary of Art and Artists*. 7th ed. London: Penguin, 1997. You will use it constantly.

Vasari, Giorgio. *Lives of the Artists*. Trans. by George Bull. London: The Folio Society, 1993. 3 vols. A one-volume edition has been available from Penguin Books. Vasari was the first historian of Italian art and a friend of Michelangelo. His biographies are delightful to read, informative, and often even reliable. Essential in this or the following translation.

————. *Lives of the Most Eminent Painters, Sculptors, and Architects*. Trans. by Gaston Du C. de Vere, ed. by Kenneth Clark. New York: Harry N. Abrams, 1979. 3 vols. An alternative translation.

Voragine, Jacobus de. *The Golden Legend: Readings on the Saints*. Trans. by William Granger Ryan. Princeton, NJ: Princeton, 1993. 2 vols. The lives of the saints are rarely to be found in the Bible, but they were the constant source of material for artists. This medieval compilation was the standard source for those artists and for us.

Supplementary Reading:

Ahl, Diane. *Benozzo Gozzoli*. New Haven: Yale University Press, 1996. A reassessment of a painter usually regarded as having produced only one great work, the chapel in the Medici Palace. This definitive volume is the first comprehensive book in English on the artist in a century.

Ames-Lewis, Francis. *The Intellectual Life of the Early Italian Renaissance Artist*. New Haven: Yale University Press, 2000. Fine study of how Renaissance artists fought for professional and social recognition and for recognition of painting as one of the liberal arts. As aspiring intellectuals, they wrote art treatises and poetry. The author explores social history as art history.

*Baldini, Umberto, and Ornella Casazza. *Brancacci Chapel*. New York: Harry N. Abrams, 1992. Out of print but still available through used and rare book sites. Highly recommended.

Barolsky, Paul. *Michelangelo's Nose: A Myth and Its Maker*. University Park: Pennsylvania State University Press, 1990. Erudite discussion of literary aspects of Renaissance biography.

————. *The Faun in the Garden: Michelangelo and the Poetic Origins of Italian Renaissance Srt*. University Park: Pennsylvania State University Press, 1994. See above.

Bertelà, Giovanna Gaeta. *Donatello*. New York: Scala/Riverside, 1991. Well illustrated and inexpensive.

Bertelli, Carlo. *Piero della Francesca*. New Haven: Yale University Press, 1992. First publication after the long restoration of Piero's Arezzo frescoes; excellent plates.

Borsi, Franco, and Stefano Borsi. *Paolo Uccello*. London and New York: Thames and Hudson, 1994. Complete catalogue, splendidly illustrated.

Borsook, Eva. *The Mural Painters of Tuscany*, 2nd ed., rev. and enl. Oxford: Oxford University Press, 1980. Excellent study focusing on fresco painting.

Brown, David Alan. *Leonardo da Vinci: Origins of a Genius*. New Haven: Yale University Press, 1998. The best study of the earliest works of Leonardo and of his development. Thoughtful, imaginative study by a leading expert, clearly presented.

Brown, Patricia Fortini. *Art and Life in Renaissance Venice*. New York: Harry N. Abrams, 1997. An excellent, concise introduction to Venetian art and culture.

————. *Venetian Narrative Painting in the Age of Carpaccio*. Reprint ed. New Haven: Yale University Press, 1990. Covering the period 1470–1530, this book includes a catalogue of the cycles of narrative painting. Explores the sociopolitical context of these works.

Burckhardt, Jacob. *The Civilization of the Renaissance in Italy*. Oxford: Phaidon, 1965. Also published in paperback by Penguin Classics, 1990. A classic that was first published in Switzerland in 1860, this is still an important work on life and manners in the Renaissance, despite 150 years of intensive scholarship and scholarly argument.

Burke, Peter. *The Italian Renaissance: Culture and Society in Italy.* 2nd rev. ed. Princeton, NJ: University of Princeton Press, 1999. Highly recommended.

Butterfield, Andrew. *The Sculptures of Andrea del Verrocchio.* New Haven: Yale University Press, 1998. *Catalogue raisonné.* Best study of an artist whose quality is not always fully appreciated. Important also for the author's wide-ranging information on related topics.

Cadogan, Jean K. *Domenico Ghirlandaio.* New Haven: Yale University Press, 2001. Essential for an understanding of the functioning of his famous workshop, of Florentine patronage, and of the place of the artist in Renaissance society. Also a *catalogue raisonné.*

Camesaca, Ettore. *Mantegna.* New York: Scala/Riverside, 1992. Recommended, inexpensive.

Casazza, Ornella. *Masaccio.* New York: Scala/Riverside, 1990. Best illustrated low-cost survey of his work.

Castiglione, Baldesar. *The Book of the Courtier.* Trans. by George Bull. New York: Penguin Books, 1976. Famous book by a Renaissance gentleman.

Chastel, André. *The Sack of Rome, 1527.* Princeton, NJ: Princeton University Press, 1983. Bollingen Series. Trans. by Beth Archer. The standard work on the subject, unlikely to be surpassed. Dramatic reading; historical writing at its best.

Cole, Bruce. *Masaccio and the Art of Early Renaissance Florence.* Bloomington, IN: University of Indiana Press, 1980. Highly readable, concise.

———. *The Renaissance Artist at Work: From Pisano to Titian.* Boulder, CO: Westview Press, 1984. Packed with valuable information on techniques, materials, and workshop practice.

———. *Giotto: The Scrovegni Chapel, Padua.* New York: George Braziller, 1993. An excellent short introduction to one of the central monuments of Western art.

Deimling, Barbara. *Sandro Botticelli.* New York: Taschen America, 2000. A good, short overview.

Fossi, Gloria. *Filippo Lippi.* New York: Scala/Riverside, 1989. Good and reasonably priced.

Franklin, David. *Painting in Renaissance Florence, 1500–1550.* New Haven: Yale University Press, 2001. Obviously valuable on early mannerism, as well as High Renaissance painting, it begins with Leonardo's return to Florence and concludes with Vasari's paintings. Among the dozen artists studied are Perugino, Michelangelo, Rosso Fiorentino, and Pontormo.

Freedberg, Sydney Joseph. *Painting in Italy, 1500–1600.* 3rd ed. New Haven: Yale University Press, 1992. Pelican History of Art. Standard work by one of the greatest scholars of Renaissance art.

Goffen, Rona. *Giovanni Bellini.* New Haven: Yale University Press, 1989. With many beautiful color plates and a thorough, readable, and sensitive text, this is the definitive study.

Hartt, Frederick, and David Finn. *Donatello: Prophet of Modern Vision.* New York: Harry N. Abrams, 1973. A massive volume notable for its beautiful, if eccentric, photography by Finn.

Haskell, Francis, and Nicholas Penny. *Taste and the Antique: The Lure of Classical Sculpture, 1500–1900.* New Haven: Yale University Press, 1981. This volume is both fascinating and endlessly useful in the study of the history of art at any point where classical sculpture made its presence felt—that is to say, nearly all the time. It is the only easily accessible corpus of photographs of classical sculpture.

Hay, Denys, and John Law. *Italy in the Age of the Renaissance, 1380–1530.* London: Longman, 1989. Useful Renaissance history survey

Hearder, Harry. *Italy: A Short History.* Rev. ed. Cambridge: Cambridge University Press, 2001. A readable, authoritative history for those who want the full historical sweep.

Hibbard, Howard. *Michelangelo.* 2nd ed. Boulder, CO: Westview Press, 1985. A perceptive, sensitive study that relies much on Michelangelo's own words.

Hills, Paul. *The Light of Early Italian Painting.* New Haven: Yale University Press, 1990. This book is concerned mostly with the Trecento, stopping about 1430. No other specific book on this subject has been written. Clear and full of cogent observations.

———. *Venetian Colour: Marble, Mosaic, Painting and Glass, 1250–1550.* New Haven: Yale University Press, 1999. The subtitle shows the valuable range covered by the author; in addition, he pays close attention to the natural light of Venice. Includes 160 color plates.

Holmes, Megan. *Fra Filippo Lippi, the Carmelite Painter*. New Haven: Yale University Press, 1999. Praiseworthy book on a complex, contradictory artist. The interaction of patronage, religion, and art is clarified.

Hood, William. *Fra Angelico at San Marco*. New Haven: Yale University Press, 1993. A volume much praised for its scholarship, writing, and quality of reproductions.

Howard, Deborah. *The Architectural History of Venice*. New York: Holmes and Meier, 1981. (The 2002 edition includes added color plates by Sarah Quill.) A concise survey of the city's architectural context.

Humphrey, Peter. *The Altarpiece in Renaissance Venice*. New Haven: Yale University Press, 1993. Sumptuously illustrated and well organized. Venetian Renaissance art is traced through the evolution of major altarpieces.

―――. *Painting in Renaissance Venice*. New Haven: Yale University Press, 1997. An excellent single-volume survey.

Janson, Horst W. *The Sculpture of Donatello*. Princeton, 1957 (reprint, 1963). Standard catalogue of his work. Ultimately indispensable, despite the grainy black-and-white reproductions in the reprint edition.

Jones, Roger, and Nicholas Penny. *Raphael*. New Haven: Yale University Press, 1987. Especially valuable because it is the best general, affordable corpus of photographs of Raphael's work.

Kanter, Laurence B., and Tom Henry. *Luca Signorelli: The Complete Paintings*. London and New York: Thames and Hudson, 2002. For those who want to learn more about his work, an erudite and satisfying text with large color reproductions.

Kent, Dale. *Cosimo de' Medici and the Florentine Renaissance*. New Haven: Yale University Press, 2000. An important study of Medici patronage.

King, Ross. *Brunelleschi's Dome*. New York and London: Penguin Books, 2000. Immensely readable, reliable, and about much more than the dome.

―――. *Michelangelo and the Pope's Ceiling*. New York: Walker & Co., 2003. Superbly researched and written. Not just about the ceiling, but also Pope Julius II, Raphael, and the vivid history of the time, this book deserves to be read and reread.

Ladis, Andrew. *The Brancacci Chapel, Florence*. New York: George Braziller, 1993. Great Fresco Cycles of the Renaissance Series. Sensitive, imaginative text.

Lavin, Marilyn A. *Piero della Francesca: The Flagellation*. Reprint ed. University of Chicago Press, 1990. Thorough and provocative study of a famous puzzle.

————. *Piero della Francesca: San Francesco, Arezzo*. New York: George Braziller, 1994. Concentrated look at the cycle in this valuable series.

————. *Piero della Francesca*. Oxford: Phaidon, 1999. Authoritative overview.

Lightbrown, Ronald. *Sandro Botticelli: Life and Work*. 2nd ed. New York: Abbeville Press, 1989. The definitive study.

Lloyd, Christopher. *Fra Angelico*. 2nd ed., rev. and enl. London and New York: Phaidon Press, 1992, Colour Library. Recommended, reasonably priced.

Marani, Pietro C. *Leonardo da Vinci: The Complete Paintings*. New York: Harry N. Abrams, 2000. Available in a reasonably priced compact paperback, this book provides all the essential images needed for study.

Meiss, Millard. *Painting in Florence and Siena after the Black Death*. Princeton: Princeton University Press, 1979. Real history, demonstrating the interaction of art and all other aspects of life.

Michelangelo. *Complete Poems and Selected Letters of Michelangelo*. Trans. by Creighton E. Gilbert. Princeton: Princeton University Press, 1980. Standard translation, invaluable for Michelangelo's thoughts on art, life, religion.

Muir, Edward. *Civic Ritual in Renaissance Venice*. Princeton: Princeton University Press, 1986. Important for understanding the importance of Venice as a *subject* for Venetian art.

Néret, Gilles. *Michelangelo*. Köln and New York: Taschen, 2000. Handy, short guide.

Olson, Roberta J. M. *Italian Renaissance Sculpture*. World of Art Series. New York: Thames and Hudson, 1992. Excellent and reasonably priced.

Osborne, June. *Urbino: The Story of a Renaissance City.* Chicago: University of Chicago Press, 2003. Highly recommended.

Paoletti, John T., and Gary M. Radke. *Art in Renaissance Italy.* New York: Harry N. Abrams, 1997. Organized by city-states, this book's strength is in patronage and local style. Best used in conjunction with Hartt and Wilkens (see Essential Reading), because it can be difficult to follow the careers of individual artists. Good supplemental material, such as extensive contemporary quotations.

Paolucci, Antonio. *Luca Signorelli.* New York: Scala/Riverside, Library of Great Masters, 1990. Good coverage in an inexpensive book.

Partridge, Loren. *Michelangelo: The Sistine Chapel Ceiling.* New York: George Braziller, 1996. Well-illustrated overview.

———, et al. *Michelangelo: The Last Judgment, A Glorious Restoration.* New York: Harry N. Abrams, 2000. The best and most detailed look at the stupendous fresco.

Pedrocco, Filippo. *Titian.* New York: Scala/Riverside, 1993. A reasonably priced introduction.

———. *The Art of Venice.* New York: Scala/Riverside, 2002. Covers the entire history of the city's art, with much on the Renaissance. Reasonable.

Pignatti, Terisio, and Filippo Pedrocco. *Giorgione.* New York: Rizzoli, 1999. Authoritative.

Pope-Hennessy, John. *Introduction to Italian Sculpture.* Part I: *Italian Gothic Sculpture*, Part II: *Italian Renaissance Sculpture*, Part III: *Italian High Renaissance and Baroque Sculpture.* London: Phaidon Press, 2000 (4th ed.). These volumes are available separately, in hardback and in paperback. After more than 40 years, they remain the standard study.

Riess, Jonathan B. *Luca Signorelli: The San Brixio Chapel, Orvieto.* New York: George Braziller, 1995. The current authority writing in this important series.

———. *The Renaissance Anti-Christ: Luca Signorelli's Orvieto Frescoes.* Princeton: Princeton University Press, 1995. Full treatment of the chapel.

Rosand, David. *Painting in Cinquecento Venice: Titian, Veronese, Tintoretto.* New Haven: Yale University Press, 1982. Standard book on the subject

Santi, Bruno. *Leonardo da Vinci*. New York: Scala/Riverside, Library of Great Masters, 1990. An inexpensive and well-illustrated introduction.

———. *Raphael*. New York: Scala/Riverside, 1991. Well illustrated, inexpensive.

Settis, Salvatore. *Giorgione's Tempest: Interpreting the Hidden Subject*. Chicago: University of Chicago Press, 1990. Essential for those who *must* know more about the painting.

Seymour, Charles Jr. *Sculpture in Italy: 1400–1500*. New Haven: Yale University Press, 1976. Pelican History of Art. A classic survey of the subject.

Spike, John T. *Fra Angelico*. New York: Abbeville, 1997. Rewarding for the informed reader.

Steer, John. *Venetian Painting: A Concise History*. World of Art Series. London and New York: Thames and Hudson, 1970. Useful and reasonably priced.

Steinberg, Leo. *Leonardo's Incessant Last Supper*. New York: Zone Books, 2001. The last word on the painting, by a brilliant scholar and superlative writer.

Sueur, Hélène, et al. *The Little Book of Michelangelo*. Paris: Flammarion, 2003. Part of a first-rate, inexpensive series.

Temperine, Renaud. *The Little Book of Leonardo da Vinci*. Paris: Flammarion, 2002. Another in this admirable series of reasonable introductions.

Tolnay, Charles de. *Michelangelo: Sculptor, Painter, Architect*. Princeton: Princeton University Press, 1975. A one-volume distillation of the monumental multivolume study by the leading Michelangelo scholar of the 20th century.

Vespasiano. *The Vespasiano Memoirs: Lives of Illustrious Men of the XVth Century*. 7th ed. Trans. by William George and Emily Waters. Toronto: University of Toronto Press, 1998. Brief lives by a contemporary observer. Look also for a used copy of the 1963 Harper Torchbook paperback (*Renaissance Princes, Popes and Prelates*). Fascinating.

Wallace, William E. *Michelangelo: The Complete Sculpture, Painting, and Architecture*. Westport, CT: Hugh Lauter Levin Associates, 1998. A broad consideration of Michelangelo's work by a highly esteemed scholar.

Welch, Evelyn. *Art in Renaissance Italy, 1350–1500.* London: Oxford University Press, 2000. A wide contextual view of the period, including decorative art and interiors, as well as painting, sculpture, and architecture. Thoughtful and stimulating.

White, John. *Art and Architecture in Italy, 1250–1400.* New Haven: Yale University Press, 1973. Pelican History of Art.

*———. *The Birth and Rebirth of Pictorial Space.* London: Belknap Press, 1987. Unfortunately, this landmark book is out of print. It is a brilliant book on the subject, richly and clearly written. It demands and repays close attention. Try to find it at your library or on interlibrary loan. You may also find it from secondhand dealers, but it will be expensive.

Zöllner, Frank. *Leonardo da Vinci.* New York: Taschen America, 2000. A basic introduction to the artist, containing many reproductions of his work.

———, and Johannes Nathan. *Leonardo da Vinci: The Complete Paintings and Drawings.* Part I: Text, Part II: *Catalogue Raisonné,* Part III: Drawings. Taschen, 2003. Costly, but 600 pages, oversize, hardcover, excellent reproductions.

Zuffi, Stefano, ed. *Art in Venice.* New York: Harry N. Abrams, 1999. A beautiful photographic survey at a bargain price.